Stratification and Inequality Series
The Center for the Study of Social Stratification and Inequality,
Global COE Program
Tohoku University, Japan
Volume 9

Fluidity of Place

Stratification and Inequality Series
The Center for the Study of Social Stratification and Inequality,
Global COE Program
Tohoku University, Japan

Inequality amid Affluence: Social Stratification in Japan
Junsuke Hara and Kazuo Seiyama

Intentional Social Change: A Rational Choice Theory
Yoshimichi Sato

Constructing Civil Society in Japan: Voices of Environmental Movements
Koichi Hasegawa

Deciphering Stratification and Inequality: Japan and beyond
Yoshimichi Sato

Social Justice in Japan: Concepts, Theories and Paradigms
Ken-ichi Ohbuchi

Gender and Career in Japan
Atsuko Suzuki

Status and Stratification:
Cultural Forms in East and Southeast Asia
Mitsuhiko Shima

Globalization, Minorities and Civil Society:
Perspectives from Asian and Western Cities
Koichi Hasegawa and Naoki Yoshihara

Fluidity of Place: Globalization and the Transformation of Urban Space
Naoki Yoshihara

Series Editor: Yoshimichi Sato, Tohoku University

Editorial Board: Koichi Hasegawa, Ken-ichi Ohbuchi, Toshiaki Kimura, Kunihiro Kimura, Yoshimichi Sato, Naoki Yoshihara, Mary C. Brinton, Jeffrey P. Broadbent

Stratification and Inequality Series
The Center for the Study of Social Stratification and Inequality,
Global COE Program
Tohoku University, Japan
Volume 9

Fluidity of Place

Globalization and the Transformation of Urban Space

By

Naoki Yoshihara

Translated by
Minako Sato

Edited by
Miriam Riley

First published in Japanese in 2008 by the University of Tokyo Press as *Mōbiritii to basho: 21-seiki toshi kūkan no tenkai*.

This English edition first published in 2010 by
Trans Pacific Press, PO Box 164, Balwyn North, Melbourne, Victoria 3104, Australia
Telephone: +61-3-9859-1112 Fax: +61-3-9859-4110
Email: tpp.mail@gmail.com
Web: http://www.transpacificpress.com

Copyright © Trans Pacific Press 2010

Designed and set by digital environs, Melbourne. http://www.digitalenvirons.com

Printed by BPA Print Group, Burwood, Victoria, Australia

Distributors

Australia and New Zealand
DA Information Services/Central Book Services
648 Whitehorse Road
Mitcham, Victoria 3132
Australia
Telephone: +61-3-9210-7777
Fax: + 61-3-9210-7788
Email: books@dadirect.com
Web: www.dadirect.com

USA and Canada
International Specialized Book Services (ISBS)
920 NE 58th Avenue, Suite 300
Portland, Oregon 97213-3786
USA
Telephone: 1-800-944-6190
Fax: 1-503-280-8832
Email: orders@isbs.com
Web: http://www.isbs.com

Asia and the Pacific
Kinokuniya Company Ltd.

Head office:
3-7-10 Shimomeguro
Meguro-ku
Tokyo 153-8504
Japan
Telephone: +81-3-6910-0531
Fax: +81-3-6420-1362
Email: bkimp@kinokuniya.co.jp
Web: www.kinokuniya.co.jp

Asia-Pacific office:
Kinokuniya Book Stores of Singapore Pte., Ltd.
391B Orchard Road #13-06/07/08
Ngee Ann City Tower B
Singapore 238874
Telephone: +65-6276-5558
Fax: +65-6276-5570
Email: SSO@kinokuniya.co.jp

All rights reserved. No production of any part of this book may take place without the written permission of Trans Pacific Press.

ISBN 978-1-920901-53-0 (Hardback)
ISBN 978-1-920901-59-2 (Paperback)

Photos reproduced with gratitude to G. McKay and I. Wallace (Photo 4.1), D. Ziv (6.1), J. Marshall (7.1), and H. Leisch (7.2 and 7.3). Cover Photo: JupiterImages.

The National Library of Australia Cataloguing-in-Publication entry

Author: Yoshihara, Naoki, 1948–
Title: Fluidity of place : globalization and the transformation of urban space/ Naoki Yoshihara.
ISBN: 9781920901530 (hbk.)
9781920901592 (pbk.)
Series: Social stratification and inequality series; 9
Notes: Includes index.
Bibliography.
Subjects: City planning.
Urban renewal.
Globalization.
Dewey Number: 307.1216

Contents

Figures	vi
Photos	vi
Tables	vii
Acknowledgements	ix
Prologue	1
Part I: Urban Space and Place in Fluidity	
1 Ambiguity of Modernity and Globalization	11
2 Between Regions and Fluids: On Metaphors of Globalization	25
3 'Cities Beyond Society' and Postmodernization	38
4 'Global Civil Society' and Narratives of Place	53
5 Local Governance and 'Open Urban Space'	71
Part II: Urban Spatial Turns in Asian Megacities	
6 Urban Asia: The Case of Jakarta	89
7 The Gated Community and the Slum	106
8 Islam in Bali	123
9 Bali and the Japanese	141
10 Coordinate Axes of the Post-Global City: Urban Spatial Turns in Contemporary Asia	160
Epilogue: The Question of Place	174
Notes	184
Bibliography	212
Index	224

Figures

3.1:	Tokyo Midtown	50
6.1:	Jakarta at around 1885: historical dual structure	100
7.1:	Location pattern in Jabotabek, DKI Jakarta	116
7.1:	continued	117
8.1:	Location of batik factories	129
9.1:	Organizational structure of the Japan Club in Bali	146
9.2:	Changes in the estimated long-stay population (by age group)	204

Photos

3.1:	The Shin-Marunouchi Building viewed from the Yaesu side	47
4.1:	A rural fair	57
6.1:	The Golden Triangle	96
7.1:	Kampung Kandang	111
7.2:	The gate at Lippo Karawaci	119
7.3:	A streetscape at Lippo Karawaci	120
8.1:	Tents inhabited by KIPEM	130
8.2:	Batik factory worksite (taken by author)	131
8.3:	Shack-like housing inhabited by batik factory workers (taken by author)	132
9.1:	Japan Club in Bali (taken by author)	145
9.2:	*Tile Book Print Kecak*	148

Tables

4.1:	Distribution of the Overseas Chinese, 1989–1997	60
5.1:	Definitions and characteristics of governance	74
7.1:	Distribution of slums in DKI Jakarta, 1998–2002	110
8.1:	Shifts in overseas tourist numbers, 2001–05	126
8.2:	Changes in Bali's workforce by industry, 1970–2004	128
8.3:	Population shift by religion, 1996–2006	134
9.1:	Changes in the number of Japanese residents in Bali	143
9.2:	Numbers of Japanese residents by area, 2006	143

Acknowledgements

This book is published as the ninth volume of the Center for the Study of Social Stratification and Inequality's series. I am much honored to have the chance to publish this book through a grant offered by the CSSI. The original version of this book was written in Japanese and published by Tokyo University Press in 2008. It has a long history. In the lengthy gestation period, I have read Henri Lefebvre, Manuel Castells, David Harvey, John Urry and so on, polemically, and developed my thinking about their works. My concern has focused on the theme of 'modernity, time and space' historically. I was walking on the road of the so-called 'spatial turn' in my observations. My book, *mobiliti to basho* ('mobility and places,' now published as *Fluidity of Place*) was the product of my 'spatial turn,' but it is likely that it will not reach a lot of readers in Japan. Our academic societies have become too unfamiliar with and indifferent to this 'spatial turn.' It is expected, therefore, that this translation will be a contribution to the development of the 'spatial turn.' Of course, this book highlights various forms of inequality and difference in the globalized society, built in space and place, and so offers insights into and understandings of 'globalization and localities,' for instance.

I would like to acknowledge the many friends and comrades with whom I jousted over the theme of 'modernity, time and space' and shared the experience of engaging in the 'spatial turn.' Especially, I benefited from heated discussions with members of *kukanronkenkyukai* (the society for space theory), who introduced me to postmodernism, cultural studies, complexity theory and much more. They are too numerous to list individually here.

I also thank intellectuals of good intentions for their support and enthusiasm for publishing this book. Professor Yoshio Sugimoto, one of them, offered more concrete ideas on the title and entire composition of the book. Minako Sato and Miriam Riley, others of them, translated my sentences filled with metaphors into clear English and proofread the translation phrase by phrase. This book would not have existed without Sugimoto's initiative and Sato's and Riley's intellectual endeavors.

Naoki Yoshihara
17 December 2009

Prologue

Why 'Fluidity and Place' Now?

> I was at a loss what to do, for I durst not return to the same landing-place. (Swift 1965: 279)

The way the question 'fluidity and place' is framed is clearly contradictory in the master narrative of modernity, as under modern dichotomies or developmental models fluidity is at the opposite extreme from stasis of place and therefore out of phase with it (or at least not on the same plane). Accordingly, we must first exit the narrative of modernism if we are to frame our question in this way. The trouble is, thus far hardly any rearrangement/reexamination has been done on the subject of either fluidity or place on the theoretical horizon of 'unthinking social science' (Wallerstein). Both have been explained within conceptual frameworks premised on the modern nation-state until now. Whether it is inter-regional or inter-class fluidity or place, all have been addressed within the modern framework of 'the territorial.' Needless to say, it was globalization that blasted a hole in this situation and sowed the seeds of a paradigm shift in modern social theory. In fact, fluidity and place are frustratingly entangled under globalization and, in order to understand them, new types of social theory are beginning to emerge—for example, theories centering on complexity or the emergent.[1]

However, if I declare my departure from the narrative of modernity here at the beginning, even if I use phrases that reflect the climate of the times and in some cases get closer to the substratum of cultural transformation, I will probably end up obscuring the destination of my discussion. Therefore I would like to set aside the problematic inherent in the framing of the question of 'fluidity and place' itself for the time being. Instead, I shall begin with a close observation of the advance of globalization and ask 'why "fluidity and place" now?' by setting the axis of our vision on a spatial turn in contemporary urban space, as established in the subtitle of this book.

The new experience of time and space

When lively debates over global cities were under way, it was *Dual City: Restructuring of New York*, co-authored by Castells and Mollenkopf (1991) that added powerful momentum to the discussion. This text describes the polarization that began in the 1980s in the literally global city of New York through the contradistinction of 'haves' and 'have-nots.' This polarity had the basic characteristic of a 'dichotomy observed between nodes of flow space interlinked by globalization and disparate and weak locales of social community' (Takahashi 1993: 243). While I shall leave the discussion of the theoretical impasse of such a dichotomy until Chapter Six, the dichotomy itself has lived on in the form of the global-local binary identified by M. P. Smith, namely the position which 'ha[s] equated the "global" with the space of top-down political-economic power relations and reduced the "local" to a site of either class polarization or ineffectual cultural resistance to the inexorable march of global capitalism' (2001: 10).

A new point to note here is that this position has branched out into two separate views of place: one emphasizes 'the variations of place' for capital and the other regards placeness as the basis for one's identity (see Chapter Four for details). Without going into detail, the two arguments share a continuum called 'proximity' beyond their marked superficial differences. In other words, the former is characterized by the pursuit of 'propinquity' based on the capitalist instinctual drive to gain profits from 'being close' and the latter features a yearning for 'propinquity' stemming from anxiety about 'not being close.' Coupled with this, the premise shared by these two arguments is what Harvey (1989) calls the 'new experience of time and space.' He describes this new experience as a new round of 'time-space compression.'[2] It represents short-lived and transient time and fragmented and pulverized space and constitutes the bedrock of 'flexibility' in the period following the crisis of Fordism stressed by Harvey. To Harvey, flexibility is observed in five dimensions—labor processes, labor markets, state policy, geographic mobility and consumption processes—and positioned in confrontation with Fordism.[3] Fordism is marked by underlying rigidities, which in turn are underpinned by 'alternating time' and 'geometrical systematic space.' Fordism went into crisis after 1973 and gave rise to widespread flexibility.

In any case, it is possible to take the first step in discussing 'fluidity and place' by subjectively reading and inquiring into what is called the 'new experience of time and space.'

The mechanism of instantaneous time[4]

By the way, the time and space of Fordism characterized by rigidities, especially the mechanism of time, is best represented by none other than clock-time. According to Adam, clock-time is 'time that is abstracted from its natural source; an independent, decontextualized, rationalized time' and 'time that is almost infinitely divisible into equal spatial units, [...], and replaced to as time *per se'* (1995: 27). Lefebvre states that the rule of clock-time over society has expelled all forms of livable *kairos* time, that is 'the sense of time when it is said that now is the time to do something irrespective of what any clock indicates' (Gault 1995: 155). Certainly, clock-time has been the center of modern social structures and practices. Harvey argues that clock-time is being replaced by short-lived and transient time following the crisis of Fordism, especially coupled with the emergence of new technologies that are closely associated with 'time-space compression.' His argument is characterized by the view that the shift from clock-time to short-lived and transient time is a 'state' as well as something that conjugates the ambiguity of modernity (a 'condition' of post-modernity).[5] However, while his argument suggests that new technologies are dramatically transforming opportunities for the mobility of people, information and images and their constraints, it does not provide an explicit account of how they form the basis of flexibility.

In this regard, the concept of 'instantaneous time' described by Urry is useful as it elicits such mobility by following the process of re-ordering our experience of 'duration (*dureé*)' (Bergson 1889)[6] in an 'instantaneous' or 'virtual' form, even though it is a similar time-space metaphor. Urry summarizes its elements as follows.

> [F]irst, new informational and communicational technologies based upon inconceivably brief instants which are wholly beyond human consciousness: second, the simultaneous character of social and technical relationships which replaces the linear logic of clock-time characterized by the temporal separation of cause and effect occurring over separate measurable instants; and third, a metaphor for the widespread significance of exceptionally short-term and fragmented

time, even where it is not literally instantaneous and simultaneous. (2000: 126)

Under the instantaneous time woven by these elements, 'the end of geography' (Gregory 1985) expressed on the basis of physical scales such as national and local becomes inevitable. The destruction of spatial boundaries causes not only the compression of 'physical distance' but also that of 'aesthetical distance' that exists in the form of enhanced immediacy, impact, sensation and synchronicity. The aforementioned mobility was not necessarily assumed to be synonymous with the collapse of territoriality. Incidentally, when these things slid into discourses about globalization, they tended to converge on master narratives such as the 'structuring of the world by capitalism' (Hall) and the fragmentation/dissolution of the local. The approach to 'impersonate globalization as a single unit in a way' (Yoshihara 2004: 175) observed in this discourse appeared to deny territoriality but it was in fact based on *modified* territoriality by way of annexation/ domination of 'the small' by 'the large.' In other words, it cleverly stood on the foundation of territoriality while pretending to deny it.[7]

Fluidity and place

Fluidity addressed together with instantaneous time, however, no longer permits an ambiguous intervention/invasion by territoriality. In fact, it stands upon global complexity which nullifies territoriality. I shall present more specific discussion in Chapter Two, but it is essentially comprised of the global flows and hybrids of people, things and events that are constantly roving and challenging boundaries. It exists as an indicator of the constellation of globalization described by Appadurai 'as fundamentally fractal, that is, as possessing no Euclidean boundaries, structures, or regularities' (1996: 46). Under this fluidity, the flow of images continues to gather speed and the 'placeless' state comes to the foreground. For this reason, our mode of representation of the world to ourselves becomes increasingly dependent on images, which prompts us to use all five senses in the search for our identity. Harvey describes it as follows:

> […] in a world where image streams accelerate and become more and more placeless. Who are we and to what space/place do we belong? Am I a citizen of the world, the nation, the locality? Can I have a virtual existence in cyberspace…? (1996a: 246)

In any case, it is easy to understand why some people regard place as the basis for stability or unproblematic identity. However, what we must remember is that mobility that coexists with instantaneous time is in fact an internalized form of the capitalist instinctual drive which in itself has a high level of mobility.[8] Certainly, no matter how 'the present' of said mobility is depicted, the undeniable fact is that the abstraction of space by capital, that is, 'active production of locales' by capital, is a decisive factor after all. On this basis, it is easy to agree with the view that emphasizes 'the variations of place' to capital.

At the same time, what we are witnessing in mobility that coexists with instantaneous time is the open nature of place and space, so to speak. In short, this implies the 'opened contradictions of capitalism' (Lefebvre), but it is essentially a question of how to discern the dynamism lurking at the base of 'the variations of place.' Going back to the aforementioned mobility, what attracts our attention here is the meaning of place/placeness contained in the following statement.

> [W]hile cross-border cultural flows may undermine nationhood, they also activate a multitude of other identities, introducing potentially greater flexibility into inherited forms of citizenship. As the boundary between the native and the foreigner becomes more porous, a generalized diasporic condition emerges from the margins, encouraging the formation of a new "public sphere" composed of "transnational coalitions outside state and market systems." (Morris-Suzuki 2000: 65)

What Massey calls the 'alternative interpretation of place' emerges as an indirect extension of this description.[9] Massey states as follows:

> In this interpretation, what gives a place its specificity is not some long internalized history but the fact that it is constructed out of a particular constellation of relations, articulated together at a particular locus. If one moves in from the satellite towards the globe, holding all those networks of social relations and movements and communications in one's head, then each place can be seen as a particular, unique point of their intersection. The uniqueness of a place, or a locality, in other words is constructed out of particular interactions and mutual articulations of social relations, social processes, experiences and understandings, in a situation of co-presence. (1993: 66)

Needless to say, place is viewed as a situation in which social relations and understandings are woven into a rhizomatous network which is open to the outside world. If so, the next question is how to single out the function to extract the complexity though chaotic energy inherent in this network itself. On this point, the concept of 'quantum reality' coined by Zohar and Marshall is helpful.

> Quantum reality[...] has the potential to be both particlelike and wavelike. Particles are individuals, located and measureable in space and time. They are either here or there, now and then. Waves are "nonlocal," they are spread out across all of space and time, and their instantaneous effects are everywhere. Waves extend themselves in every direction at once, they overlap and combine with other waves to form new realities (new emergent wholes). (Zohar and Marshall cited in Urry 2000: 122)

The key term here is 'new reality,' which in this case implies 'the emergent.' I shall discuss this in detail in Chapter Two, but briefly, it is the basis for the 'web of meaning' (Lefebvre)—a de-integrative and non-organic existence in itself—which is formed when people articulate and weave instantaneous incidents.

In search of a new type of human nature

At this point, we realize that we are ultimately searching for what Harvey calls a 'new type of human nature.' It is blessed with specific sensitivity to instantaneous time and equipped with the ability to transform 'from an urbanism based in exploitation to an urbanism appropriate for the human species [...] it remains for revolutionary practice to accomplish such a transformation' (Harvey 1973: 314). By the way, Chicago School sociologist Robert Park once formulated the concept of human ecology by drawing on the world of the *laissez-faire* in human nature.[10] Park's human nature was completely assimilated into the mechanism of *laissez-faire*. As far as Harvey was concerned, it was a new type of human nature compatible with Fordism as 'total lifestyle,' that is, an 'urbanized human nature' (1985). Then, after the crisis of Fordism, what is the 'new type of human nature' created under mobility coexisting with instantaneous time as discussed above?

Needless to say, the global flows and hybrids of people, things and events that are wandering and constantly revising boundaries exist alongside the abstraction/emptying out of various urban subjects and 'degradation of collectivity organizing and structuring people's activity' (Urry 2000). Consequently, when a 'new type of human nature' is considered here, naturally, it must be closely linked with the dynamism lurking at the bottom of the aforementioned 'variations of place' which turns this 'degradation of collectivity' *from something broken into something newly formed.* Of course, it is in practice an extremely difficult task to identify the course of dynamism filled with the momentum of such transformation. However, for the very reason that the McDonaldization of the world and the state of mixed desire and fear for the indigenous (Iyer 1989) are spreading in 'the present,' we cannot avoid this issue.

Come to think of it, we are now surrounded by impulsion toward the aforementioned 'propinquity' generated/induced by various states of collectivity, including race, ethnicity, religious creed and neighborhood. And we live as we face the process of homogenization through them. It can be said that the variations attached to the aforementioned instantaneous time and mobility which are constantly shifting toward *différance,* and the fractal structure which repeatedly assembles and dissembles, do implicitly nurture our approach to *subjectively* deal with such cases. A 'new type of human nature' cannot exist after all without the 'physicalization' of this approach.

In the rest of the book, I shall elaborate and expand on the state of 'fluidity and place' roughly sketched above from respective phases. Just as Gulliver says, '[w]hen all was ready, and the day came for my departure...' (Swift 1965: 276).

Postscript

In fact, it is essential to explore the meaning of deepening hybridity and/or complexity promoted by the advance of globalization if we are to consider and develop the theme of 'fluidity and place.' Urry pursues this earnestly. According to him, with the help of complexity theory that 'did not imply [...] conceiving of humanity as mechanical, but rather instead conceiving of nature as active and creative,' or 'laws of nature compatible with the idea of events, of novelty, and of creativity' and after all '(scientific analysis) based on the dynamics of nonequilibria, with its emphasis on multiple futures, bifurcation and choice, historical dependence, and [...] intrinsic and inherent uncertainty resonates' (Wallerstein 1966: 61–64), '[g]lobal systems can be viewed as interdependent, as self-organizing and as possessing emergent properties. I suggest that we can examine a range of non-linear, mobile and unpredictable "global hybrids" always on the "edge of chaos"' (Urry 2003: 14). I cannot go into detail here due to limited space. Please see Urry (2003) and Chapter Two of this book for details.

Part I
Urban Space and Place in Fluidity

1 Ambiguity of Modernity and Globalization

> ...when we cease to think in categories we see that, in fact, experience makes of each of these contrary terms a substitute for the other...
> (Lefebvre 1984: 123)

Introduction

What really *was* the debate about the postmodern, which so invigorated the world of criticism and produced one extremely stimulating proposition after another? Was it merely one phase in the conventional pattern of 'knowledge' creation, involving the eclipsing of a new variety of argument by a newer version? Or was it simply one variant among the strains of meta-knowledge produced by Enlightenment 'knowledge' of Modern Western Europe in its ebb and flow? In either case, amid a vortex of criticisms and counterarguments ranging from 'the superficial' to 'denials of humanism,' the debate about the postmodern took center stage in a contest of all sorts of 'knowledge.' Now that the 'party' has passed into history, of all things, hard holism ('theory of totalization') and utopian thinking that sets salvation (the Messiah) against the 'miseries of the world' are coming back to life. If anything, we are witnessing an emerging situation in which discourses of postmodernism are carefully separated from the postmodern phenomenon and blamed unilaterally for the chaotic state of 'knowledge' with no clear direction.[1] The same old pattern is being repeated all over again. It looks as if we have gone back to square one. Is this what is really happening?

I do not intend to discuss distinctive, purely theoretical features of the various discourses of postmodernism here. Rather, I would like to point out that *as a consequence of* their exposure to a wide spectrum of reactions ranging from positive to negative, these discourses have revealed the dynamic nature of modernity and led to a spatial turn[2] accompanying interdisciplinary de-territorialization. Based on a common understanding of discourses of postmodernism, their most resolute quality is to have highlighted 'the present' of modernity by the use of the prefix 'post' beyond the so-called contrastive and contrapositive approach. At the same time these discourses have attempted to reveal the horizon of the conflict between continuity on one hand and discontinuity on the other, constituting dualistic phases of history that could fall into the trap of modernism with just one false step.

What is important here is, whether discourses of postmodernism swung to the continuity phase or the discontinuity phase, they were already out of range of modernism based on a linear view of history and free from the schemata of 'structure and subject' and 'center and periphery' which were major features of modernism. Come to think of it, whether Giddens (1990), Beck et al. (1994) or Harvey (1989), all tried to transcend the emerging conflict between continuity and discontinuity and to elucidate it according to the process of interpenetration between rejection and reversal.[3] If such attempts have managed to reach the depths of modernity, it was made possible by clever avoidance of the abovementioned schemata. In other words, they have in essence refuted the argument that an opposing reaction to modernity was automatically generated whenever it reached the critical phase/final stage, be it rejection or reversal.

The main aim of this chapter is to reveal the state of modernity, which historically has a highly equivocal character based on the modern mechanism of space and time, and discover the source of social potential inherent in it. In addition, the transformation phase of modernity under globalization is explored in light of the contemporary situation in which reconsideration of a 'master narrative' is called for.

Ambiguity of modernity

The following statement made by Baudelaire drew my attention for its significant contribution in explaining the equivocality or ambiguity of modernity.

> By "modernity" I mean the ephemeral, the fugitive, the contingent, the one half of art whose other half is the eternal and the immutable. (1981: 12)

What is suggested by this statement that is seemingly very tautological is the ambiguous nature (of modernity) beyond the question of whether postmodernity is one form of modernity or its negative aspect. It highlights through postmodernity the state of modernity as being a paradoxical whole.[4] Incidentally, the nature of the ambiguity/ equivocality (equivocality to blur dichotomy, in a way) of modernity becomes clearer when we look back to Western European modernity, which was the starting point/primordium of modernity.[5]

While it is not easy to describe the state of Western European modernity with clarity, it is undeniable that it held a strange balance between nostalgia for classical and ancient times and assimilation into something homogeneous, such as progress or evolution (usually related as a moral of the Protestant ethos). Take Descartes, for example; he is often referred to as the founder of modern rationalism but he attained universal rationality and rational subjectivity in his attempt to find clear evidence of Aristotelian rhetoric. He laid his hand on the door of modernity while dipping his feet deep in the classics. Western European modernity was really a multi-faceted and multi-layered historical ensemble which moved forward as it stepped backward. Another of its characteristics was that this duality or ambiguity was set on a sympathetic relationship involving multiphasing and segmentation between the elite class immersed in dialogues with the classics and those in the substratum of society who had planted their roots firmly in daily living without turning to the classics and established another way of life different from that of the elite.

However, our usual image of Western European modernity has been the 'modern age' which was guided by the French Revolution and the Industrial Revolution and evolved into something of a developmental stage. When it was given a universal historical position, civil society, which was moving forward while carrying the middle ages on its back, had no choice but to seek refuge with the project of the 'modern age' so as to shed itself of a very 'Western European' ethnicity and historicity and homogenize the whole based on a time axis converted from rationality. What provided this modern practice with veneer and foundations was the modernistic aesthetic sense that was only comprehensible to the elite, and the logic and imagination of the everyday lives of people in the social substratum were largely blocked/distorted by this projection. Thus, modernity was established as a 'totality, some set of thoughts and practices having enough in common over space and time to encourage us to generalize' (Cooke 1990: 4). At the same time, Western European modernity as a multi-layered space containing multiple historical experiences retreated to the background of society. It can be said that Western European modernity bolstered by the glorification of progress and ideologies of industriousness and frugality became 'something eternal and unvarying' and enveloped/defined modernity other than Western European. Needless to reiterate, 'the concerns of minorities, local identities, non-western thinking, a capacity to deal with difference, [and] the pluralist culture' (Cooke 1990: x) were depreciated or disregarded in this constellation. For example, the only position given to an 'Oriental' being was that of the other. In other words, a discourse about its being was permitted solely in relation to Western European modernity as the only regime.

However, the present world in which we live appears to be witnessing a definite fading of such modernity stemming from the Western European form, or in a way, experiencing a radical discontinuity from such modernity. In fact, what has emerged extensively after the disconnect is the sentiment 'to close the gap between high and low culture, to communicate in symbols which the untutored citizen may be better able to understand and enjoy, and, above all, to replace the monolithic, homogeneous universality [...] with a more heterogeneous, locally sensitive and inclusive language which entertains as it parodies the pretensions of the past' (Cooke 1990: 109).[6] It is widely known that criticism for radical Orientalism, cultural studies and microhistory study have gained momentum in the meantime in conjunction with, or in support of, such sentiment.[7] Nevertheless, is this trend sufficient proof that the aforementioned discontinuity is in fact the same as that highlighted in certain quarters of postmodernism? This question must be considered carefully because the observed discontinuity, going hand in hand with the continuity, appears to constitute none other than the ambiguity of modernity. Let us now consider this in light of temporal and spatial experiences of modernity.

Modernity and temporal and spatial experience (1)

As we have seen so far, there have been various discourses about the 'knowledge' of Enlightenment that is heir to Western European modernity that have been built upon the denial of its inherent duality or ambiguity. If we are to use one transcendent rhetorical device, they can be converged on a 'master narrative'—an 'endless narrative' constantly swallowing up 'new narratives'—used by Lyotard in his *La Condition Postmoderne* (1979). It can also be said that this master narrative is made up of various elements such as hierarchy, mastery/ logos, creation/totalization/synthesis, genre/boundary, hypotaxis, signifier, *grande histoire*, master code, origin/cause and determinacy as suggested by Hassan (1985). Historically, however, it was no doubt contemporaneous with the formation, development and spread of the modern nation-state and could not have existed without the emergence/involvement of a theory that favored the nation-state as the 'arbiter of important social changes' (Appadurai 1996: 4).[8]

The characteristics of time-space perception of the Enlightenment that emerged hand in hand with this trend can be summarized as follows:

> More than anything, it has been pointed out that it was based on homogeneous time (objective time) and "unequivocality" of space. The Enlightenment mythology, established as the concept of modernity, espoused "a linear, homogeneous and continuous time" (Bourdieu) that was in itself within the Newtonian view and severed time from social time and prompted "the breaking down of time into small units," "the timetabling and mathematization of social lives" (Lash and Urry) and after all, the development of Greenwich Mean Time. It gave absolute priority to "clock-time," which was perceived as change from an orientation to task to an orientation to time by Thompson following Sorokin and Merton. At the same time, it developed space from an "accurate map" (Harvey) based on the exclusion of "otherness" and backed by "cold rationality" which vanished the rich diversity of trajectories/spatial narratives of discontinuous (atypical) practices into the "continuous space of geometry" (Bourdieu). This perception of Enlightenment unmistakably represented a quality of "totalization" and the "tyranny" of perspectivism. (Yoshihara 2002: 18)

The origin of homogeneously flowing 'absolute time' and 'continuous space of geometry' at the core of this time-space perception of the Enlightenment can be traced back to the Age of Discovery. This was the beginning of an age when the world and time were divided into equal parts while church-woven time and worker-woven time clashed with each other. It was the arrival of a 'world in which the distance between cities was determined based on measurable distance units and human time was measured by mechanical clocks' (Matoba 2007: 34). It should be noted again that 'absolute time' and 'continuous geometric space' thus conceived spread in perfect agreement with national integration/division and territorialization by the nation-state, and therefore these aspects themselves had the effect of making people's bodies pulsate to the 'center–periphery' rhythm.

By the way, Benedict Anderson (1983) and others have already argued lucidly that the above 'absolute time' and 'continuous space of geometry' were the fundamental factors in the imagining of the nation and the dissemination of the nation as a form and therefore

I shall not go into detail here. I would simply like to discuss this briefly in relation to the creation of Modern Japan. It can be said that 'continuous space of geometry' and 'absolute time' greatly contributed to the formation of the nation-state narrative through the creation of a national territorial space beginning with cartography at the end of early-modern times and the embedding (physicalization/regularization) of the clock-time mechanism in people through the media (fields) of factories, schools, the military and cities respectively (Yoshihara 2004).[9] In any case, 'absolute time' and 'continuous space of geometry' in a sense played major roles in locating people in the enclosure of 'nation' without achieving social integration.[10] Come to think of it, the aforementioned elements of modernity proposed by Hassan, which have been extracted as things 'eternal and unvarying' by Enlightenment 'knowledge,' also converge on the 'center and periphery' movement of the nation-state for which 'absolute time' and 'continuous space of geometry' are decisive/operative factors.

The fact that the abovementioned temporal and spatial perception of the Enlightenment originates in a dualism that separates natural and social time and, after all, nature and society, becomes an issue is because the one powerful predisposing factor for the tendency of Enlightenment 'knowledge' toward a linear developmental model can be found right there. It is also apparent that this is an underlying cause of the 'bias towards time without space' (Soja 2003) of epistemological dominance[11] at the base of the 'structure and subject' approach. Setting aside the details, it serves as the starting point both in tracing the origins of an approach that views the temporality and spatiality of social life as something neutral and homogeneous/uniform, and in searching for the source of 'the political metanarratives of emancipation' guided by 'the rational individual or centered subject whose imagined autonomy'—'Enlightenment rationality'—is a 'being-outside-the-world,' so to speak (Poster 1990: 14–18).

A further inquiry into the time-space perception that gives an absolute and privileged status to both time proceeding at a uniform and constant speed and dead, solidified space will no doubt take us to the dark shadow of Enlightenment 'knowledge' and the dichotomy[12] deeply rooted in such 'knowledge.' This situation can be found in the perspective of 'totalization' based on the schema of 'structure and subject' in the most intensive form, but the most important property of Enlightenment 'knowledge' is actually apparent in the fact that 'structural conflict or strategic conduct were conceptualized as internal to each society, whose boundaries were coterminous with the nation-state' (Urry 1995: 3) unveiled under this perspective. As aptly pointed out by Poster (1990), however, the subject assumed by the perspective of 'totalization' is now in flux. At the same time, the experience of time that has been deemed as singular quantitative change or event transition is now recognized as highly variable and, together with a stronger sense that space is filled with contradictions, the argument focusing on 'spatiality' is gaining force. We shall look at how it actually manifests itself in the next section.

Modernity and temporal and spatial experience (2)

Lately, there has been much talk about the temporal and spatial senses of people who are not necessarily connected with the temporal and spatial perception of the Enlightenment discussed thus far. As the movement of people and images and the electronic media are gaining critical importance especially under advancing globalization, people are becoming aware of the existence of multiple constellations of time and space outside of the rhythm and history of their own society and coming to understand the diversity of 'lived time'[13] by sensorially sharing the paths and patterns followed by various societies at various times. In the context of my earlier discussion, this parallels the weakening of people's fixation on the territorial of the nation-state (i.e., de-territorialization but more importantly, there is a deepening of the perception under these circumstances that modernity is highly heterogeneous in an historical sense. In short, it is the perception that the 'global cultural economy has to be seen as a complex, overlapping, disjunctive order' (Appadurai 1996: 32).

Needless to say, with the deepening of these perceptions, doubt is cast upon the aforementioned argument that globalization will lead to a loss of local cultures.[14] In addition, the advance of globalization has prompted a reexamination of the argument that time is increasingly sped up, rationalized and used as a scale for measurement (clock-time) and that consequently time as a social interaction, so to speak, of people living subjectively through it will be damaged—the argument that the shrinking of the world by globalization will expand a uniform and standardized space which will swallow up sensorily and qualitatively living 'spatial time' connected to human bodies.

In reality, the situation in which 'the isomorphism of people, territory, and legitimate sovereignty that constitutes the normative character of the modern nation-state is itself under threat from the forms of circulation of people characteristic of the contemporary world' (Appadurai 1996: 191) is cultivating an awareness of time that is passing 'plurally.' With this increasing awareness, theorists are showing a deep interest in the theoretical position of Heidegger (1929) who considers that man is fundamentally a temporal being who tries to find meaning in the temporal characteristic of being; or that of Bergson (1889) who sees time as 'time of becoming' and connected to the physical; or that of Mead (1959) who focuses on time embedded in actions, events and roles and emphasizes 'the emergent of the present' in *The Philosophy of the Present.*

These positions can be summarized as an inquiry into 'internal time.' This can be roughly described as follows in terms of what Husserl (1966) proposes as the phenomenology of internal time, for example. The past reproduced in the memory is stored as the re-written memory of the present, not as a certain fact of the past. Similarly, the future exists as something that *changes as the present changes*, not as something transcendental that is autonomous from the present. Such 'internal time' is of course clearly different from 'absolute time'/'external time' equally divided into the past, the present and the future. It is not derived from the chronological question of where to draw lines between past, present and future. The past acts like, say, a drawer from which the present can freely take out and put in. The future is something that can only be realized by the present. In this way, 'internal time' is deeply set in the present, which is people's 'lived time' (Matoba 2007).

The above trend in relation to the perception of time naturally also laps against the perception of space. In terms of globalization, it manifests as the perception that the uniformization and homogenization of space are taking place, heavily mixed with internal differentiation and segmentation and expressing multiphase and non-isomorphic properties. By the way, the multitieredness of space highlighted in this conceptualization is variously interpreted. For example, Harvey (1989) includes the diversity brought on by the reinforcement of locales by capital in the multitieredness of space[15] and Bachelard (1957) includes differentiation that bestows the quality, not the quantity, which flows homogeneously against time. Alternatively, Lefebvre (1991) sees space as a carrier of meaning rather than a 'blank page'[16] and states that it not only arises in the midst of social activity but also reproduces it. Urry expands on Lefebvre's view and argues that space is not a simple 'space' but all sorts of spaces, and after all, involves spatial relations and spatialization. In any case, what has come to occupy the center of people's perception is a space with movement, propinquity, idiosyncrasy, sensation, symbolism and meaning—what Massey (1994) calls 'spatiality.'

The new point of discussion here is how to define place or placeness in relation to the differentiation and multitieredness of space as we have seen above. Such discussion has been active in recent years, with, for example, Harvey (1989) characterizing place as a place to attract capital and Tomlinson (1999) defining it as a countervailing base against globalization—'home' and 'living room.' However, place or placeness here implies locality described by Appadurai as follows along the lines of Massey's 'spatiality' above.

> I view locality as primarily relational and contextual rather than as scalar or spatial. I see it as a complex phenomenological quality, constituted by a series of links between the sense of social immediacy, the technologies of interactivity, and the relativity of contexts. This phenomenological quality, which expresses itself in certain kinds of agency, sociality, and reproducibility, is the main predicate of locality... In contrast, I use the term "neighborhood" to refer to the actually existing social forms in which locality, as a dimension or value, is variably realized. Neighborhoods, in this usage, are situated communities characterized by their actuality, whether spatial or virtual, and their potential for social reproduction. (Appadurai 1996: 178–179)

It is considered that the reality of place or placeness emerges as part of 'spatial time' or 'lived time.' The key point of such discussion is, needless to say, the perspective from which to see modernity not as a mere transition from 'one state' to 'another state' under the historical understanding that 'the very epoch of the nation-state is near its end' (Appadurai 1996: 19), that is, progressive historical time, but as a 'complex, multitiered and divergent order' adrift between the two.[17] From this perspective, place can no longer be anything but 'non-place.' However, the equivocality or ambiguity of modernity has not been elaborated adequately even in this position. I shall examine this in the next section.

Reflexivity of modernity and its destination

As it has become clear from our discussion so far, 'absolute time' and 'continuous space of geometry' prevailed as modernity advanced but 'spatial time' and 'lived space' continued to exist and strengthened their influences as they went in parallel with or alongside 'absolute time' ('linear time') and 'continuous space of geometry' ('homogeneous and uniform space') in 'the present' of modernity. Whether to call 'the present' high modernity or hyper modernity or late modernity is not particularly important here.[18] What is required here is the confirmation that the 'spatial time' and 'lived space' that are attracting close attention in 'the present' have not been attained by following a path built on the denial of 'absolute time' and 'continuous space of geometry' but, if anything, rose up reflexively in recurrent clashes and through merging with the latter.

The point of this discussion is, again, the fact that reflexive 'spatial time' and 'lived space' may not simply regress to times prior to modernity colored by Enlightenment 'knowledge.' Rather, they remain rooted in time-space dynamics, which were not inherited by modernity. 'Spatial time' and 'lived space' at least span a far longer period than what is usually called the modern age, and the aforementioned dynamics is considered to continue/operate in the substratum even in 'the present'—a comprehensive and historical transition period in which globalization is developing literally globally. Needless to say, the horizon of conflict between continuity and discontinuity and the process of interpenetration between rejection and reversal mentioned at the beginning of the chapter start making sense only in this context.

Let us take Maffesoli's 'communities of the emotional and affective dimensions' as an example. 'They are usually understood in the postmodern context of network (personal connections) formation based on the structuration of habitus of large cities' (Hotta 2002: 18) on the premise of the redundancy of individualism. They are themselves founded on 'spatial time' and 'lived space.' Although Maffesoli himself refers to 'communities of the emotional and affective dimensions' as 'tribes,'[19] it does not mean a return to the so-called community in which imagination as a collective social fact operates dialogically with rituals and creates daily social norms (1991). As Appadurai says, 'communities of the emotional and affective dimensions' are rather peculiar to a post-electronic society found in 'the mutual contextualizing of motion and mediation' (1996: 5).

Yet, the imagination central to 'communities of the emotional and affective dimensions' has been carved and polished through practices of daily living that have preceded and survived social domination by 'absolute time' and 'continuous space of geometry,' that is, habitual daily activities that people practice physically. Imagination of course existed as something unique to the special space of expression of brilliant individuals in the age commonly referred to as pre-modern. In the comprehensive historical transition period of 'the present,' it existed, and still exists, as something pervading the consciousness in the daily lives of ordinary people. The difference is not important. What is important is the understanding that the imagination found prior to the bordering by the nation-state and that found in the current age of de-bordering certainly have different forms of expression, but they are connected at the substratum level of social form. In any case, there is no doubt that 'communities of the emotional and affective dimensions' is an expression of one narrative of time and space woven by individuals, groups, states and societies on the horizon of conflict between the continuity and discontinuity of modernity or with the process of interpenetration between the rejection and reversal of modernity; and it is in itself a representation/appearance of modernity that is a 'complex, multitiered and divergent order.'

It is also true, however, that the aforementioned reflexivity of modernity is becoming less obvious at the current stage where globalization is progressing *beyond* the level of global development and entering a 'state of history' which no longer conceives any alternatives. Now, globalization at least appears to have completely engulfed a 'complex, multitiered and divergent order,' which is one alternative introduced by the narrative of enlightenment and progress. This alone appears to make the advancing Western European modernity, or the narrative of enlightenment and progress, all the more conspicuous again. It can be said that a 'master narrative' bringing the whole world in severe competition is developing without any distortion, that is, in a purified form under 'the present' of modernity.

As is clear from the above discussion, globalization has demonstrated the very ambiguity of modernity (a post-electronic society is one example) by placing the 'master narrative' in the foreground of society while nurturing the collectivity that restricts its self-indulgent development from within. In the end, however, globalization has taken a more purified form in which the former denies the latter or the former permits the latter to have only minimal substance. Therefore, in view of the current situation in which globalization has developed across the board in the form of neoliberalism and, as Harvey (2005) points out, the crest of the wave has reached as far as China, it cannot be completely wrong to think that only the original, first narrative of enlightenment and progress, that is, 'absolute time'/'external time' and 'continuous space of geometry,' has survived. However, as will become apparent from discussions in the following chapters, the reflexivity of modernity has not been extinguished by the 'master narrative.'

In closing

I would like to make some remarks about the problematic involving positionality when establishing our perspective on the ambiguity of modernity based on the above discussion.

First of all, the disciplination or bordering of 'knowledge' which took place along the development and dissemination of modern progressive thinking has run into a wall. Come to think of it, the 'theory of totalization' led by Enlightenment 'knowledge' was constructed on the basis of 'society' sharing the same borders as the nation-state and 'the rational individual or the centralized subject that have been imagined to be autonomous' as absolute prerequisites, and the disciplines functionally allocated by it have supported the so-called 'meta-narrative of liberation' or Messianistic utopia (Poster 1990). The schemata of 'structure and subject' and 'center and periphery' have also largely constrained/framed each discipline. Needless to say, however, it is gradually becoming more difficult to determine the *raison d'être* and scope of the 'theory of totalization' and the disciplines derived from it as various social norms and rules assumed by them are rapidly going out of date and, above all, society itself is turning into a simulation zone.

The next point that should be mentioned in relation to the above is that the validity of the schemata of 'structure and subject' and 'center and periphery' is being questioned sharply. This has already been pointed out in debates about Giddens' theory of structuration (1984) and Bourdieus's habitus (1977),[20] but the limitations inherent in the above schemata are undeniably as long as modernity is a paradoxical totality and a 'complex, multitiered and divergent' whole. The trouble is, there is not yet a clear alternative theory. The question now is how to establish a polynomial explanation grounded on the notion of flow or uncertainty, that is, chaos, rather than the notion of the past involving order, stability or systematicity, in the face of a world swept up in divergent and non-isomorphic global flows (Appadurai 1996). This is closely linked to the issue of how to reorganize the 'theory of totalization' using a fractal metaphor instead of a Euclidean narrative style. On this point, however, it is interesting to see the direction of the spatial turn mentioned at the start of this chapter, but it is still at a very early stage.

The final point I would like to emphasize is the impasse of the approach that sees the development of modernity as a successive process. For example, the 'new international division of labor' theory and the world-systems theory, considered to be the first to call the 'theory of totalization' into question, clearly cannot escape such an impasse after all. Their perspective on the experiential transformation of time and space by the action of capital is, in the end, still an external formularization and not free from the afterglow of the 'theory of totalization' (Yoshihara 2002: 7). Even an argument such as Giddens' high modernity that has been frequently referred to in the modernity debate is still under the heavy influence of the aforementioned successive approach.

Returning to the abovementioned reflexivity of modernity here, what needs to be developed is a retrospective approach that can close in on the dynamism of modernity that constantly goes backward whilst moving forward.[21] Of course, this is at this point only a possibility and several requirements must be met in order for such an approach to be developed. I shall mention just two of them for the moment. One is the development of a viewpoint from which the aforementioned horizon of conflict between continuity and discontinuity or the process of interpenetration between rejection and reversal of modernity can be interpreted in a reflexive/circulative manner. One of the keys in achieving this is the issue of how to treat the contingency of history. Using narratology as an analogy, this is related to the issue of how to extract another narrative that is visible through the gaps in one narrative. In short, it is necessary to affirm that history's contingency has opened and keeps open the possibility to choose/consider various narratives without being limited to the currently lived one.

In relation to the above, the second requirement entails the establishment of a method by standing in 'the present' of modernity to dislocate, text-dependently in the meantime, and reformulate the observed divergent structure and the phases of social experience constituted by fluid and indeterminate interactions. In connection with narratology, this will be pursued from the perspective of textual action theory but, in the meantime, I would like to state that the resolution of resentment toward various arguments about postmodernity (look at postmodern bashing of recent years!) is an urgent task.[22]

As the twentieth century was drawing to a close, twenty years after Lyotard declared 'the end of a master narrative' in his *La condition postmoderne*, Baudrillard pointed out that the world was still caught up in the postmodern problem formulation by stating, 'The whole problem is one of abandoning critical thought, which is the very essence of our theoretical culture, but which belongs to a past history, a past life' (1999: 17). Come to think of it, we are certainly faltering in the midst of this question.

In the chapters that follow, the equivocality or ambiguity of modernity is analyzed from various angles based on the current state of spatial turn and 'the present' of globalization. The diversity of surfaces exposed in the analysis is ultimately the diversity of modernity. At the same time, some pathways to develop social theory as spatial theory should be revealed. While there is a profusion of various flowers in the field of spatial theory, they are all growing from a rhizome that is modernity itself. However inept it may be, this thesis will attempt to demonstrate this problematic.

2 Between Regions and Fluids: On Metaphors of Globalization

> Social reality does not exist in the sum of people's behaviors, but in the overall pattern of situated behaviors. (Meyrowitz 1985: 42)

Introduction

Transition to the postcolonial era and a decline in the status of the nation-state accelerated considerably as globalization spread at the end of the twentieth century. This development was an alternative to modernity to some, and a sign that modernity had reached some kind of critical phase to others. In reality, globalization has been progressing under the influences of decisive factors such as a series of economic processes and the political ones that guide and accelerate them and has entailed an extremely irregular transfiguration of the time-space structure. Standing on the doorstep of the twenty-first century, Held asked whether globalization was 'a set of processes which alter the spatial form of social activity... [or] a fully developed global system' (Held (ed.) 2000: 170). While Urry later repeated that 'the global is often taken to be both the "cause" of immense changes and the "effect" of those changes' (2003: ix), Negri and Hardt (2000) discussed the trajectory of globalizing society heading toward the end stage of globalization in their highly controversial *Empire* as if in response to Held's question. According to them, the empire embodies a new sovereignty paradigm other than the modern sovereignty and exists as a consequence of the advancement of globalization. In other words, this new sovereignty is a single global order that replaces the nation-state and exerts unlimited pervasive control that is spreading across society. At the same time, Negri and Hardt theorize that the empire will give rise to a mobile 'other' called 'the multitude' (2000; 2004).[1] They clearly position globalization at 'the end of history' from the perspective of convergence theory. In their view, globalization is as a whole conceptualized as something of an inevitable, integrated mechanics, just as the empire is an absolute being 'outside of history.'

This view of globalization is hardly new. The perspective that there is a dichotomy between the global and the local and that the former will eventually swallow/eclipse the latter is an archetype of the above convergence theory. The view that addresses the global and the local in a so-called 'domination-subordination relationship' focuses only on the aspect of static interconnection between the global and the local and emphasizes either forced adaptation to globalization or liquidationist resistance/rejection by the local against it at most. However, such a simple dichotomous/lineal interconnection model, that is, convergence theory, of globalization has in recent years become less influential due to the emergence of a view focusing on the dynamism of globalization. Now, what is the actual state of discussion about globalization? And what are the current keystones and trends in globalization research approaches?

In asking these questions, it is of course essential to clarify the logical composition and analytical framework of the issue of globalization. The starting point is, however, how to go about interpreting the present, vivid state of world order. In other words, clarification of the logical composition and analytical framework is required as part of the task of highlighting the dynamic change mechanism of globalization and the resultant problematic. I shall address this point later. Firstly, let us look briefly at how globalization has been discussed to date.

Between the global and the local

To put it plainly, there have been competing positions surrounding globalization: one that simply affirms the present condition; one that flatly rejects it on ideological grounds; and one that sides with neither of these views and describes phenomena on an empirical basis (Held and McGrew et al. 1999).

The first position essentially views globalization as part of an inevitable process of social development that no one can resist. This is what Held and others call the 'hyperglobalist position' (Held and McGrew et al. 1999: 2) that considers market forces to be all-powerful promoters of the development of democracy. In this case, the free market and democracy are based on North American standards. This perspective unconditionally endorses informatization supported by new technologies ('scapes,' to be discussed later) and agents organized at the global level. It has the keystone of neoliberalism and is undoubtedly founded on the intersection where modernity is replaced by globality, but it continues to drag developmentalism and the mechanism of integration that are at the root of modernity.[2] Needless to say, the impacts of globalization on the local are seen only unambiguously from this position and the significance of deviations or distortions caused at the local level is ignored. In other words, this position accepts the global as given and sees that the local 'are transformed in linear fashion by this all-powerful "globalization"' (Urry 2003: x). From this position, described by Stewart as being caught in the 'trap of linearity' (1989: 83), 'globalization (or sometimes global capitalism) has come to be viewed as the new "structure," with localities, regions and so on as the new "agent"' (Urry 2003: 121).

The second position asserts that globalization is concealing the reality of the tri-polar world order by establishing global standards in parallel to North America's political hegemony and constitutes an ideological anti-assumption to the first position. This is what Held and others call the 'sceptic position' (Held and McGrew et al. 1999). It is at the other end of the spectrum (from the first position) in that it completely rejects North America's political hegemony underlying globalization which is completely affirmed by the first position. More significantly, however, is the distinction that the second position sees globalization as a mythology where the existing social framework is essentially maintained, whereas the first stance assumes that globalization is outside of the existing social framework. Still, it has a close but distant relation with the first position in that their structures of argument are not based on analysis of the changing reality; it is a mirror image of the first position.

In any case, the first position, which is an *ex post facto* view of globalization as something that has already *changed*, and the second view that flatly rejects the former are poles apart yet still situated on the same plane. By contrast, there is another position that proposes from a totally different logical plane that globalization is *changing* at this very moment. According to this third position, globalization exists as what Tomlinson considers 'the rapidly developing and ever-densening network of interconnections and interdependences' (1999: 2), which is something that is extremely unstable and full of unpredictable contradictions. It sympathizes with the first position only to the extent that it assumes the 'fluctuation' of the existing social framework. The difference between this position and the first in terms of their argumentation structure is far more marked than any similarity. Details aside, in the first position the ideology of neoliberalism is the antecedent condition and the reality is fitted into this framework. In the third position, the contingency of networks with unknown destinations is traced up from the level of empirical phenomena and, for example, the ideology of neoliberalism is reconciled with the reality *retrospectively*. Nevertheless, the difference between these two positions is not that simple. Let us focus for the moment on the aspect of connection between the global and the local in order to consider the meaning of this difference.

From the perspective of the first position, dominative global power is exerted on the local uniformly and homogeneously. However, as Beauregard aptly points out, the concatenation from the global to the local is not formed by a vertical static link alone; it rather originates in a number of spatial scales and is expressed through the medium of various actors that exist in each of the scales (1995). If such origination/mediacy of the spatial scales/actors does 'reorganize them [the multiple processes that we recognize as globalization] and redirect them toward new ends' (Negri and Hardt 2000: xv) as well as resisting globalization, the perception of the multistaged and multitiered nature of the concatenation between the global and the local is extremely important. However, this perception does not directly relate to the perception of the concatenation between the global and the local underlying the third position. We are reminded of what Urry calls a 'strange attractor' here. This entails 'parallel processes through which globalization-deepens-localization-deepens-globalization' (Urry 2003: 15). According to Urry, 'the global and the local are bound together through a dynamic, irreversible relationship, […]. Neither the global nor the local can exist without the other' (2003: 15).

Being somewhat relevant to the above perception, Kellner positions globalization as an amalgam of homogenizing forces and heterogeneity, variation or hybridity (2002). As the latter constitute the *basso continuo* of the third position, combined with Kellner's view this position is able to make a major contribution to the extraction of a dialectic momentum ('strange attractor') hiding behind the concatenation between the global and the local. On this very point, a definitive distinction is drawn between the third and first positions. Incidentally, the aforementioned notions (classification) of 'structure' and 'agent'[3] found in the first position are rejected in the third. Yet, this position itself also remains at the level of phenomenal description as mentioned above. It therefore has not fully developed an insight into the state of irregular constellation between the global and the local that is lacking in the first position.

Have the conflicts between these three positions, especially the first and third, revealed anything about globalization? To what extent have they shed light on its historical phase? These questions require further consideration. Let us address them from a slightly different point of view.

From regions to fluids

Urry deals with 'regions' and 'fluids' as metaphors of globalization in his *Sociology Beyond Societies* (2000). He argues that globalization is engaged in a competition with 'societies' over regions. In other words, globalization is seen as the conquest of nation-state/society bound regions by global economic and cultural regions. Urry points out that economic and social globalization is accompanied by a relative decline in the power of 'societies' that in this case have clear and controlled borders. The battles between global and societal regions are won by the former in the end. That is, some larger regions take over smaller regions called individual societies. Naturally, it is considered that actions and motives are also framed by a global culture released from the yoke of individual 'societies' rather than produced and reproduced within particular regional collectives. Incidentally, Urry later states that the metaphor of 'regions' overlooks a mutually constitutive relationship between the global and 'societies' and is caught in what Brenner calls a 'territorial trap' (Urry 2003: 44).

What is notable here is the assumption that global culture is highly homogeneous. In other words, it is envisaged that globalization is a narrative of cultural homogenization and integration. This is a distinct characteristic of the scholars who expound globalization using the metaphor of 'regions' to associate it with the 'American century.' This type of argument organized around the metaphor of 'regions' was more common in early stages of the debate on globalization.

However, in recent years this line of argument has quieted down considerably. What has taken its place in recent years is the position that explains globalization using the notion of 'fluids.' The center of attention concerning globalization has shifted to this position. The focus of this metaphor of globalization is literally on global movements. What draws Urry's (2000) attention in relation to these global movements is the development of infrastructure across societal borders and the computerization-driven technological advancement that promotes it. These technologies enable people, objects, money and images to flow instantaneously beyond the limits of regions, or 'societies.' According to Urry, these technologies that exist as a constant in globalization 'do not derive directly and uniquely from human intentions and actions. [They are] intricately interconnected with machines, texts, objects and other technologies'; and therefore, '[t]here are no purified social structures as such, only hybrids' (2000: 33).

In any case, the metaphor of 'fluids' that is interested in the flows of people, objects, money and images crisscrossing regions in nanoseconds and in an unpredictable manner has become predominant in the recent globalization debate instead of that of regions. In this metaphor, it is of course essential to assume that global movements/flows are extremely heterogeneous and fragmentary and have a high level of hybridity. Another point to note is that the transition from the metaphor of 'regions' to that of 'fluids' is simultaneously a transition from one of 'structure' to that of 'network.' Let us discuss this point briefly, once again based on Urry's argument (2000).

The metaphor of 'regions' assumes, in short, that societies have integrated institutions and clear and controlled borders. Needless to say, these societies are characterized by a closed structure consisting of vertical hierarchies and formal and informal elements. This characteristic gives rise to the metaphor of 'structure,' so to speak. Accordingly, the metaphor of 'regions' is interchangeable with that of 'structure.' Conversely, the metaphor of 'fluids' is clearly different in nature to that of a vertical and closed structure. As mentioned earlier, fluids relate to networks that are characterized by heterogeneous and unpredictable hybrid movements/flows. Therefore, the metaphor of 'fluids' is necessarily equivalent to that of 'networks.' Obviously, the focal point of the 'network' metaphor is on its dynamic and open structure. Details aside, Urry arranges this argument as above and effectively superimposes the transition from the metaphor of 'regions' to that of 'fluids' on the shift from that of 'structure' to 'network.'

It is clear that this attempt for a comparison of metaphors provides a certain frame of reference for the conflict between the first and third position discussed above. So, what new dimensions has this attempt added to our knowledge of globalization? Simply put, it has shed light on the facts of the momentum for de-territorialization and the hybridity of global flows at the social morphological level. However, a closer examination will reveal the existence of a historical phase that cannot be represented as a simple transition from territorialization to de-territorialization or homogenization to de-homogenization. We shall discuss this in the following sections.

From de- to re-territorialization (1)

We have already seen that, among four metaphors of globalization, 'regions' resonates with 'structure' and 'fluids' corresponds to 'network' and that in recent years the focus of interest has shifted from the former to the latter respectively. At the substratum of this interest are de-regionalization and the contingency and hybridity of 'fluids.' They may be similar in substance, but they have indeterminable directions and forms and are highly paradoxical. They entail borders that quickly appear and disappear and relations that never break but constantly change. The fact that these fluctuations and changes of borders and relations no longer represent differences between places makes the configuration of globalization extremely complex. For the moment, we shall discuss the contingency and hybridity of 'fluids' in terms of de-territorialization.

Firstly, the implication of de-territorialization based on the above discussion is the spreading of 'a world of mixtures' (Mol and Law 1994: 660), which is created by the acceleration of global flows of people, objects, money and images. This is the world of fluids, with no distinction between inside and outside and no beginning or end, where connect and disconnect easily occur. The progression of this condition firstly weakens the societal power called the state more than anything else. It becomes extremely difficult 'to draw together its citizens as one, [...] and to speak with a single voice' (Urry 2000: 36–37). Rather, de-integrative, multitiered and disjunctive orders emerge in and out of the existing societies and more forcefully prompt a decline of the state as well as the hollowing-out of existing societies. In other words, this condition is generated through the stimulus to '"de-totalise" each national society' (Urry 2000: 43) provided by the aforementioned pluralistic and contingent flows of various kinds that take/follow hypertextual patterns. Nevertheless, the state does not become completely powerless. In fact, it comes to play the important role of 'regulatory state.' '[S]tates increasingly act as catalysts of networks of countries operating at the regional or interregional level and hence function as one class of agencies in a more dynamic system of unpredictable global complexity' (Urry 2003: 110).[4]

By the way, the aforementioned de-territorialization is itself even more multifaceted. One particularly noteworthy aspect is that which is perceivable indirectly from the context of locality as non-place involving the transformation of social relations among people. We need to now pay attention to the advancement of de-territorialization that mainly entails the process of disorganization-reorganization of communities. It appears together with the expansion of all sorts of networks that bring distant events, places or people closer (Tomlinson 1999: Latour 1987)—for instance, a cosmopolitan network from below and afar that uses human shields as its main strategy in response to the al Aqsa intifadah, as noted by Gilroy (2005: 80). Castells describes this community disorganization-reorganization process as 'the displacement from community to network as the central form of organizing interaction' (2001: 127). Needless to say, the community referred to here is what Ingold (1993) calls the local community, which is characterized by clear territorial division, geographical proximity, cooperation based on sharing/blending of work/dwelling, and a sense of habitation rooted in the 'land.' Conversely, the network is a virtual community, or what Rose describes as communities that 'exist only to the extent that their constituents are linked together through identifications constructed in the non-geographic spaces of activist discourses, cultural products and media images' (1996: 333).

Needless to say, identities that have been derived from a close association with towns, villages and national borders and have always belonged to the national can no longer exist in this network/virtual community. Rather, the network/virtual community can launch across societal regions from the end point of the old local identity. For example, what Castells calls 'resistance identities' (1997: 356)[5] have been nurtured self-contradictorily in the womb of the global flows that are driving de-territorialization. Of course, various attempts are being made to revive local identities through impregnation of various ethnic traditions and indigenous customs *from above* against 'resistance identities.' It is curious that many of these attempts are also making full use of the machines and technologies of globalization.[6] I shall discuss this point later but in the meantime, let us take a brief look at the process of cultural organization/integration accompanying de-territorialization. As discussed below, this mainly entails transformations in human social relations.

According to Albrow and others who follow on from Appadurai, the foundations for the formation of social relations are not longer tied to traditional communities and there is an absence of localness in a hybrid space that is highly de-territorialized and inhabited by a jumble of insiders and outsiders (Albrow et al. 1997). To borrow Appadurai's expression, the struggle between cultural homogenization and heterogenization in this space generates complex, multitiered and disparate relationship modalities that are not embedded in communities at the level of individual and collective action. As is widely known, Appadurai explains these relationship modalities in terms of five cultural dimensions: ethnoscape, technoscape, financescape, mediascape and ideoscape (1996). What is important here is that these relationship modalities are deeply rooted in complex associativity created by cultural integration. This interpretation is of course largely constrained (defined) by an objective world observed by those such as Albrow and Appadurai. Nevertheless, it is clear that cultural integration that is severed from historical roots and conveyed through media constitutes the substance of relationship modalities that no longer form bordered regions.[7]

At the same time, it becomes apparent that these relationship modalities are taking on some kind of regionality when observed from another perspective. This situation is caused by the leakage of people's active and experiential-world out of the limited space of the local as a result of the collapse of local communities, that is, a phase shift from de-territorialization. I shall elaborate on this point below.

From de- to re-territorialization (2)

As mentioned above, Castells turned his attention to 'the displacement from community to network as the central form of organizing interaction' (1997: 356) as an activator for change in people's everyday social relations. According to him, this is the appearance of new sociability patterns rooted in individualism, and in addition, the emergence of new regional constellations from a concentration of this change in social relations and interconnections between places brought on by transport systems equipped with the latest computer networks/links and the like (2001). From here, Castells finds the codes of meaning generated by pluralistic communicative forms based on the interactions occurring at the intersection of the so-called 'space of flows' and 'space of places.' This understanding certainly departs from the notion of de-territorialization to highlight regionality generated by interactions, although at the social morphological level.

Conversely, another faction has emerged suggesting a trajectory from de-territorialization to re-territorialization from a different perspective to that forwarded by Castells. Advocates of this thesis adopt micro-phenomenological methods. One of them, Dürrschmidt, uses the concept of 'milieu' to describe some kind of regionality generated from human involvement in various situations (1997). The milieu here represents an aggregate of individual tendencies in the constellation of social relations and the actions of individuals who are engaged in various situations. According to Dürrschmidt, familiarity is fostered through repetitive use of certain communication routes in the process of integration between multiple places that occupy meaningful positions within the milieu. He devises the notion of 'familiarity' from the dimension of the subjective reconfiguration of place and does not necessarily use it to mean regionality connected to fixed space. It is clear, however, that Dürrschmidt's conceptualization is situated on placelessness and implies some kind of territoriality.

Whether it is based on social morphology or micro-phenomenological methodology, there are already some discourses foreseeing a move towards re-territorialization after de-territorialization. Come to think of it, both the third position in relation to globalization theory and the argument reliant upon the metaphor of fluids more or less appear to keep re-territorialization within theoretical range, only it is not as evident as in the aforementioned arguments of Castells or Dürrschmidt.

Here, I would like to once again ask what constitutes the key evidence for the occurrence of a shift from de- to re-territorialization. Based on our discussion so far, the answer would probably be placelessness and social relational regions. Placelessness referred to here signifies that one's living in a place is disconnected from the culture and history nurtured and marked by that place. Social relational regions signify fields of relations where various safety nets are constructed/reconstructed around such placelessness in order to satisfy the conditions of living in that reality. In such regions, various codes of meaning are exchanged mediated by cultures with different social-historical backgrounds, and they are constantly moving and changing. This is possible because places are not limited by any fixed spaces, or 'neither boundaries nor relations mark the difference between one place and another' according to Mol and Law (1994: 643). Some forms of organization that exhibit an extremely strong cohesive property such as that surrounding what Castells calls 'resistance identities' are in fact deeply rooted in placelessness and social relational regions.

At any rate, as de-territorialization is one of a diverse range of social forms brought about by global flows, re-regionalization is one of the social forms contingently brought about by de-territorialization in its own process of fluctuation. In this sense, an exploration of the shift from de-territorialized regionalization to re-territorialization will lead to a fundamental review of the framing of the 'from regions to fluids' question outlined above and furthermore, a deeper investigation of the problematic of 'a dialectic momentum hiding behind the concatenation between the global and the local' mentioned above. I have only briefly discussed the substance of the aforementioned shift here, and have only made a few remarks about its shape in a metaphorical dimension. Several issues in need of further consideration have been highlighted in doing so. I would like to conclude this chapter by touching on these points.

Conclusion

One point in need of consideration is that, while the social relational regions that are the cornerstone in the trajectory from de- to re-territorialization are assumed to constitute a so-called open system, they are fraught with the ever-present danger of reversion to a closed system. It is quite conceivable that social relational regions may suffer internal collapse as clear divisions based on class, hierarchy, race, ethnicity, region, gender and so on come into being and enclose them into geographical spaces in the form of ecological segregation or differentiation. In that case, 'differences' that are mutually accepted by people who are grounded in networks become something to be sorted and screened and must completely transform into distinctiveness. In fact, these reversals are beginning to become reality. It is interesting that these reversions resonate partially with the aforementioned attempts to rediscover local identities through impregnation of various ethnic traditions and indigenous customs *from above* (that is, *the other type of re-territorialization*).

There are many possible factors that are promoting sympathy between the reversal of re-territorialization and *the other type of re-territorialization*, but a series of risks brought forth by the abovementioned global flows appear to be a major influencing factor. Many people believe that these risks, described by Urry as 'the spread of AIDS [...] the growth of environmental risks [...] "nuclear monsters" [...] the loss of national sovereignty' (Urry 2000: 36) may be reduced but will never disappear. Consequently, many experience endless anxiety about these infinite risks which cannot be resolved by individuals. Surrounding this feeling of anxiety, social relational regions develop from sociation-type communities open to the outside and also nurture them on one hand while contributing to the formation of the reversal on the other. Because social relational regions are founded on unstable and unpredictable global flows, it is not impossible to understand that individuals become motivated to attempt to construct/re-construct all sorts of safety nets and at the same time develop a strong tendency to seek 'societies' that do not permit 'differences.'

At first glance this reversal, rooted in spatial heterotopy of placelessness and existing on its denial, does not appear to intersect with *the other type of re-territorialization*, that is, a tendency to seek local identities, traditions or 'authenticity' of place at first glance, but they are both situated on the same plane in that they are both opposed to assumptions against heterotopy. More troublingly, now there is a growing tendency to discuss both forms together, or re-territorialization and *the other type of re-territorialization* to be exact, as a set of 'new opportunities' or 'new activities' created by globalization (Urry 2000: 36–37). Details aside, this trend is symbolic of an extremely irregular relationship between the global and the local.

My second point in relation to the previous is the question of how to establish a logical composition and analytical framework for globalization. In this chapter I have attempted to shed light on globalization from the angle of metaphors. It is doubtful how successful this attempt has been, however much of this approach has been borrowed from Urry. Urry argued for the effectiveness of metaphors by quoting Lakoff and Johnson's theory that 'human conceptual systems are metaphorical in nature and involve an imaginative understanding of one kind of thing in terms of another' (1980: 194). I use metaphors in this chapter and many other parts of this book. Looking back at this point, however, I feel that metaphors alone cannot provide us with a fully realistic interpretation of the present, vivid state of world order; and unfortunately, the metaphorical approach does not reveal the logical composition and analytical framework of globalization very clearly.

As is apparent from our discussion thus far, the economic process and the political process that promotes it are the decisive factors of globalization. Whether it is the placelessness or social relational regions at the core of the above discussions, for example, it is impossible to deny that they are in principle structured and regulated by global relations that exist as mimicries of personal interests and predominant market relations. At the same time, it is true that they 'are richly filled with combined sensitivity of the body which is not always determined by the dictate of exchange value and the logic of the market' (Yoshihara 2005: 8). This multiple sensitivity is deeply involved in the case of Appadurai or Tomlinson mentioned above and acts as the source of imagination/practice for agents while functioning as a medium for 'the active' in the conscious action process. However, neither Appadurai nor Tomlinson consciously explore how this conscious action process is associated with the aforementioned economic and political processes. They only mildly sense that they may be connected by the presentation and signification of information technologies.

In this case, information technologies are substituted by the mediation function of a culture to formulate meaning codes. The culture's symbolization action appears, however, to have concentrated on the aspect of power, including guidance or persuasion 'from above,' and the aspect of interactions between variation and differentiation that underlie cultural integration does not appear to have been much discussed. Exploration of this feature would provide an extremely important moment for the clarification of the dynamic change mechanism of globalization based on the emergent that appears on the waves of various kinds of action or collectivity, in addition to the understanding of the logic that mediates the aforementioned economic and political processes and conscious action process. Incidentally, the emergent[8] referred to here can be considered, for the time being, as the following type of wave motion described by Zohar and Marshall in terms of physics as they observe the abovementioned nonlinear global order, where 'outputs provide inputs into a circular system' (Urry 2003: 16).

> Waves are "nonlocal," they are spread out across all of space and time, and their instantaneous effects are everywhere. Waves extend themselves in every direction at once, they overlap and combine with other waves to form new realities (new emergent wholes). (Zohar and Marshall 1994: 326)

This in fact resonates with what Urry describes as 'a huge array of islands of order within a sea of disorder' in reference to Prigogine (2003: x).[9]

Let us just say that the above problematic is one manifestation of pressing issues that need to be addressed in order to expand the applicability of metaphors.[10]

3 'Cities Beyond Society' and Postmodernization

> Being amid the changing city, being used to seeing the transformation, we don't take much notice of it and time passes through it. (Tayama 1981: 99)

'Neo-medieval society' and the emergence of empires

With the advance of globalization, the networks and flows that easily slip through porous national borders are appearing in the foreground of society. As globalization takes on the characteristics of a fluid consisting of 'complex mobile hybrids' (Urry 2000: 61),[1] the foundation of existence of 'society' that has been thought of as self-replicating is gradually being eroded so that a decline in the ability of 'society'/the nation-state to maintain its borders is becoming widely apparent. In this situation, 'the social' is being interpreted by reference to mobility instead of 'society' and the role of national citizenship, the public sphere and, above all, the state as 'coordinator' is being reexamined. People are taking renewed interest in the role of multiple 'performative citizenship' (Albrow 1997: 178), highly media-oriented public arenas, or the state that 'striate [delineate and sectionalize] [...] all of the flows traversing the ecumenon' (Deleuze and Guattari 1986: 59). (See Chapter Four for details.)

The above situation means, in plain terms, that the power of 'society' to unite citizens, give them a national identity and *speak in one voice* has declined, that is, the relationship between the nation, state and society has weakened. What is noteworthy is the emergence of the argument that the globalized world expanding in front of our eyes is a 'neo-medieval society' based on the recognition of this situation (Billig 1995: 20–21). According to this argument, the globalized world is regarded as a parallel to the medieval world of complex and mobile hybridity where multiple sovereignties and identities overlap and compete with one another. This argument unequivocally heralds the end of the paradigm of modern sovereignty.

By elaborating on the paradigm of imperial sovereignty that replaces the modern version, Negri and Hardt make the following points (2000). According to them, an empire exerts boundless control; it is a regime which invades every part of the 'civilized' world and is not subject to temporal constraints that only permit it to exert its control momentarily in the course of history. In other words, an empire according to this view is a regime that is situated outside or at the end of history and bears influence over all areas of social order by wielding its power to the depths of all social lives. Such an empire is described as a 'double eagle,' which is a legal structure/ power operated by the mechanism of life-politics (biopolitique)[2] as well as a pluralistic multitude consisting of multiple change agents. In describing empire this way, Negri and Hardt finally set their focus on change agents based on 'unity/diversity' or 'commonality/disparity' who 'reorganize them [the multiple processes that we recognize as globalization] and redirect them toward new ends' (2000: xv).

This point aside, I would like note that, in rivalry with the empires of the medieval world, 'new empires' such as Microsoft and Coca Cola and the cities teeming with their headquarters are increasingly drawing attention as fields incorporating various powers which may connect to multiple intersecting networks and social lives, interpret, absorb and rearticulate them and compete with one another and link with pluralistic language communities. Today, cities are re-'emerging'/ appearing with new social connotations under dynamic relationships between various processes of globalization.

Globalization and urban restructuring

Since the 1980s, globalization swept across many areas of not only economics but also politics, society and culture. As far as its impacts are concerned, the destructive, negative and marginalizing aspect has been emphasized as much as its innovative, positive and dynamic feature. Nevertheless, there is already an almost common understanding of the restructuring which took place when cities left the general framework of one-country–one-society and turned towards a world society lured by globalization. I shall present the arguments of Castells and Sassen to provide an example of such an understanding.

Firstly, Castells (1989; 1996) argues that economic restructuring is not possible without progress in the informational mode of development for which information processing activity in various production, distribution and management processes is of critical importance. He explains the appearance of 'space of flow' which achieves interactions between various organizational units via a series of communication flows while driving decentralization of economic and social organizations and centralization of decision-making and knowledge-creation activities simultaneously under the informational mode of development. What Castells calls 'informational cities,' or world cities, are situated at these nodal points in information networks which overcome the need for spatial propinquity and enable the global-scale decentralization of business activity. The most significant characteristic of these informational or world cities can be found in their 'structural duality' which is represented by: (1) non-complementary processes of 'informational growth' and 'industrial decline' (a mismatch between the gradual abolition of labor and the demand for new labor); (2) the information-based formal economy and the 'relegated work'-based informal economy; and (3) a polarized occupational structure within the advanced service and high-tech sector.

Sassen (1991) introduces a similar understanding and key concept (service intensive mode of production) to that of Castells and presents a 'global city' argument in a more refined form aligned with New York, London and Tokyo. According to Sassen, global cities are, first of all, cities in which a high concentration of giant multinational corporate headquarters is found and the signs of global economic restructuring are appearing, intensely exhibiting the following characteristics. That is, global cities are the 'control tower' with a high intensity of top-level decision-making and management tasks and act as the 'center' where essential producer services of the international financial core are traded and processed daily, raising such producer services to the status of new key industries. The cornerstone of this understanding is the fact that global cities are teeming with not only the corporations that manage and control their worldwide network of factories, offices and R&D facilities but also companies of various sizes which provide essential business and producer services to these corporate activities. This indicates that the condition of employment opportunities and labor demands expresses itself through an extremely polarized aspect of social restructuring in global cities situated at nodal points in the world's hierarchical urban system, formed according to the management strategy of multinationals called the 'new international division of labor.'

According to Sassen (1991), this new division of labor firstly manifests itself as occupational separation between highly paid professionals with a good command of high technologies in sectors such as finance, insurance and accounting, and bottom-level employees such as office cleaners and maintenance workers and providers of personal services to the aforementioned professionals. While the residential districts with high-wage technocrats undergo increasing gentrification, the areas inhabited by bottom-level workers—where a large influx of migrant workers usually occurs—are left out of development processes and fall into decay. In this way, this polarization trend in employment opportunities and labor demands in the producer services sector is deeply embedded in the spatial structure as the 'center and periphery' geography of global cities. Sassen's position resonates with Castells' aforementioned argument, however its notable feature can be found in its attempt at a retrospective examination, in a spatial dimension, of the state of social restructuring occurring in parallel with its economic counterpart. If we suppose that the stratification surfacing in cities today entails not only an economic gap but also lifestyle differences, a division of social interactions as well as spatial habitat segregation, then Sassen's 'global city' argument does provide a prototypical theory on stratification.

What draws our attention here is the fact that these informational cities/global cities have been, and are still being, formed by way of the creation of accumulation spaces under neoliberal policies. It is now obvious to everyone that what underlies informational cities/global cities is the market principle governed by profit-maximizing multinationals and a series of neoliberal policies that support it. In fact, what we see through informational cities/global cities are the spreading of 'flexible production' and the reorganization of industrial relations in the form of a capital offensive against labor. The endless labor-market deregulation, large-scale wage and employment restructuring and, above all, weakening of income distribution effect due to the abandonment of welfare states make it inevitable that progress in the polarization of complex and various divides is etched into the bodies of informational cities/global cities.

From 'cities within society/the state' to 'cities beyond society'

Informational cities/global cities are infused with neoliberal policy trends and contain multitiered and segmented polarization: how do they stand as they are surrounded by the 'informational mode of development'/'service intensive mode of production' that permeates all corners of the world? The first thing that comes to mind in relation to this question is the fact that cities have for a long time functioned as joints/links which organize national societies hierarchically and topographically under the modern nation-state system. Let us elaborate on the 'cities within society/the state' derived from this formulation.[3]

It is a matter of common knowledge that the modern nation-state has been built on self-sufficient labor organization within a single national economy and has 'centralized' various divisive factors in it and dissolved them into the 'uniformity and integration' movement. Within this nation-state, the fantasy of national society was nurtured and various moves toward differentiation and hierarchization within society were integrated into the 'nationalization of civil society.' The so-called 'civil public sphere' played an important role in this process of integration. Specifically, it took the form of intermediate groups connecting the modern civil society and the political state, including public institutions such as labor unions, employers' associations, professional associations, churches, local governments and political parties, and traditional collegial organizations represented by local communities, families and religious organizations, and provided forums for the alleviation and adjustment of various private and interclass disagreements and conflicts in civil societies (Saitō and Iwanaga 1996: 246–247). Cities performed a greater function as the 'integral institution' (Yazaki 1963) or the 'nodal institution' (Suzuki 1957) formed on the 'civil public sphere'[4] rather than on a simple locational medium. Incidentally, Urry's comment that the city has become a metaphor for a structure which 'involve[s] a center, a concentration of power, vertical hierarchy and a formal or informal constitution' (2000: 33) is easier to understand in this context.

Society's hierarchical order was certainly carved into its regional structure quite clearly in the modern urban spatial structure. For example, the 'downward explosion of world cities' described by Engels in *The Condition of the Working Class in England*, or the 'zone of transition' commonly addressed by the early Chicago School, shows that the divides of cities are marked by classes and hierarchies. However, the situation did not develop into the complete dismantlement of cities basically because of a certain level of progress made in social policies and beneficent social reform for poor-relief measures according to the logic of 'uniformity and integration' and the maintenance and preservation of the aforementioned 'civic public sphere.' In other words, the (internal structure of the) city as the 'integral institution' was partitioned and joined together within a single national society. This is why the resultant division of areas of habitation did not turn into the mobilization of an entire society. Modern cities were 'cities within society/the state' after all.

The configuration of 'cities within society/the state' did not easily break down while the metropolis remained inside the framework of the mechanics of modernity, even during the 1950s and 1960s when suburbs, created by the 'division of labor between monopoly capital and the state' (O'Connor 1973) as a form of built environment in advanced industrial countries, prompted segregation in the metropolis while exploiting poor urban centers. Or at least, the pattern of conflict in 'affluent suburbs and poor urban centers' peculiar to the metropolis was dissolved into a growing and expanding frame of the metropolis itself as the logic of 'uniformity and integration' and 'equality and development,' that is, a Fordist adjustment framework, functioned effectively.[5]

What provided a vital transformational impetus to the 'cities within society/the state' which were locked in the cycle between 'center and region' or 'center and periphery' taking place within the framework of a single sovereign state was none other than globalization. With the advancement of globalization, it became difficult for the 'society'/nation-state to maintain its borders as before and the boundaries of the axes of conflict that existed within the framework of nation-state began to fluctuate. Thus, the foundation of the 'center-region' or 'center-periphery' structure that had persisted as a 'domestic phenomenon' was undermined. In this situation, cities, especially those which have transformed into informational/global cities, have found themselves on a plane where various networks in the transnational social space are loosely intertwined and integrated as the role of the nation-state diminishes. On this very plane, the 'space of flow' mediated by multiple networks of the air and electrons is created and, through this creation, globalism by which distance and territorial expanses are instantaneously dissolved is nurtured while the cities themselves are decontextualized and hyperspatialized. In any case, 'cities within society/the state' underpinning the centralized planned authoritarian system can no longer survive and 'cities beyond society' containing the impetus for all kinds of conflict and synergy/cooperation and subsuming the states are leaping forward to replace them. 'Cities beyond society' thus emerge as the driving force for the 'de-totalization' of national frameworks on a foundation that is different from the configuration of the power/knowledge of 'cities within society/the state.'

When we consider the position of 'cities beyond society' in line with the changing role of the state (from the 'gardening state' to the 'gamekeeper state,' so to speak), we notice that it functions as a 'catalyst' for the disjuncture and eccentric articulation of the 'periphery' rather than a guiding light in the engulfing of the 'periphery' by the 'center.' 'Cities beyond society' are embedding their roots deeply at the points of intersection of various flows of people, images, information, money and so on that are expanding hypertextually, so to speak, irrespective of bordered 'society,' and at the stationary and mobile nodal points of machines, technologies and organizations which promote the formation of scapes[6] as they relay such flows. As a result, diasporas that are located at the 'periphery' and tend to be associated with victimization, forced deprivation or inward wounding from severe persecution, for example, in 'cities within society/the state' come to occupy central positions in 'cities beyond society' as global beings free from territorial boundaries, have full command of multiple languages and build bridges between the global and the local. This situation, which Cohen (1992) calls the 'diasporaization' of the world more than demonstrates the 'currency' of global cities which acts as the bases for heterogeneity, difference and the mobility of various things.

Of course, we must not overlook the fact that as their 'diasporaization' continues 'cities beyond society' are manifesting various divides that have not been seen in 'cities within society/the state.' 'Cities within society/the state' were saddled with various disparities and inequalities as mentioned earlier but these were basically 'domestic phenomena' attributable to the 'center-periphery' cycle. Incidentally, national citizenship played no small role in reducing such disparities and inequalities. However, 'cities beyond society' are developing many internal cracks because there is significant imbalance regarding access to various types of mobility and the configuration of social resources, and national citizenship is not always effective in alleviating these problems. (See Chapter Four for details.)

The advancement of postmodernization

In the sphere of 'cities beyond society' today, the condition of postmodernization is being generated in wide-ranging arenas. It is taking place extensively in cities as it expands what Castells calls the 'space of flow' and the mobilization of the subject. Let us briefly look at the way the 'space of flow' and the mobilization of the subject are made manifest.[7]

'Cities beyond society' exist also as 'informational cities' (Castells) that are equipped with various information and telecommunications tools. They turn themselves into a field of intersecting and accumulating databases by setting up ubiquitous networks organized by media technologies in all directions and promote the conversion of the demand-network system into a spectacle space. Here, while borderless and real-time communication has become possible, the penetration by decontextual and self-referential electronic media everywhere is altogether destroying intimate human relationships distinctively found in the traditional civil public sphere and forcing individuals into the darkness of isolation. For this very reason, people form their identities in urban space in the absence of communicative relationships with others by relying entirely on a set of information and telecommunications tools containing vast amounts of information and knowledge. In other words, '[h]uman powers increasingly derive from the complex *interconnections* of humans with material objects, including signs, machines, technologies, texts' (Urry 2000: 14; emphasis added).

In any case, because urban space creates the possibility of unforeseeable 'events' or new 'connections' on one hand and constantly severs social relations and shreds their surface structure on the other, it gives rise to the subject consisting of a consciousness and body that are standardized but constantly being dismantled, de-integrated/de-centralized and endlessly dispersed. While media technologies played an enormous role in marketing 'visual' and 'audio' communications and commoditizing desires, senses and even human bodies throughout the modern age as aptly argued by Yoshimi (1995), they are now driving the 'space of flow' and the abstraction of the subject to the extreme. This situation demonstrates the openness ↔ non-exclusivity inherent in a heterogeneous space that is rhizomatous rather than tree-like but, at the same time, entails increased surveillance unique to an amorphous and chaotic space as discussed below.

What looms out of all these factors is urban space as a hybrid with no apparent focal point, organizing principle or hierarchy (peculiar to 'cities beyond society') in which images are distributed at increasing velocities and social life is ever more governed by the media, and where the momentum for underlying contingent and disjunctive ordering is hidden. This occurs 'in between zones where all ties are suspended and time stretched to a sort of continuous present' (Braidotti 1994: 18). In urban space filled with de-territorialized mobility and 'an image of a complex of mobilities' (Lefebvre 1974: 93), it is the *planeur* (glider), not the *flâneurie* (stroller) that leaps onto the stage (Chambers 1990).

It is noteworthy that a condition called postmodernization is advancing along with the appearance of the 'space of flow' and the abstraction of the subject discussed above. According to Zukin, this condition can be understood as the space of 'liminality.' This space of 'liminality' is a landscape in which public and private, culture and economy, and place and market are harshly scrambled, and in each case the former is gradually being replaced by the latter (Zukin 1991). This refers to the 'built environment' resulting from what Barber calls 'malling' (Barber 2001) which promotes 'privatization'/ commercialization. At first glance this space appears to have the multifunctionality and multiutility appropriate for a public space but it is fundamentally a 'privatized public space'[8] in which a ruleless giant lump, or a super-high rise, has become 'the vernacular' (J. Saitō 2005).

Conversely, Harvey points to the mode of consumption in which '[t]he relatively stable *aesthetic* of *Fordist modernism* has given way to all the ferment, instability, and fleeting qualities of a postmodernist *aesthetic* that celebrates difference, ephemerality, *spectacle*, fashion, and the commodifications of cultural forms' (Harvey 1989: 156) as a projection/reflection of the condition of postmodernity under the flexible accumulation system. In this consumption mode, people wear T-shirts, listen to CDs, open web pages of organizations, purchase video clips of their idols and gradually give themselves over to a 'sense of vicarious or fluid "network-membership"' (Urry 2000: 44).

Actually, postmodernization taking place on this side of the Pacific Ocean is clearly different in its topology from that of the other side. For example, postmodern cities incorporating town walls are connected with rural villages through a common texture in France. CBDs with hordes of postmodern deco high rises strangely resonate with sprawling suburbia in the United States. In Tokyo, however, all the view corridors that had been preserved until the economic bubble period are now blocked and 'mall'-type spaces with mere cosmetic diversity or plurality proliferate. In fact, these spaces are spectacle spaces, as oft pointed out, but they only permit nonpolitical, authorized performances. As a result, postmodernization has created, for example, a landscape with the amorphous intersection of a glass-walled building (on the Yaesu side) and a stone-clad structure (on the Marunouchi side)

Photo 3.1: The Shin-Marunouchi Building viewed from the Yaesu side

Source: *Nikkei Architecture* (11 June 2007).

on either side of Tokyo Station which only amplifies a 'bleak urban landscape' with no vision or ideology (see Photo 3.1). The only thing found there is the arbitrariness of power that treats public space with embedded memories as if it were private property. Of course, this is done through the intermediary of so-called critical infrastructure connecting commodities and consumers such as editors, the media, architects and planners.

Despite these differences, however, the topology of postmodern cities found in 'informational cities'/'cities beyond society' is essentially 'a representation of landscapes formed by the supplantation of places by markets *through the cultural* and the erosion of public spaces by private spaces, and the borderless spaces of spectacle or simulacre characterizing it' are themselves the product of 'a social structure created by the system of flexible accumulation of capital' (Yoshihara 2005b: 158). One cutting-edge and symbolic phase of such topology of postmodern cities is gentrification. It virtually exists on the 'space of flow' as the deformed commoditization of space, the spatialization of consumption and the mobilization/abstraction of the subject.

The topology of gentrification

The term 'gentrification' referred to here certainly carries the common connotation of an 'upgrading' of areas around urban centers to become middle/upper class spaces through private capital, resulting in the displacement of the working class as well as the poor and migrants. More directly, however, it refers to the gentrification from the 1990s onwards which has been observed along with the advance of global-scale neoliberal urbanism.[9] Neoliberal urbanism is well characterized by the unchecked deregulation and privatization of urban services (i.e., re-marketization of 'the public' in the case of Japan) and underlies globalization, global cities and gentrification. This gentrification under neoliberal urbanism, with urban entrepreneurialism at its core, has developed and continues to develop in parallel with a relative weakening of the state's role more than anything else, and a strengthening of the relationship between local government and capital. It contains the process of raising the value of labor for elites such as yuppies (young upwardly-mobile professionals) to the extreme while lowering that for newly arrived informal workers to rock bottom levels.[10] For this reason, the more brightly and, oddly, flatly the gentrification is portrayed in cultural discourses and presentations, the less visible the minority becomes.

The phenomenon of gentrification has been a theoretical and ideological plateau on which numerous debates have been fought, with politico-economic analysis solely focused on the constructive effects of capital on the urban environment at one end of the spectrum and on the other end a postmodern perspective which finds aesthetic elements in 'urban spaces as works' as the subject of visual consumption. Now the perception that the process of gentrification, a cultural novelty in itself, is directly linked to the geography of globalization involving the political and economic reorganization of cities is suddenly gaining strength. In other words, gentrification is clearly recognized as 'one of the major "leading edges" of contemporary metropolitan restructuring' (Hamnett 1991: 174).

Again, this raises the question of 'postmodern geography' that lies unevenly at the base of gentrification. Postmodern geography mostly overlaps with postmodernization as discussed above but, according to Soja, it is an urban pattern that is 'fragmented yet homogenized' and 'confusingly arranged into a contingently ordered spatial division of labour and power' formed by an accumulation and concatenation of offices, malls and residences (Soja 1989: 244). This urban pattern inevitably required a mechanism to integrate fragmented social spaces, or a coordinating pattern, for this very reason. Soja locates this pattern in the formation of spaces from 'lived spaces' covered with many opaque layers, that is, the formation of 'compensatory spaces' created by adding virtual images and graphics to real spaces. The key to the formation of such 'compensatory spaces' is (an expansion of) the role of global capital and the neoliberal supply-based urban policies that support it, but the presence of urban inhabitants who sympathize with these factors by participating in the aestheticization of cities through visual consumption is also essential. Haraguchi points out that this is how 'complicity' between global capital and urban inhabitants in 'compensatory spaces' comes into existence (Haraguchi 2005).[11]

Today, multifunctional towns providing highly enjoyable migration opportunities are being created under this 'complicity.' No matter how magnificent, spectacular and fascinating they appear, or if like Disney World they appear to be 'the happiest place on earth' (Soja 1989: 246), they are after all towns where possessive individualism and fake freedom of choice reign supreme. Being 'a world of pseudo-satisfactions' (Harvey 2005: 170), these towns are hardly public spaces in substance. Tokyo Midtown, which opened in March 2007 based on the development concept of 'diversity on the green,' is an ultimate example. The premise/core concept of this complex is 'open network interactive,' meaning a gathering and exchanging of all sorts of people and information, as well as ' migration enjoyed on foot' derived from greenery[12] (Figure 3.1). However, these seemingly open and multicultural spaces are governed by the reinforced code of possession and are under security surveillance at every turn. In other words, Tokyo Midtown represents spaces minutely controlled by mechanical eyes and spaces filled with exclusivist desires to prohibit enclaves or ghettos which have emerged together with the advancement of neoliberal gentrification/privatization of public spaces. For this very reason, Tokyo Midtown can be regarded as an ultimate form of gentrification.

Figure 3.1: Tokyo Midtown

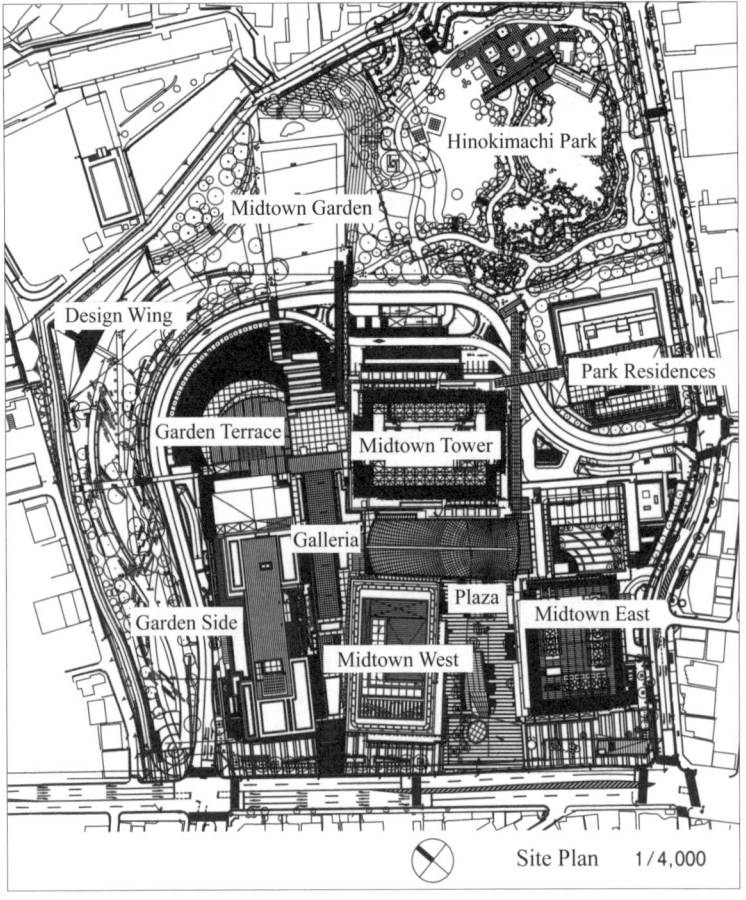

Source: *Nikkei Architecture* (11 June 2007, p. 29).

To regain 'dwelling'

It is clear from the above discussion that 'cities beyond society' are structured and regulated by global relations that are basically mimicries of private interests and dominant market relations and that the more dynamic and open the space is, the stronger the tendency for its inherent potential chaos (including polarization/division) to be interpreted as a risk to be controlled, and its removal becomes unavoidable. In the case of Tokyo Midtown, however, this is kept largely invisible, suggesting its 'leading-edge' position. Conversely, it is true that 'cities beyond society' have the potential to create new 'connections.' While the ambiguity of 'cities beyond society' found in their openness and exclusivity indicates their unpredictability and complexity, it also entails their appeal, which is their potential, at the same time.

Come to think of it, one of the major issues for the 'cities beyond society' is whether they are able to play the role of 'regulator' which turns the trend towards increasing social inequalities after the state's exit and increasingly multitiered polarization/division, and whether they can bring the hybrid networks of various sizes crisscrossing over these inequalities and polarization/division to the foreground of society. Frankly speaking, this is an extremely difficult task in light of the present situation thoroughly imbued with the machinations of neoliberalism. Details aside, the first thing that is required of 'cities beyond society' is, provided that they 'are equipped with a centrifugal vector to resist centripetal integration' (Saitō 2005: 145), to build a place which articulates diverse functions rhizomatously and acts as a strong foothold for fighting the privatization of cities and returning them to the public without falling into the trap of an excessively abstract sense of belonging or 'privatization' by what Sennett (1974: 337) calls 'intimate tyranny' or without denying the present condition of urban space marked by segregation and division. To achieve this, 'cities beyond society' must maintain their highly fluid tolerance of collective identification, then demand a place that guarantees the enjoyment of 'diversity' by everyone without limiting access to certain people. The construction/realization of what Arendt (1958: 57) calls 'the common meeting ground of all' now looms as the most important challenge for people living in cities. It is not that complicated. It means that it is important for people to meet total strangers or others and talk to people whom they have never met before.

The collapse of towns as a result of gentrification has led to the collapse of communities that are supported by the illusion of intimacy and identity. To coincide with the disintegration of these communities, cross-border, multi-constructional networks that are completely accustomed to a globalized perspective are emerging. Fortunately, there is an undercurrent of some form of 'synergy' in such networks which comes from the meeting and interacting of strangers. Of course, there has been no move on the plane of 'synergy' to prevent the instinctual drive of capital from turning all humanity into property or no sign of an emerging coalition of various ethnicities, classes or occupations to achieve this so far. However, we are now able to foresee a stage where mutual strangers immerse themselves in a mixed flow of conflicting beliefs, habits and tastes to cultivate culture over a long period of time and slowly open a path to publicness underpinned by what Sennett calls civility.

After all, although the 'cities beyond society' are situated amid the instinctual drive of global capital and the mechanism of neoliberal entrepreneurialism, they are preparing to move in the direction of non-capitalist, autonomic spaces based on 'dwelling (*l'habiter*),' so to speak, not corporate spaces whose operation is managed.[13] This is why we need to ask ourselves now how to regain and practise '*l'habiter*' within the multitiered and disjunctive structure of globalization.

4 'Global Civil Society' and Narratives of Place

...men are united more firmly by good will than by pacts, by their hearts than by their words. (More 1989: 87)

For reexamination of 'society'

Globalization is causing an unprecedented upheaval of not only sociology but all forms of 'knowledge' today. What is called professional 'knowledge' has in some ways been 'knowledge in a particular area.' In other words, it has been considered to occupy an exclusive and privileged place. Now, it has become difficult for 'knowledge' to find its own position in such an advantageous place. Rather, there is a deep need for it to step out of its position.

As for sociology, it has begun to redefine its own position as it conducts a fundamental reexamination of 'society,' which has been a given assumption, and locates mobility at the center of the sociological problematique. At the same time, de-professionalized 'knowledge,' which traverses the boundaries of individual professional 'knowledge' arenas in its inquiry into the global, has emerged and suddenly triggered speculation about its direction. People are turning their attention to what can be called the 'marginality' of 'knowledge' as 'society' crosses its borders. The challenge for this marginal 'knowledge' is to articulate disparate areas of professional 'knowledge' rather than to combine them.[1] In other words, it is strongly required to exercise *spécificité* instead of professionality.

By the way, the reexamination of 'society' has been conducted around themes such as 'center and periphery' and 'global and local' using keywords such as nation-state, public sphere and citizenship. Dichotomic views that the latter (periphery, local) would be swallowed up by the former (center, global) were predominant until very recently. These views have now retreated to the background or have been relegated to the margins. As shown by the prevalence of the view that the advancement of globalization (centralization) will deepen localization (peripheralization), the argument that emphasizes the complementarity and/or ambiguity of globalization and localization is becoming mainstream. There is another emerging argument which explains globalization using the metaphor of a fluid, that is, in terms of a series of symbiotic, conjunctive and unstable relations formed by flows of people, objects, money, information, images and so on, and in terms of the instantaneity/synchronicity/reflexivity of such relations. (See Chapter Two for details).

Based on this trend in sociology, this chapter will first discuss the state of 'global civil society' that is being whispered at its cutting edge in relation to the transformation of citizenship. Then, it will consider the current position of the local and place in which 'global civil society' is deeply rooted. In recent years, calls for the 'strengthening of place' have been heard from various sides but they tend to lack analysis of the dynamic relations surrounding globalization. This chapter will raise a reflective viewpoint on this tendency. While I recognize the need to mention the notion of 'virtual community' that has come under the spotlight in recent years, I shall only discuss it secondarily in the context of the reformulation of community.[2]

Global citizenship and 'global civil society'

From national to global citizenship

Globalization is being discussed from various angles. I shall thrash out sharply conflicting arguments surrounding two positions later but I would first like to point out that globalization has left 'society' with the burden of mutually incompatible allegiances and incommensurable obligations and made its position as a 'territory' untenable. In the past, 'society' brought citizens together, gave them a national identity, that is, exclusive citizenship based on a single bordered space, and made it possible to 'speak in one voice' through it. According to Marshall and Bottomore (1992), this expansion/strengthening of national citizenship has markedly reduced inequalities caused by social stratification, especially class-based income and asset disparities.[3]

However, this national citizenship functioned/functions effectively only on the assumption of a hierarchical structure under the nation-state. Globalization has weakened this hierarchical structure by promoting global flows and networks that detour around the national government and developing de-territorially arranged infrastructure,[4] and at the same time undermined the foundation of national sovereignty. With regard to this point, it is notable that various forms of obligations and rights are developing as the aforementioned flows and networks are expanded and infrastructure is upgraded, and that a state of imbalance in the level of access to them and resultant new inequalities and disparities are appearing. Further, the blurring of boundaries between 'domestic' and 'foreign' issues is occurring as symbolized by an increase in waste problems and health risks. These situations are notable because in conjunction they make it difficult to maintain national citizenship and bring about a new configuration of power/knowledge.

Now, what form of citizenship has emerged to replace national citizenship? Soysal literally refers to it as 'post-national' citizenship (1994), while Yuval-Davis calls it 'differential multi-tiered citizenship' (1997: 12) and Urry terms it 'citizenship of flow' (2000: 173). I shall call it global citizenship for the moment. What is important here is that this global citizenship is 'pressing hard against modern forms of centralist political control' (Cooke 1990: xiii) and that it exists as 'performative citizenship' (Albrow 1997: 178) from below embracing obligations based on conscience. Details aside, this suggests that this global citizenship partially sympathizes with the role of the state as a 'coordinator' of global flows and networks and that it has its roots deep in the system of localized consciousness and action which interacts with these flows and networks.

I shall discuss the former in the section titled 'Reexamination of a national framework,' but I would like to touch on the latter briefly here. The state is no longer a social space in which people who (have to) ascertain their own positions within global flows and networks—whether they are subsumed by them or excluded from them—can imagine that they are fellow citizens. People living in the present are in the middle of complex and multiple movements everyday even if this motion is imaginary (virtual travel on the computer, for example), and therefore they tend to form complex identities rather than to amplify their sense of 'purely national self.' Of course, people living in the everyday world may simply go about their mundane activities with very little awareness of how their actions will affect the global. However, their repetitive actions are incorporated into global flows and networks and connect to *other worlds* through recurring 'disjuncture' and 'competition.' They also expand multiple alternative identities rather than a fixed one by developing temporary and incidental relationships beyond 'bordered territories.' It goes without saying that these identities support and add depth to the system of de-territorial local consciousness and action.

In any case, these identities in themselves have a highly disjunctive and 'appearance-correspondence' nature, but they do not fit into the nation-state system or the concept of clearly bordered, exclusive national citizenship. Interestingly, they occupy an extremely important position in 'global civil society' discussed below.

What is 'global civil society'?

While the advancement of globalization has given rise to the development of diverse fluids with no clear beginning or end and the prevalence of the identities discussed in the previous section, a new type of civil society that is cosmopolitan and hybrid has emerged. According to Jones, this is creating new opportunities for new forms of learning, the formation of new counter cultures, changes to the meaning of copyright and privacy, and direct democracy (1995: 26). However, this form of civil society does not include the creative subject and it does not aspire to be a utopia based on the idea of progress and development; it helps geographically distant people form close ties but its members merely engage in intermittent 'appearance-correspondence.' Transnational democracy observed among its members obscures relations/boundaries between private and public, front (stage) and back (stage), and far and near, and prompts the conversion of public sphere to public stage characterized by visibility. Accordingly, such a 'global civil society' features what Heidegger calls 'a de-severance of the "world,"' which is a transformation of spatiality through which private is transported to an unreachable larger world and distance and remoteness are removed (Scannell 1996: 167). Civil societies organized by nation-states are rapidly outdated and about to be replaced by civil societies formed by CMC (computer mediated communication).

Another notable point is the occurrence of what Cohen calls 'diasporaization' across the globe. This literally refers to diasporas that are 'deterritorialized, multilingual and capable of bridging the gap between global and local tendencies... [and] become more integrated into the cosmopolis...' (Cohen 1992: 176),[5] and a certain kind of transnational sense of unity is arising as this situation spreads. This sense of unity is nurturing citizenship that is relatively free from the state as well as promoting the formation of the aforementioned 'global civil society.' This 'diasporaization' is another clear sign that the concept of a single, stable and comprehensive national identity, that

Photo 4.1: A rural fair

Source: McKay (1996: 37).

is, the idea of civil society composed of a single nation, is no longer realistic (Urry 2000: ch. 7).

Nevertheless, 'global civil society' cannot be realized solely through the growth of global cosmopolitans who freely flow in and out of the aforementioned fixed identities. We cannot ignore the influences of various sociations appearing on the public stage partially mediated by these diasporas/global cosmopolitans, and the reciprocal relations developing between them. The sociations here include 'new tribal' communities (to be discussed later) such as self-help groups, direct action groups and environmental NGOs as well as what Mckay (1996: 11) calls a 'loose network of loose networks' such as free festivals, rural fairs and Peace Convoys (see Photo 4.1). Details aside, these interweaving communities are forming 'global civil societies' although they may be partial, incomplete and incidental. At the same time, we cannot overlook the role of the state as a 'social coordinator' (to be discussed later) who supports and regulates a certain type of horizontal spread of these borderless networks. This is because the condition of 'global civil society' built on the resistance to globalization and the utilization of the global as described by Castells (1997) can only arise on the premise of this role of the state.

Given this perspective, we necessarily come to face the fundamental question of how to understand globalization. Since I have already elucidated the structural framework/overall picture of globalization in Chapter One, I shall provide a minimal description of globalization here in order to avoid gilding the lily. The key to such a description is the question of how to apply Brodie's (1998) argument that a small perturbation in a system can lead to an unpredictable and chaotic divergence of said system to the explanation of the 'global-local paradox.'

Local evolution of the global

Flow and network—metaphors of globalization

Today's current of globalization debate can be mainly explained by two opposing positions. One is the position that interprets globalization literally as the advent of a new age, that is, a borderless utopia. Advocates of this view point out that the flows of people, images, information and money moving not only inside national borders but also across them are creating new opportunities for the people. The second position asserts that the fluctuation of the national entity leads to a return of medievalism,[6] that is, a retrogression to the pre-modern West, or a dystopia. Both camps recognize that the aforementioned flows yield new risks (for example, spread of AIDS and increased environmental hazards) and new inequalities of access as by-products. What differentiates the two positions is the tone of their argument, the former optimistic and the latter pessimistic.

These two discourses have so far produced neoliberal reactions on one hand and communitarian reactions on the other.[7] These responses become apparent as different stances to the question of whether the global will actively assimilate a restructuring of impersonated capital, so to speak, or passively live with 'enclosed at-homeness'/ aboriginal identity in its evolution/*différance* into the local. Actually, this difference leads to two disparate positions concerning the local/ place to be discussed later. What I would like to point out here is the emergence of another position from a negative entanglement of the aforementioned positions which sees de-centralized, complex, multitiered and conjunctive effects (of globalization) embedded inside the existing 'society.'

The basis of this position is the perception that the order and system of globalization take the form of a network or fluid or hybrid society rather than a territorial one, regardless of the metaphor of globalization. The story of a larger territory swallowing up smaller territories can no longer fully illustrate globalization. For this reason, metaphors based on structures which 'involve a center, a concentration of power, vertical hierarchy and a formal or informal constitution' (Urry 2000: 33) are rejected as inappropriate. Giddens' process of 'disembedding–transfer–reembedding' which occurs between 'the distant' and 'the imminent' cannot be envisioned easily without the metaphor of network (1990). However, it is undeniable that network-type systems are prone to give rise to control through incitement or persuasion by information manipulation (i.e., surveillance society) because they are not reliant upon political action backed by power.

Reexamination of a national framework

While global flows and networks are generating diverse local forms in reality through their varied influences, what is more noteworthy than anything else is the fact that they are promoting 'de-totalization' of the traditional national framework. According to Castells, one-to-one correspondence is no longer found between the logic of power formation within global networks (i.e. very non-homogeneous and fragmented flows of people, objects, money, information and images which travel across territories at high speed in the form of unpredictable fluids) and the logic of national association and presentation observed in individual societies (1997: 11). At least, it is undeniable that corporations, brands,[8] NGOs, multinational 'states' and societies such as that of the Overseas Chinese (see Table 4.1) no longer match the boundaries of nation-states and that 'bordered territories' are no longer central to people's identity formation/the self-definition of a nation. Does this necessarily mean that the increasing divergence of 'social space,' in which people imagine their citizenship, from the state will extend 'borderless communities' while uniformly rendering all states powerless?

Bauman has made an interesting comment on this point. According to him, the nature of the state is changing/returning from that of 'gardener' to 'gamekeeper' (1987). In other words, the role of the state is changing from that of gardener who identifies the optimal growing condition for individual plants and determines which plants are productive or non-productive in maintaining the garden to that of gamekeeper who controls the mobility of animals and secures hunting conditions in individual hunting grounds for hunters (i.e., coordinates resources for hunting). This metaphor of gamekeeper precisely captures a shift in the state's role from a direct supplier of goods and services to a regulator of goods and services supplied by a diverse range of private, voluntary, quasi-public and public institutions, or in other words, it encapsulates the state's specialization in coordination work such as activity monitoring and standardization. At the same time, it can be said that the gamekeeper metaphor faces up to the reality in which the nation-state can no longer maintain its own society

Table 4.1: Distribution of the Overseas Chinese, 1989–1997 (Unit: '000 people)

Country/Region	1989	1997
World	27,260	32,840
Asia (except Japan)	23,690	25,281
Southeast Asia	23,305	24,959
Malaysia	5,200	5,445
Singapore	2,090	2,311
Thailand	6,100	6,358
Indonesia	6,500	7,310
The Philippines	1,200	1,030
Brunei	55	45
Vietnam	1,000	1,000
Cambodia	300	300
Laos	10	160
Myanmar (Burma)	850	1,000
Asia except SE Asia	385	323
Japan	100	234
Anglo-America	1,860	3,643
USA	1,260	2,723
Canada	600	920
Latin America	460	1,096
Europe	870	1,938
Oceania	290	528
Australia	200	372
New Zealand	32	111
Africa	90	120

Source: Based on Amako et al. (eds) (1999: 116) and Ma and Cartier (eds) (2003: 13–16).

as its garden because the flows of people, objects, money, information and images are slipping through its control so easily. By the way, Deleuze and Guattari provide the following explanation about the 'gamekeeper' nature of the state in the context of the coordination of space spreading across national borders in view of the emergence of giant world-machines[9] and neo-tribal societies[10] that exist 'outside' the state.

> One of the fundamental tasks of the State is to striate the space over which it reigns...It is a vital concern of every State not only to vanquish nomadism, but to control migrations and, more generally, to establish a zone of rights over an entire "exterior," over all of the flows traversing the ecumenon. If it can help it, the State does not dissociate itself from a process of capture of flows of all kinds, populations, commodities or commerce, money or capital, etc... the State never ceases to decompose, recompose and transform movement, or to regulate speed. (Deleuze and Guattari 1986: 59–60)

The state draws lines in a space to partition (striate) it and coordinates smooth and de-territorialized flows in this way. Of course, it does not mean that the state will be conquered by global flows; it rather suggests that the state will perform an even more important function for various networks as a midwife/catalyst. The state is able to act as a 'social coordinator' in this way thanks to digitization of computer control and because the state has revealed itself as part of a complex system.

It is clear that decision-making by state power does not entail physical coercive measures as much as before and that it has become difficult to envision a purely national environment that enables the nation-state to establish order and perform coordination activities while acting as a gardener. Nevertheless, it is also true that the state is coming to perform even more diverse functions for global flows. We need to keep in mind, however, that this factor makes the 'social coordination' function of the state more dependent on new forms of computer-based information collection, search and provision, or in other words, it has to become highly media-oriented. Details aside, what looms ahead is a surveillance society similar to what Power calls 'audit society' (1994).[11]

Setting aside this transition to 'surveillance society,' it is clear that while giant world-machines and neo-tribal societies interact to evade state control or increase resistance to the state as Deleuze and Guattari suggest, the state is at the same time changing from what can be called a Foucauldian endogenous coordinator of the nation to an exogenous action term which reacts to various flows and transforms them. As mentioned above, it is rapidly becoming difficult to imagine a society, and citizens peculiar to said society, within securely guarded national borders.

Diverse forms of the local

With the aforementioned reexamination of the national framework/ transformation of the nation-state into a 'social coordinator,' what local forms are emerging as the 'legitimate children' of global flows and networks? Harvey and Castells present contrasting arguments on this point.

As we know, global flows and networks entail their own peculiar temporal and spatial transformation. Harvey finds it in 'time-space compression' involving the following (change of) feeling.

> [I]n a world where image streams accelerate and become more and more placeless. Who are we and to what space/place do we belong? Am I a citizen of the world, the nation, the locality? Can I have a virtual existence in cyberspace...? (1996b: 246)

According to Harvey, this 'time-space compression,' or a diminution of the impact of temporal and spatial barriers, has unmistakably been brought about by the creative destructive force of capital (1989). What is noteworthy is the view that there is a stronger incentive for differentiation of the local by capital, especially mobile capital, or put plainly, that an intensifying scramble by capital to secure the local appears to strengthen locality. This view constitutes one of the more powerful positions in place theory to be discussed later. However, Harvey has pushed this interpretation of the local in connection with capital strategy to the background and come to explain the local in the context of individuality/ *spécificité* emphasized by cultural studies in recent years (1996b).

Conversely, Castells sees the expression of the local in the form of resistance to global order and systems (fluids). He mentions various environmental NGOs, women's movements dealing with the impacts of the global market on women and children in the Third World, New Age-ists and religious fundamentalists as examples of such resistance. At the core are 'resistance identities' and the following virtual communities formed around them, that is, communities of which 'their constituents are linked together through identifications constructed in non-geographic spaces of activist discourses, cultural products and media images' (Rose 1996: 333).

Needless to say, this understanding originates from the view of globalization as a fluid, that is, the view that situates a non-human hybrid in the pivotal position of social relations. At the same time, it conceals an irrepressible urge for 'propinquity' even though it is a non-place, no matter how the advocator denies it. While this understanding also underlies the aforementioned understanding of the local proposed by Harvey, it is also true that it partially resonates with another trend in theory which regards the local as the basis for stability and intimacy. Yet, it is not reduced to a so-called dichotomy between global and local on the same plane. The aforementioned view of Castells is situated on the theoretical horizon that interprets globalization using metaphors such as networks or fluids and is therefore in direct opposition to the usual perception of globalization as a process of homogenization by which the world is painted uniformly by something immaterial. The argument which consolidates globalization into a single dimension of cultural imperialist coercion is based on a gaze that *transcends* context, time and even the body, and therefore sees the local as a field simply waiting for visual consumption. After all, it is still within the Cartesian tradition of monocular geometricization of the world in the context of temporal-spatial theory.[12]

The local that is pointed to by Castells, and Harvey in recent years, is undoubtedly outside of this tradition. In other words, it belongs to a different dimension from 'the world imaged as a globe' (Ingold 1993: 32) that is 'the detached disinterested observation of a world apart' (Ingold 1993: 40), and follows as an extension of joint involvement (resistance) in global flows and networks. While some level of inclination toward communitarianism such as an 'urge for propinquity' is observed here, the local thus constructed basically attempts to confirm the content of 'promises' of globalization as the local by activating 'a multitude of other identities, introducing potentially greater flexibility into inherited forms of citizenship' (Morris-Suzuki 2000).

Now, what are the specific narratives of place that have emerged from these arguments about the local?

Narratives of place and the reformulation of community

Competing narratives of place

Today's debate over place is evolving by way of questioning the reality through what Urry calls 'Academic mobility across disciplinary borders' (2000: 210). Geography and sociology have joined phenomenology in an investigation into 'creative marginality' surrounding theories of place. An example of phenomenological approaches to place is the conceptualization (of place) by Yi-Fu Tuan as human 'experience' that differentiates space, that is, 'so to speak, a surrounded and humanized space' (1977: 54). This understanding of place as an 'inside space' is deepened by Relph as a phenomenon linked to the 'lived world' founded on human experience. Relph highlights such a place by contrast with the 'placeless,' a space that has been excessively standardized/homogenized and has lost its identity (typically, planned cities) (1976). It appears that narratives of place are beginning to take a form of evolution/turn from the interpretation of the local we discussed in the previous section as the starting point based on this phenomenological understanding as the prototype.

One of the leading narratives of place is formulated on the basis of 'the notion that a place has a single intrinsic identity, the notion that the identity of a place—a sense of place—is constructed from the introverted history based on the past that is excavated in search of an internalized origin' (Yoshihara 2004: 177). This is founded on what Massey calls 'a progressive sense of place' due to 'a diversion from the progressive dimension of Time as Becoming' (1993: 63). Borrowing Ingold's (1993) expression, it is aligned with the context of a Gemeinschaft that appears after *reformulation*, so to speak, in contrast with a somewhat global Gesellschaft. Heidegger's idea of 'delineated' place is an example of this.[13]

The other is a narrative formulated on 'the position which considers a place as part of the earth's surface developed in a manner desirable to capital and concerns about the variations of place created in the world after the formation of space homogenized by flows of capital and information' (Onjō 1998: 214), which largely overlaps with Harvey's argument about the local in the previous section. To borrow Ingold's expression again, this view bases its argument directly on the 'global Gesellschaft.' It goes without saying that there are no signs of physicalized, multi-sensory local relations here.

These two positions have been in competition with one camp under the banner of humanism and the other Marxism in geographical terms, to put it rather crudely. They have formulated polar opposite narratives that have a sharp mutual tension between them. However, their relationship is fundamentally 'far, but near.' Incidentally, while the former has clearly kept its feet on 'stability and problem-free identities' at the visible level, the latter has had its eyes on the stability and intimateness of place amid the 'strengthening and replay of play' by capital beginning with the 'annihilation of space by time.'[14] This is why these two positions oscillate between the 'identity of place' and the 'mechanism of place' as the former transforms into the latter and the latter reverts to the former while in sharp opposition. In other words, both positions attempt to travel along the phenomenological approach but they do not see the multidimensional vector presented by it and converge *together* on the metaphor of territory, so to speak, which proposes the 'lived world' as a picture.

As the constellation of globalization, which is seen 'as fundamentally fractal, that is, as possessing no Euclidean boundaries, structures, or regularities' (Appadurai 1996: 46), comes to the foreground of society, the understanding of place as something that 'is constructed out of particular interactions and mutual articulations of social relations, social processes, experiences and understandings, in a situation of co-presence' (Massey 1993: 66) is gathering momentum to contend with, or even surpass, these two positions. Massey calls this understanding of place that is 'attained with a mind to the way networks of social relations and understandings are rhizomatously articulated and open outwardly' (Yoshihara 2004: 179) 'an alternative interpretation of place' (Massey 1993: 66). In any case, given that the only prerequisite for the 'network membership' is to 'intermittently come together to "be with" others in the present, in moments of intense fellow-feeling' (Urry 2000: 44) under global fluids and hybrid mobility, the 'view of place as a field of opportunities for condition-dependent events which contains conflicts and cooperation between individuals and groups' (Onjō 1998: 215) has emerged as a position appropriate for this situation. This understanding is deeply rooted in the diversity of people's senses and 'lived experiences' and consequently contributes to the liberating of the aforementioned phenomenological approach from the metaphor of territory.

Place mediated by the body

Ingold (1993) focuses his attention on the physicalization, with all senses, of 'connection' and 'events' that are the key to the above understanding of place. In other words, place found under global fluids and hybrid mobility is linked to the building of 'successive stratified and tangled networks' by people as they involve themselves with various elements of 'dwelling' through their five senses in their (highly contingent) practical life activities (events) (Lefebvre 1974: 403). Here, place is understood as bringing human interaction (communion) into existence through inhabiting, staying, resting, relaxing, and after all, 'dwelling' while existing 'as multiplex, as a set of spaces where ranges of relational networks and flows coalesce, interconnect and fragment' (Urry 2000: 140).

We are reminded of the following criticism about existing materialism and idealism made by Marx and Engels in *Theses on Feuerbach*.

> The chief defect of all hitherto existing materialism—that of Feuerbach included—is that the thing, reality, sensuousness, is conceived only in the form of the object or of *contemplation*, but not as *human sensuous activity*, *practice*, not *subjectively*.... idealism does not know real, sensuous activity as such. (Marx and Engels 1964: 665)

The human sensuous activity referred to here underlies what Marx points out in *Ökonomisch-philosophische Manuskripte* as practical possession of the world through five senses (i.e., totality of 'dwelling' or reacquisition of various conditions of human existence by humans themselves) (Yoshihara 2004: 147).

> Man appropriates his total essence in a total manner, that is to say, as a whole man. Each of his human relations to the world—seeing, hearing, smelling, tasting, feeling, thinking, observing, experiencing, wanting, acting, loving—in short, all the organs of his individual being, like those organs which are directly social in their form, are in their objective orientation or in their orientation to the object, the appropriation of the object; the appropriation of human reality. (Marx 1959: 93)

This represents a state that is the polar opposite of what Fabian calls 'visualism'[15] (1992): the state of 'physical experience' generated by complex entanglement of cooperation and reciprocity between visuality and other senses. Places are woven into this physical experience and in turn weave it in them, and therefore they are primarily felt via five senses. There is no longer any distance between people and things in places.

Of course, it is undeniable that place has an aspect that is structured and regulated by global relations (being mimicries of private interests and dominant market relations themselves) codified by vision technology, just as the local does. At the same time, it is true that place is filled with multiple sensitivity of the physical that slips through the order of exchange value and the logic of the market. In the end, '(place) can be viewed as the particular nexus between, on the one hand, propinquity characterized by intensely thick co-present interaction, and on the other hand, fast flowing webs and networks stretched corporeally, virtually and imaginatively across distances' (Urry 2000: 140). For this reason, it is possible to say that place becomes a foothold for resistance against the global on one hand and keeps its feet deep inside the global world on the other (Castells 1997).

Following on from the above discussion, I would like to point out further, if I may, that narratives of place are woven from physical relations by which 'each "I" and all others subsume and reflect one another' (Mita 1984: 33) by '[t]he touch of the unknown' (Canetti 1973), not from a sense of belonging or aboriginal identity that are helplessly carried away to national traditions or iconic history.

At this point, the reformulation of community again comes to the fore as an important issue as it resonates with the reexamination of theories of place. As we all know, a diverse range of views have been exchanged over the issue of community in the field of sociology, but now the reformulation of community is stirring up debate as the discipline crosses its own boundaries in its efforts to reform. Let us consider in the next section how a reinterpretation of community is taking place in the wake of the above discussion of place.

Reformulation of community

It is clear from our discussion so far that communities based on the sense of propinquity/'connection' rooted in places are reemerging as they sympathize with various global networks and flows rather than being in the process of disintegration. Conversely, the validity of the concept of distinctly bordered community is being sharply questioned.

The concept of community in sociology has broadly had such connotations as 'regionality,' 'communality' and 'communion.' The first one usually refers to a particular habitat based on geographical propinquity; the second means cross relationships between social groups or local institutions having a certain level of coherence; and the third entails interchange among people characterized by ties, a sense of belonging and warmth derived from personal contact between members (Bell and Newby 1976). In this case, the third connotation of 'communion' is especially significant for the concept of community. It is considered these days that 'communion' can be engendered in the absence of geographical propinquity or bordered cross relationships from a point of view that stresses social relations in the aforementioned global flows and networks and coexistent habitats. This means that people *can imagine* that they are members of a community even if they do not see each other daily and they are not present in the same space physically, and that they are neither engulfed in the nation-state altogether. This is why we must formulate a completely new definition of community.

In doing so, we must examine the following two points reflectively as a prerequisite for the reformulation: (1) an overemphasis on 'regionality' and 'communality' commonly found in community theories has been camouflaging unequal social relations within each community and its extraordinary hostility toward outsiders; and (2) blatant indifference to the fact that community is felt by the body/ woven in the body's experience. The form of 'communion' with *outsiders* that is felt through/across borders has been ignored because of the excessive importance attached to enclosed and bordered people and interactions among them. What has come about as a result is 'the use of the term "community" which can falsely imply that the locality is based upon warm, consensual, face-to-face relations of communion' (Urry 2000: 140).

Based on the above points, the key notions for a discourse on community now are that it (community) will never 'return' to geographical propinquity and that it is grounded on mobile communion that is 'constructed in communicative processes rather than in institutional structures, spaces, or even in symbolic forms of meaning' (Delanty 2003: 187). It is considered that this 'communion' can restore non-geographic propinquity through a better integration of listening, touching, tasting, seeing and moving. This type of community is fundamentally intentional and freely selected beyond national borders even if it may form its own space or place and therefore retain traces of memory of all sorts of social groups. In any case, it has become extremely difficult to speak to communities in the single voice of the nation-state (just as it has to the local and places). At the same time, deciphering the topology ('currency') of association emerging in various forms using a new community paradigm has become inevitable.[16]

In relation to the reformulation of community discussed above, I would like to point out here that the dichotomous view that assumes some kind of global Gesellschaft in contraposition to some local Gemeinschaft which still persists in this circle is an extremely simplistic approach. This is because uncritical acceptance of this type of dichotomous scenario involves the risk of allowing the aforementioned propinquity and communion to be returned to the closed national community, instead of 'global civil society.'[17] It is fundamentally a question of whether one can maintain a flexible gaze upon the situation in which global flows and networks are open to the outside and forming magnetic fields for physically mediated communities (Delanty 2003) while insatiable marketism is undermining localized 'regionality' and closed 'communality.'

In search of an alternative

I have proposed a reinterpretation of globalization by examining the phase of global flow and network and stated that the accumulation of these flows and networks is promoting the formation and evolution of 'global civil society.' I have also explained that this 'global civil society' nurtures the collectivity/relationship that is disentangled from a particular national context and that this is where the local and places are situated. The increasingly media-oriented civil society of today is filled with bottomless anxiety caused by virtuality. It has no choice, however, but to land on that plane in the meantime and reconcile with place which has been damaged by futile debates between communitarians and libertarians. This subjective questioning will make a new 'reading,' or narrative, of place possible. All in all, this chapter has only presented part of what is understood about the narrative of place and it must be said that the narrative of place has only just begun in this sense.

Nevertheless, 'global civil society' that is evolving as it enfolds us appears to lead us to an increasingly unpredictable and chaotic system. Transnational cooperation between citizens which tends to be spoken of *together with* 'global civil society' these days may have overcome many divides, but it appears to create several times as many new divides.[18] We cannot rule out with absolute certainty the possibility that the fractals underlying global flows and networks which are activating 'global civil society' may revert from the mechanism of de-ordering to that of re-ordering to act as a stepping stone for the configuration of certain forms of power/knowledge, or that place may regress from a plural and multidimensional 'reading' to one which is *deemed orthodox*.

I have already stated that it has become difficult for the nation-state to sustain its power. However, it is easily conceivable that the state will refine its function as the 'social coordinator' in the direction of the deepening of 'surveillance society' to coincide with the aforementioned reversal of 'global civil society' or the 're-reading' of place. What alternative can we propose to counter the resurgence of skepticism toward globalization (liquidationist negativism) then? I must say that the challenge left to us is enormous and far-reaching.

5 Local Governance and 'Open Urban Space'

> Man himself is an organism whose existence is dependent upon his maintaining the delicate balance that exists between all forces of nature, physical and organic, from sunlight and the soil, the bacteria, the molds, and growing plants right up to the complex interaction of thousands of species. (Mumford 1953: 173)

Introduction

Coupled with the advancement of globalization, communitarianism, as well as neoliberalism, has been spreading in recent years. To coincide with this trend, we see the emergence of a movement on the platform of liberal nationalism overseas and in Japan we find one that distinguishes true conservatism from reactionary conservatism and realigns liberalism with the former. These movements are expressions of irregular situations that cannot be organized fully along the conventional coordinate axes, but I shall not go into details here. In this chapter, I would firstly like to look at the social implications of an orientation towards the 'closed community' that is surfacing along with the spread of communitarian thinking prompted by the advancement of globalization.

The 'tyranny of intimateness' accompanying the 'closed community' has been aptly discussed by Young (1990), who elucidates the social topology of gated communities, and later by Junichi Saitō (2000). In this context the focus is on the compatibility of the 'closed community' with neoliberalism. I argue, however, that the pathology of the 'closed community' is presenting intensively in 'safe and secure city planning' today in terms of its sympathies with neoliberalism. Since I have already discussed this point elsewhere (Yoshihara 2007), I shall not elaborate here. Together with the idealization of community, 'forced conformity' found in 'safe and secure city planning' creates a situation in which walls and boundaries are established on the outside while zero tolerance of deviance is fervently pursued on the inside. This generates a contradictory relationship in that community members watch each other in order to smoke out 'different others' while wishing to enjoy personal contact among them. This echoes with what Sennett once called 'the fall of the public man.' Sennett (1974) sharply criticizes the move to idealize the homogeneous and 'closed' sphere of intimateness by pointing out that the glorification of community based on assured safety and collective identity is spoiling the public nature of 'the city as a whole.' Young also looks critically at the situation involving a combination of the desire for 'closed community' and the denial of the city as a 'big public world' (1990).

Let us now turn to the state of urban space which is the opposite of the 'closed community' and actively approves differences instead of forcing 'conformity.' Let us tentatively call it 'open urban space.' Simmel has been the forerunner in illuminating this aspect of urban space. He considers urban space as an 'inter'-communal world dominated by individual uniqueness or individuality, which is 'qualitatively unique and not interchangeable with others,' and individual differences (1957). This portrayal is homologous with his conceptualization of the monetary world where individual freedom is one of its cornerstones (Simmel 1990). Simmel's interest in the 'open nature' of urban space resonates with Jacobs' (1965) perspective where the dynamics of urban living are found in the interplay of differences and diverse values and Dahl's (1973) gaze that tries to discover the true value of democracy in a complex *mise en abyme* of units of various sizes. While my argument in this chapter clearly 'inherits' the viewpoints/interests of Simmel, Jacobs and Dahl in urban space, it attempts to examine the possibility of 'open urban space' that is not reclaimable by 'closed community' with reference to local governance as a coordinating pattern operating between multiple subjects, so to speak.

I have commented on local governance elsewhere (Yoshihara 2002, 2004) and I shall therefore refrain from going into details here. However, I would like to clarify the following points with regard to governance, summarized in Table 5.1.[1]

1. Governance appears in the shape of the formation of formal/ informal self-organizing networks by various forces/sectors that are (regarded to be) somewhat autonomous, including local governments, corporations and various intermediate groups, which set and share some specific objectives, in an environment which requires the designing of new institutions/thought experiments between existing organizations and the execution and processing of complex and overlapping tasks and issues in view of the 'contemporary paradox'[2] (Held) followed by the 'failure of the system.'
2. The appearance of this form is founded on highly voluntary political processes, which is a mode of governing that differs from conventional government based on mutual relationships by which

'differences of opinion can be discussed and negotiated' and on dependency relations (Held 2007: 84).
3. In addition to the underlying mode of governing that defies the term 'national,' governance is a means to establish new approaches and conceptual frameworks and to pose questions and propose visions.

At the same time, I would like to add the following.

4. As Harvey has been pointing out from time to time in recent years (2005), local governance has become a theme of discourse under the influences of neoliberalism, that is, the infiltration of neoliberal policies which restrict the nation-state's intervention (regulation) in the market (liberalization) is in the background.

With these points in mind, in this chapter I would like to explore the mode/form of existence of local governance from the operational aspect of urban planning and discuss the possibility of 'open urban space.'

What is governance? Problem setting and approach

In short, governance is a new mode of governing/governability and, moreover, a method of considering new approaches/issues and presenting visions for the future. It is the idea of institutional design/conception. There have already been numerous attempts to formulate governance but the important question is how to set a logical and realistic agenda which would otherwise lack persuasiveness without the use of the word 'governance' as a counter model. In this case, the first thing to consider is how to reconcile it with the political parlance that was, and still is, integral to the governing framework of the nation-state, that is, concepts such as sovereignty, constitution, citizenship and democracy.[3] I must point out that it is, however, virtually impossible to find conceptual linkage with these terms because governance is fundamentally based on the multitiered and disparate governing function of the global and the local.

For this reason I shall abandon the idea of 'conceptualistic alliance' (Endō 2003: 252), with 'government' representing hierarchy for the moment, and try to shed light on aspects that can only be expressed by the term 'governance.' The key to this is the principle and strategy that guide the new mode of governing and the situations/arenas in which governance is thematized in relation to this. All of these factors can only be considered in light of the reality in which transnational/global institutions on one hand and local subjects on the other perform part

Table 5.1: Definitions and characteristics of governance

Definition	Characteristics
Jessop, B. Diverse modes of heterarchy (or self-organizing)	• Self-organizing individual human networks • Consultation-based inter-organizational coordination • Decentralized and context-mediated inter-system operation
Stoker, G. Various modes of mutual cooperation	• (Principal-agent) relationship • Inter-organizational negotiation • Systematic cooperation
Rhodes, R. A. W. Self-organizing inter-organizational networks	• Interdependency between organizations • Continuous interactions between network members • Competitive interactions • Relative autonomy from the state

Sources: Jessop (1998), Stoker (1998), and Rhodes (1996).

of the governing function in the context of de-nationalized states and consequently form a governing structure comprising of a multitiered and multidimensional spatial scale. I shall explain these points step by step below, but I would first like to mention my idea of the 'form of operation' of governance (organizational and interorganizational relationships). This articulation can be summarized as follows.

> [T]he shape of the formation of formal/informal self-organizing networks by various organizations/groups that are relatively autonomous, including local governments, corporations and various intermediate groups, as they set and share some specific objectives, in the situation of "system failure" which increasingly demands the designing of new institutions, the execution of tasks and the processing of issues among the existing organizations. (Yoshihara 2002: 96; 2004: 98)

This formulation has been derived by combining and summarizing the aspects listed in Table 5.1. Our attention is drawn to the following points: that governance deeply involves coordination and '[i]n contrast with the top-down control in coordination through hierarchy and the individualized relationships in coordination through markets, (governance) involves coordination through networks and partnerships' (Painter 2000: 317); and that the basic and inherent components of governance include the object of contention, the subject (local governments, corporations and intermediate groups, including NPOs, neighborhood associations and other resident groups, local industry associations, etc.), interests (stakes), identities and the site/arena of struggle between them. In governance, these elements coexist in cycles as they form a complex entanglement.[4] At the same time, I would like to stress that these components of governance are always context-sensitive and in the process of reorganization. In the context of what Jessop sees in the substratum of governance, that is, 'the dramatic intensification of societal complexity which flows from growing functional differentiation of institutional orders' (1997: 59), this represents the very unstable nature of governance ('governance failure'), including the possibility of retrogression to government or manifestation of inbuilt faults.

Why governance now? Conditions and social implications

Let us now consider the background to the thematization of governance. This is somewhat schematic, but one possible main factor (for the thematization of governance) is that the advance of globalization has caused seismic changes (failures) in existing functional areas and regulatory systems which have resulted in an eruption of issues that cannot be resolved by inertial and closed rules and procedures (codes and regulations). In other words, governance has come to be the subject of discourse because:

1. multifaceted issues have emerged that are beyond the processing capability of the state and the market, especially the former alone, to regulate and coordinate by matching countermeasures, goals or costs based on territorial orders;[5]
2. cross-'border' issues that are discussed in multiple functional areas and spatial scales, that is, intricately-intertwined issues at global, national and local levels have become widespread; and inevitably,
3. the question of how to deal with the concatenation of single issues collectively and cooperatively has now become the greatest concern.

Needless to say, these issues are deeply rooted in multidimensional and multitiered divides—gaps found in various tiers, not only in relation to income but also gender, generation, ethnicity and so on—that are appearing at the level of ordinary individuals. In reality, they are considered to generate a synergetic effect that is amplifying the instability of existing systems. Incidentally, the aforementioned divides are tending to grow in accordance with 'an ability to access widely differing tiers or arenas of decision structures of the world (global regions), nation-states and local regions' and 'an ability to avoid constraints and social obligations established at any of these levels or arenas' (Bartolini 2003: 52) and in fact they are argued as such. What draws our attention here is the increasing number of people who are found to be excluded from political systems and strategies relating to the issues due to this tendency, even though they are party to (carriers of) these issues.

Governance created by the aforementioned background factors exists as a mode of governing that is de-territorialized, or diffused throughout the global/local levels, more than anything else. In other words, it expresses itself with a 'form of operation' that is highly pluralistic and convergent beyond the territorial and has never been enclosed in a sovereign state. Governance is rather notable for having at its base cross-border organizations and groups on one hand and on the other hand organizations and groups that are smaller than the state but not constrained by it.[6] This is why 'inter-regional coordination' in spatial scales and 'borderless disposal of issues' in functional areas are the central features of governance. Details aside, while the former takes the form of broad-area administration/narrow-area administration or global/regional/local and the latter takes the form of public/private, formal/informal or legal/social (*de jure* institutions/*de facto* institutions), it is important that they are thoroughly supported by the equivalence principle that is not reclaimed by perfunctory equality.

In any case, governance is essentially an organization of systems/a new mode of governing which is being affected at the intersection of multiple territories. It goes without saying that governance does not absolutize the hegemony or decisions over any territorial resources. Rather, it is founded on multilevel/multilayered linkages and territorial competition incorporating the diversity of resources found in each territory. This is where governance radically deviates from government which is based on decision-making within an enclosed area (political territory in a confined space), or the principle of national sovereignty, so to speak. Details aside, it again gives us a glimpse of 'the world view containing globalization and localization in a unified manner that is different from the principle underpinning the nation-state' (Endō 2003: 253).

From government to local governance

Let us discuss the instability of the existing system before moving on to the subject of governance as a new organizational mode.

The question of what a system is constitutes a very polemic issue in itself and I shall adopt the minimal definition and take it to mean 'a complex formed around interests.' In other words, a system is basically an aggregate of the mechanisms for the intermediation of interests and the establishment of orders to facilitate it. Based on this understanding, it becomes clear that a certain type of 'bias' is occurring in the interest representation circuit in relation to the problem of under-representation, so to speak. It is common knowledge that the direction of government of post-war Japan has been broadly determined by the axes of conflicts of interest between metropolitan areas and regions (cities versus rural areas), leading-edge industries and structural recession-hit businesses, corporations and labor unions and so on. These conflicting interests have been coordinated in the area of production through public works, subsidies, Non Tariff Barriers, corporatism, etc. The aforementioned 'bias' has occurred in this very process of coordination of conflicting interests; it was inextricably linked to the establishment of the 'national narrative' of 'growth' and '*sōchūryū* (Japan's pervasive middle-class mentality).'

However, as the post-war society entered the post-economic bubble period, some kind of gap opened up in these axes of conflict. This was the occurrence of what Ueki calls a dislocation, or regime shift (2000). In terms of the aforementioned 'bias,' it was no longer possible to prioritize the allocation of institutional resources to the metropolitan middle class, various classes of 'citizens'/consumers and high-tech producers and secure broad support or agreement from them (the end of the 'national narrative'). Such a seismic upheaval observed in hegemony politics can be described as a collapse of the conventional centralized hierarchy system ('government failure' from another angle).

This alterity manifests as an 'absence of legitimacy' originating from an increasing gap between law and society in the eyes of 'citizens,' and as a 'lack of efficiency' according to neoliberalist principles. In the present post-bubble period, strange scenes of *collusion* between deregulation and decentralization are playing out, but they are considered to exist upon some distorted 'sympathy' between 'absence of legitimacy' on the 'citizens' side and 'lack of efficiency' according to neoliberalist principles.[7] In any case, an extensive field for local governance is being formed in the midst of this shift (seismic upheaval) in the mode of governing as discussed below.

Let us now look at what is involved in local governance. In short, its main purpose is to intervene in hegemony politics on a local plane/scene where task execution, issue disposal and system design overlap and interpenetrate. As for the method of intervention, the following two pillars are required for the moment. One is the question of how to reinterpret the 'government failure' manifesting in the forms of 'absence of legitimacy' and 'lack of efficiency' on the local level, and the other is the question of how to present the argument for designing an alternative system. For this purpose, it is imperative to pursue the execution of diverse tasks and the designing of systems based on the configuration of material, human and institutional resources and, moreover, consider a method to appropriately deliver interests which were seldom in public in the past because of distorted mobilization systems. This means that we must pursue the issue of 'legitimacy' even if we end up setting aside the issue of 'efficiency'—that is, priority should be given to the former.

Conditions for local governance as an alternative

How can the subject of argument be set up in relation to the establishment and composition of local governance as an *alternative* (counter model)? I shall present three problematics drawing on the ideas of Yutaka Ueki, Tarō Miyamoto and others.

The first problematic involves a process of collective decision making and attendant membership space. The focus in this case is on the question of burden allocation which inevitably arises in relation to cooperative relations between multiple collective subjects, self-organizing networks and collective decision-making processes. This problematic, which manifests as membership issues/stakeholder issues, so to speak, is especially concerned with formal/informal relations within networks of collective subjects and the fringes of self-organization and 'emergence' (Itō 2007) that are anchored there[8] in relation to the state of balance/'correspondence' between decision-makers and decision-takers. Since the latter is still in the process of conceptual development, I shall refrain from discussing it in detail. Here, I would simply like to point out that the following relationship exists, or is anticipated, with regard to the former: a relationship to institutionally derive claims/benefits and deliver to the people who are significantly affected by a given issue through the formation of *informal* networks, although they are lacking 'privity,' or eligibility to be privy, to be more exact, on the *formal* level. Incidentally, this membership/stake-holder issue entails the matter of the 'trust–trustee' relationships surrounding accountability or disclosure between governance and the 'public sphere' and relates to the issue of securing 'legitimacy,' so to speak (Ueki 2000).

The second problematic is deeply linked to this issue of securing 'legitimacy' and stems from the expanding phenomenon of contracting-out (subcontracting) to collective subjects which derive and deliver claims/benefits, whether for profit not (Miyamoto 2005). Local governance presents the possibility of multiplying the means by which options are granted by multiple suppliers of collective claims/benefits to the parties of a given issue and identifies what they need for their independence by facilitating the exit of collective subjects which used to play the leading role in the derivation and delivery of claims/benefits and the new entry of the for-profit or not-for-profit sectors.[9] Nevertheless, this pluralistic governance is sympathetic with the trend of macro-level governance reorganization and the direction of market-based pluralism and is therefore yet to function definitively to raise 'privity' up to the level of a formal relationship.

The third problematic manifests more or less in connection with the above two and from the advocates of the possibility of deliberative democracy (Cohen 1997) as a counterargument against a bias in the existing election system which tends to excessively derive and deliver the interests of organized producers. In this case, it should be ensured that the institutionalization of 'deliberative democracy' takes place in the operational arena of local governance. However, deliberative democracy theory, which envisions that the issues that are ignored or the interests/claims that are inadequately transmitted under the existing electoral system are recognized as problems to be solved in the process of discussion, negotiation and mediation, has not emerged from a prescriptive model. At least, the scenario that deliberative democracy is realized once the value hierarchy at the local level is reorganized/restructured through negotiations and mediations between members in the operational area of local governance is no more than a logical expectation in the present circumstances.

Based on the above, it is clear that the primary purpose of local governance is to cause transitions of issues by focusing on the axes of conflicting interests that tended to be invisible and undervalued in the old regime and rectify the bias in the mode of delivery which favors the interests of organized producers. Needless to say, local governance postulates politics with pluralistic competition between interests/claims to support 'open urban space.' Let us shift our attention to urban planning now and consider the possibility of local governance and its latent issues.

The topology of urban planning: Harvey and Castells

Under the old regime, urban planning was basically situated within the framework of hegemony politics which perpetuated the institutional bias in a manner that was compatible with the coordination of conflicting interests in the production arena. When we trace its origin, we come to Foucault, who sought the archetype of 'good governance' of the state in cities and therefore urban planning (1982), and also to two completely different theoretical planes which oddly resonate with this view. One is the position held by Relph who proposes homogeneous spaces and their operability (to position things, events and people freely) as the premise of urban planning and above all emphasizes the predominance of 'placelessness' in urban planning (1976). The other is the radical view that homogeneous spaces have been actively created by urban planning which is characterized by 'control' and the equilibrium of interests as they lend themselves to the narratives of 'development' and 'growth' (Grabow and Heskin 1973, for example). However, these positions are within the overall framework of criticism of modernist urban planning. To identify a concrete manifestation of the abovementioned hegemony politics in urban planning, we must after all investigate its operational arena. We take Harvey's and Castells' understandings of urban planning as the starting point of our investigation.[10]

Let us first look at Harvey's argument, especially from his early work. He defines urban planning as an attempt to arrange physical components of the built environment such as houses, roads, factories, offices, schools, hospitals, water and sewer networks, etc. in an appropriate manner to create an optimal spatial mix, and argues that it is basically consistent with capital accumulation activity. In this case, there is certainly a complex interplay of various interests between capitalists, workers and property capital/land owners which cannot be unified easily, and for this very reason, urban planning in search of 'a possibility of socially harmonious equilibrium' has intrinsic value. However, it ends up contributing to the reproduction of social order that is 'harmonious' with capital accumulation activity and urban planners take part in this reproduction of social order by confining themselves to being the technically specialized practitioners of 'rationality' ('technician of value' to be discussed later) (Harvey 1985). In this way, Harvey says, the professional knowledge or technical knowledge of the urban planner plays a very positive role in 'coordinating (people's) day-to-day practices to match' 'the built environment effected by the tyrannical force of linearity.'

Castells' argument about urban planning is quite compatible/homologous with that of Harvey, at least in relation to the collective consumption theory outlined in *The Urban Question* (1972). In *The Urban Question*, Castells defines urban politics as that surrounding collective politics and tries to explain urban politics based on a dual structure consisting of urban planning which involves/regulates the conditions for collective consumption through spatial organization and the urban social movements which oppose it. What is highlighted in this case is the fact that urban planning creates the conditions for balanced 'growth' and 'development' by limiting itself to technical standardization of land use and in turn carries out suppression and adaptive absorption or integration to prevent class conflict and factional discord.

While both Harvey's and Castells' arguments appear to take a base-reductionist perspective towards capital accumulation and subordinate urban planning, they perceive the oscillations/contradictions in capital accumulation activity at the bottom of 'coordination' by urban planning and gaze at its potential to be a 'tool for flexible negotiation' that cannot necessarily be converged with capital accumulation activity. Incidentally, Harvey explains that, although capital accumulation places the responsibility for 'coordination' and 'rationality' on urban planning to its own advantage, the foundation for 'coordination' and 'rationality' is becoming unstable due to the mobilization of spaces created by capital accumulation itself ('spatial fix,' for example) and the resultant change in the interests of different classes and factions; and it creates a need for urban planning itself to find new 'legitimacy' (1985). Conversely, Castells has stepped out of his early structuralist standpoint and asserts that the opportunities for citizens to intervene in urban planning goals and strategies according to their own interests are expanding thanks to improved conditions for disclosure and participation in response to a shift in the role of urban planning from a set of predetermined rules of rationality to negotiation and strategic guidance (2002).

In any case, a great deal of attention is directed to the field where various interests of actors involved in the space become entangled and old hegemony politics oscillates widely—the plane/scene where local governance is in operation. It is of course undeniable that some kind of fluctuation is observed in the perception of urban planning itself, as discussed below.

The direction of local governance and urban planning[11]

Today, the likelihood of local governance penetrating and establishing itself in urban planning is not necessarily high. However, the deep-rooted belief that science discovers and substantiates values which has persisted in the urban planning arena since Tsuji formulated 'planning' as a 'social function connecting values and causality' (Tsuji 1954) is showing signs of instability. At the same time, the authoritarian nature hidden under the unitary value of a 'desirable condition' = 'overall interest' guided by the 'technician of value' and its affinity for government are gradually becoming apparent. More than anything else, the seemingly plain fact that values are determined in an arena of conflicting and competing claims/interests is becoming self-evident as globalization advances. It is becoming extremely important to place urban planning in this arena of pluralistic competition of interests, and Long's comment that planning 'means politics to some degree' (1965) appears to regain life in this context. (Yet, it is more important to ask 'urban planning/politics for whom?' I shall discuss this point later.)

When we attempt to discuss urban planning in relation to the organization of systems called local governance, we are reminded of Davidoff's 'citizens' participation/advocacy planning' (1965). According to Davidoff, planning was in the past more or less based on 'value neutrality.' Consequently, the question of value premise which is of primary importance for public issues was replaced by that of (choice of) technical methods for resolution, and issues such as openness and participation by plural interest groups that are truly important in planning processes were avoided. In pluralistic society, however, the planning direction is determined by the process of political debate which basically establishes how to distribute social values. For this reason, the conventional system of centralized and regimented political decision-making (i.e., government) based on one-dimensional and absolute urban planning which prioritizes value neutrality and technical viewpoints is not necessarily desirable. It is rather preferable to construct a system under which groups with different values maintain their respective claims/positions, pluralistically propose draft plans based on them and compete with each other. Davidoff recognizes the advantages of such a system for both citizens and local governments (public institutions). For citizens, it increases the opportunities to compare and analyze planning proposals and broadens the range of available information and choices. For local governments, it allows them to make comparisons with other plans which indicate the ways to improve their own plans more clearly. In addition, such a system increases the opportunity/possibility of stimulating the formulation of alternatives outside of local governments.

The role of the urban planner again becomes important in this argument. Davidoff clearly rejects urban planning in which the 'technician of value' becomes involved based on the singular value of 'overall interest.' He emphasizes instead that urban planners must represent the interests of individual interest groups and reflect them in specific planning proposals. This assertion certainly contains subtle phrasing in one sense because it does not appear to go so far as to reject the paradigm of 'rational planning' which the 'technician of value' relies on. It even appears to reinstate this assumption under the pluralistic worldview.

In any case, the point I would like to clarify here is that an urban planning model which emphasizes a planning approach based on articulation rather than hierarchy and sympathizes with local governance, so to speak, is found at the bottom of citizens' participation/interest representation-type planning. At the same time, I need to point out an impasse inherent in this argument. At which level should a mechanism to articulate competing claims/interests, or a mechanism to coordinate pluralistic interests, be established and incorporated into an institutional framework? Local governance may no longer revert to government by way of integration of 'overall interest' but serious consideration must be given to this question in order to avoid a relativistic trap into which local governance is prone to fall.

One possible direction in this case is to try to articulate/coordinate pluralistic interests and form cross-linkages with the whole in an attempt to refine such things as the form/style of perception and decision-making procedures rather than venturing to provide answers appropriate for the substance or content of a matter. To borrow Webber's expression, it relates to the assumption that urban planning (the planner) is the 'technician of procedure and process' instead of the aforementioned 'technician of value' (1978). While this direction is effected when substantive assessment of values is thoroughly abandoned, there is a danger that it can diminish the practicality of the dualistic framework contained in citizens' participation/interest representation-type planning for this very reason. Parenthetically, Nishio points out that this citizens' participation/interest representation-type planning was originally proposed as an alternative based on the interests of the low-income class in the type of planning proposed by local governments trying to promote higher levels of land use (Nishio 1975). In other words, from the outset citizens' participation/interest representation-type planning contained the question of 'urban planning/politics for whom?'

Another direction for articulating and coordinating competing claims/interests is to try to form cross-linkages with the whole in the opposite direction to the abandonment of the substantive assessment of values and on the logical plane that will never revert to the singular value of 'overall interest.' The type of dialogue espoused by Klosterman which leads to agreement through adjustment of the ethical premise of the plan ('rational dialogue') (1978) is envisioned along this line. It rearranges the ethical premise of the plan under an operational framework, establishes the obtained definition by filtering through the 'rational dialogue,' and tries to realize the recognized values through mobilization and organization of professional knowledge/technical knowledge relating to planning. For example, what underlies Rawls' theory of justice, or his inequality principle to maximize the interests of the least advantaged (1971), can become the ethical basis for planning only when it is supported by this 'rational dialogue.'

In a roundabout way, I have clarified that the conditions for the establishment of local governance mentioned above, especially the problematics involving deliberative democracy and 'legitimacy,' also constitute the cornerstones of urban planning. And we have caught a glimpse of the evidence that urban planning is nurturing some radical elements for change as well as guaranteeing the mechanism for 'open urban space' as the site of existence for local governance through the competition and intersection of various vectors.

Conclusion

As I mentioned in the introduction, the widespread influence of neoliberalism has been the background factor for the thematization of local governance in recent times. At the same time, there is a clear tendency to use the concept of governance manipulatively in terms of such things as 'cost-efficiency' and 'strengthening of the functions of municipal authorities' on the policy frontline.[12] Harvey astutely observed that neoliberalism and governance are one and the same in his recent book *A Brief History of Neoliberalism* (2005). Even without his comment, the strength of hegemony politics for decentralization based on the articulation between 'the resident' and neoliberalism and the subsumption of the former by the latter is rather spectacular. No one can now deny that decentralization proceeding in the name of 'efficiency' and linked to deregulation is causing endlessly widening gaps between regions. As for urban planning, there is an unending stream of cases in which the 'pain of others' or 'vulnerable individuals' are trampled upon unscrupulously. It would be unacceptable for the governance approach to detour around such a situation.

Come to think of it, the conditions for the realization of 'open urban space' we glanced at in the introduction appear to be increasingly less attainable today due to the strengthening of 'despotic' micro-power devised by surveillance technology. There are even some signs that they are being reclaimed by 'closed communities,' which are impregnated and directed from above and are actually *coming to the foreground*. Under these circumstances, urban planning theory addressed as part of a conceptual exercise to define the direction of local governance in the previous section has to be considered superfluous. As real-life urban planning is being completely incorporated into the neoliberal mechanism, there is even a tendency to 'use' these arguments to 'justify' this situation. In any case, the relationship between 'open urban space' and local governance as a potential is not always that of the unification of oppositions.

For this reason, it is necessary to consider the alternative conditions discussed above in view of the reality and construct a framework of local governance for supplementation, coordination and cooperation in a broad/narrow arena for each issue/task. Then, it is necessary to correct the aforementioned distortions in the mode of intermediation which enables the intervention in hegemony politics and the designing of systems that can deal with intra-/inter-regional disparities. This does not require the aforementioned detour in sympathy with neoliberalism.

In fact, what is needed here is an alternative route backed by firm ideas and a flexible sense of realism to overcome neoliberalism.[13]

Postscript

I had a chance to read Nishiyama and Nishiyama (2008) after I finished writing this chapter. The book discusses the direction of urban renewal based on the state of social enterprise in England. What is interesting is that it proposes 'another type of urban planning' by what I would call a 'public' that is not government or private and places local governance at its foundation, as we can see from the catchphrase 'from urban planning of government type to city planning of governance type.' The book obviously emphasizes the shift from government to governance but it also appears to suggest that there is an urgent need to solve the question of how to understand the mode of governing that underlies them. On this point, the book strongly resonates with my argument in this chapter and offers much to learn from.

Part II
Urban Spatial Turns in Asian Megacities

6 Urban Asia: The Case of Jakarta

> I tell you: one must still have chaos in one, to give birth to a dancing star.
> I tell you: you still have chaos in you. (Nietzsche 1993: 40)

Historical perceptions of Asian cities

Globalization has deeply engulfed Asian cities. However, its impact is manifesting in an extremely refracted manner. This process appears at first glance to be consistent with 'the history (of Asian cities) in which different cultures and heterogeneous organizations, systems, peoples and things have established harmonious order based on interdependence' (Deguchi 2005: 6), but the postcolonial condition is also at play.

For cities in Asia with a history of colonial rule, their unstable and chaotic condition has long been the focus of our attention, generating a particular view of these cities. There has been a predominant tendency 'to understand Asian cities in a negative light in contrast to Europe—very energetic but inscrutable chaos, absence of the citizenry which characterized Europe, or the mind captivated by animism-magic'; in other words, there has been a propensity 'to discuss Asian cities collectively as an anti-assumption of European cities' (Tomosugi 1999: iii). Further, 'the supremacy of primate cities has been noted and the problems of large metropolitan cities caused by migration from rural areas to primate cities have been the focus of discussion' (Matsubara 1998: i). Tasaka sums up a wide range of urban theories of this kind as follows.

> Many of the past arguments on the subject of urbanization in Southeast Asia were migration theories focusing on (the factors and forms of) demographic shift from rural villages to cities, and this was explained solely by a push factor (i.e., rural impoverishment) because cities were in the state of "urbanization preceding industrialization." Research on urban problems concentrated on analysis of "overurbanization" caused by "urbanization without industrialization," which meant the study of the informal sector from the viewpoint of employment and the study of the slums from the perspective of dwelling. (Tasaka 1999: ii)

It is notable that orverurbanization, which was given such names as 'distorted urbanization' and 'urbanization without industrialization,' more or less tended to be seen as involving societal principles inherent in the Third World (Asian societies in this case). This standpoint certainly 'recognizes to a certain extent that the socio-cultural structure of the Third World has been distorted by urbanization which historically progressed in subordination to colonial empires, but maintains that it is an indigenous social structure that is not compatible with industrialism/urbanism originated in Western Europe after all' (Yoshihara 2005c: 16). Needless to say, the indigenous social structure referred to here was interpreted as 'the backwardness' peculiar to Asia.

In social science backed by progressivism of Western origin, Asia has long been labeled primitive or ignorant. Hegel's argument on oriental despotism[1] is widely known to have impregnated and promoted the image of Asia as an underdeveloped area.

> [T]he Eastern nations knew only that *one* is free; the Greek and Roman world only that *some* are free; while *we* [the Germanic nations] know that all men absolutely (man *as man*) are free. (Hegel 1900: 19; emphasis original)

The image of the 'underdeveloped area' has been emphasized and Asia has been discussed as an object of repulsion and derision that is barbaric, unclean and raucous. Accordingly, Asia has simply been perceived as something that the West cannot understand, populated by 'others' who do not share the same values. At best, Asia has been considered to remain in a 'world that was' and must follow the path cut by the West. Geertz made the following reflexive comment about this standpoint as he pondered on his study of Indonesia during the 1950s.

> When I began, more than thirty years ago, to study Indonesia, indigenous cultural traditions were thought by all but a handful of economists, and probably by most anthropologists, to be a simple obstacle to social change, and especially to that particularly wished-for sort of social change called "development." The traditional family, traditional religion, traditional patterns of prestige and deference, traditional political arrangements were all regarded as standing in the way of the growth of properly rational attitudes towards work, efficient organisation, and the acceptance of technological change. Breaking

the cake of custom was seen as the pre-requisite to the escape from poverty and to the so-called "takeoff" into sustained growth of per capita income, as well as to the blessings of modern life in general. For the economists, the thing to do with the past was abandon it; for the anthropologists, to study it before it was abandoned, and then perhaps to mourn it. (1984: 511)

The aforementioned theories of Asian cities/overurbanization are deeply rooted in this view of an 'Asia of despotism and stagnation,' or in other words, orientalism[2] where the Third World is regarded 'as an atrocious nuisance, a culturally and politically inferior place' (Said 1993: 28).

During the 1970s, however, orientalism-based overurbanization theory gradually moved to the background. What came to the foreground then was 'dependent integration' theory which focused on the process of gradual transformation into megacities as the shift from low industrialization to overurbanization was incorporated into the 'new international division of labor.' I once described the mode of existence of a megacity as follows based on the 'dependent integration' theory.

It is gradually becoming evident that the demographic shift from rural villages to cities which is counted as one of the initiation factors of overurbanization is in fact completely bound in the global management strategy of multinational corporations headquartered in "central" cities, or in other words, it is happening via dependent integration into them. Details aside, this rural–urban migration is a product of the compound linkage between push and pull factors, so to speak. In other words, it is caused by widespread creation of surplus labor by the Green Revolution and the resultant increase in agricultural productivity (i.e., forced release "from inside"), land enclosure and relegation of farmers to wage laborers by multinational agribusinesses, and permanent destabilization of cultivation of export cash crops linked to the global market on one hand and mass absorption of low wage laborers (mainly young women from rural villages) into export processing zones which operate as factories for the global market under export-oriented industrialization policies on the other hand. In this case, the overurbanization-"peripheral" industrialization is a result of dependent integration of the world capitalist system overwhelmed by multinational corporations in "core" nations. (1988: 149)

In hindsight, while megacity theory based on this key concept of 'dependent integration' had groundbreaking significance in that it shifted overurbanization from the phase of a domestic phenomenon to that of structural concatenation with the borderless global urban system, it committed a theoretical error in that it ignored another resonant axis of globalization, which is the colonial-postcolonial perspective.[3]

Between primate cities and Asian megacities: Part I

What has been coupled with the aforementioned overurbanization in discussions is none other than the primate city. According to Jefferson (1939), a primate city is one that is far larger than other cities against the general rank and size rule. The following characteristics have been pointed out in relation to the primate city: that it consists of a plural society of multiple races with respective unique orders (Furnival 1956) and that it is a heterogenetic city comprised of peoples of indigenous cultures and heterogeneous cultures (Redfield and Singer 1954). 'Underdevelopment' and 'the parasitic' are the main features in either case, but discussions about the primate city in relation to the latter characteristic tend to emphasize that it has its origins in the colonial regime[4] and that it hinders the development of other cities and acts as a barrier to economic development. The orthogenetic city which grows out of the state of plural society and builds a unified ordered system is adopted as a model to counter this (Redfield and Singer 1954). In other words, 'the genetic' is set against 'the parasitic' (Hozelitz 1955).

By the way, the cornerstones of this type of primate city theory include the urban impoverishment paradigm and the theory of urban–rural dichotomy, and are generally marked by the following line of argument. This focuses on the problems caused by the demographic shift from rural villages burdened with overcrowding from the population explosion and the shrinkage of farming units to cities, especially excessively concentrated cities which overwhelm other small to medium-sized ones, while the urban areas lack sufficiently robust employment infrastructure in relation to the enlargement of the informal sectors (traditional sectors of urban miscellancous services) in a state of permanent semi-unemployment and the expansion of slums.[5] The premise of this argument is the perception that rural areas have become impoverished and stagnant and this situation is not easily improved and that the gap between urban and rural areas is not closing, acting as a push factor for demographic shift from rural villages to cities.

This argument/perception has the urbanism of developed countries as its model, which obviously requires industrialism as a prerequisite, and the 'ideas of difference and divison that have colonial and orientalist roots' (Breckenridge and van der Veer 1993: 11) casts a dark shadow over it. For example, Kazuyuki Konagaya focuses on differentiation between 'demographic shift without pull' and 'demographic shift only of push' and 'upper class = center' versus 'lower class = periphery' as forms of spatial occupation in primate cities and perceives these forms as lagging behind the modernity of developed countries or being pre-modern (1997). He argues that the cause of the former was 'the modern domestic industry, which grew slowly and remained weak in the large cities of developing countries whereas it responded to the post-Industrial Revolution industrialization that drove the formation of large cities in the existing developed countries such as Europe, the U. S. and Japan,' and the latter was 'similar to the original Sjoberg-type pattern which was found in the developed cities prior to the Industrial Revolution' (1997: 64). Then, he changes direction and highlights the unstable and low-wage structure of the informal sector and its weakness as an employment infrastructure as well as its provision of very poor living conditions which sometimes imposed 'subhuman subjection.'

Interestingly, on one hand the urban impoverishment/urban problem theory which gives superiority to European modernity sympathizes with the argument that 'developmental dictatorship' centering on authoritarian political systems and industrialization supremacist economic development policies that have long dominated primate cities is undemocratic and despotic. On the other hand, the subculture of poverty argument asserts that 'slum residents are culturally and mentally backward and therefore their actions lack rationality, or they do not possess sufficient skills or modern values to develop a career in the cities and therefore they are backward about reform' (Yoshihara 2005c: 23). This perception is clearly grounded in 'orientalism introduced via the West = the Occident' (Ōtsuka 2000: 8), and it stands with its feet deep in the colonial-postcolonial stratum.

What is important for the moment is the question of how to bring the colonial-postcolonial stratum up to the surface through critical examination of the aforementioned primate city argument. The key in this case is to identify the social implications of the informal sector and the slums that cannot be dissolved into the urban impoverishment/urban problem theory discussed above. The informal sector and the slums at least can be embedded in urban society only through a medium that is constructed under the historical, cultural and political circumstances of a particular society (area) that are not fully explicable using the existing center-periphery and push-pull models. Conversely, these sectors have existed/still exist as 'internal colonies'[6] not only during the colonial but also throughout the colonial-postcolonial periods.

The 'socio-cultural structure' of the informal sectors and the slums revealed by the operation of the safety net mechanism and the process of its embedding and 'disembedding' in and out of the colonial stratum must be examined from the perspective of a symbiotic relationship between urban development and Kampungs (community) at the base of the segregation between 'upper class = center' and 'lower class = periphery.' In the case of Jakarta, this symbiotic relationship can be elucidated with reference to the following process: 'the "center" is underpinned by the prestige system of the elite who acquired the European colonial style and traditional etiquette, rituals and manners which spread under Dutch colonial rule, and the urban development which took place on this basis expanded exclusive residential districts (Kelurahan Kebayoran, for example) sector by sector, weaving through Kampungs. In other words, Kampungs were incorporated into suburbs dominated by rich neighborhoods in a sprawling manner in the process of horizontal urban expansion' (Yoshihara 2005c: 24).[7] It is possible to argue that the origin of the 'activeness' inherent in the informal sectors and the slums was nurtured under this process.

Nevertheless, this 'activeness' of the symbiotic relationship between the informal sectors and the slums would revert to 'the emergent' of a spurious kind as primate cities transformed into megacities with the advancement of globalization. Let us consider this in the next section.

Between primate cities and Asian megacities: Part II

Megacities, most of which are situated in developing societies, are considered by Castells (1996) to be one of the main marks of three millenniums of urbanization. They are giant population agglomerations and act as nodal points connecting cities and the global economy. In this sense, they differ from global cities which, despite having an enormous population, are characterized by their role as control towers of the global economy and, more precisely, the accumulation of headquarters of multinational corporations. Yet, megacities are now finding their own standpoints in their continuity with global cities.[8] For instance, Lo and Yeung argue that an 'urban cloister' connecting Japan, Asian NIES (Newly Industrializing Economics) and ASEAN (Association of Southeast Asian Nations) countries was established across national borders by the mid-1990s (Lo and Yeung (eds) 1996), suggesting the aforementioned structural concatenation. For this reason, megacities are often discussed from the perspective of 'dependent integration' of the global capitalist system or the aspect of spatial economy operated by global cities at the regional level.

Certainly, a majority of Asian megacities have developed from primate cities. However, they are no longer based on labor-force mobility within a single nation. Megacities are rather based on the borderless and multitiered mobility of people, money and goods supported by 'global assembly lines' (M. P. Smith 2001). At the same time, moves towards the multilayering and articulation of the entire labor market, which are proceeding with post-industrialization and economic globalization, and the hierarchical division of the urban employment structure are occurring in both global cities and Asian megacities (Jakarta, in this instance). Homology rather than difference is increasing between these urban forms in terms of the built environment brought about by urban restructuring, for example, ARK Hills and the Golden Triangle (Photo 6.1), the shopping malls embedded everywhere in central cities, bristling condominiums for the new middle class as well as McDonaldization and Madonnaization which resonate with and underlie them.

In any case, '[t]he sense of dislocation which so many writers on the subject apparently feel at the sight of a once well-known local street now lined with a succession of cultural imports—the pizzeria, the kebab house, the branch of the middle-eastern bank' (Massey 1993: 59) is prevalent in Jakarta, and these days we hardly hear any argument which directly disagrees with the assertion that 'widespread imitative lifestyles, customs, tastes, fashion and consumerism as well as the phenomena called McDonaldization and Madonnaization of the world are observed among people with the advancement of urban restructuring driven by the philosophies of efficiency and growth which have replaced non-capitalist production systems and cultural values' (Yoshihara 2006b: 9).

Yet, extended metropolitanization in Asian megacities, especially Jakarta, contains realities that cannot possibly be discussed on the same level as that of global cities. These are appropriately thrashed

Photo 6.1: The Golden Triangle

Source: Ziv (2002: 52).

out in the theories of EMRs (Extended Metropolitan Regions) and *desakota* (urban-rural coexistence-type metropolitan regions) (McGee 1991; McGee and Robinson 1995). The latter theory entails the pool of the countless half-agricultural and half-industrial low wage population and the supply of low cost land in the *desakota* (a compound word made from *desa* (village) and *kota* (town)) with an extensive mix of agricultural and non-agricultural production which has incorporated densely populated rural villages. The former speaks of the extended metropolitanization characterized by the enlargement and functional differentiation of the metropolitan region reliant on the *desakota* and the multidirectional and catenative expansion of labor force mobility led by the new middle class.

The following points draw our attention here: that Jakarta can no longer be a primate city, which are 'cities that they labeled a pre-1970s urban population expansion in the absence of capital accumulation as "pseudo-urbanization"' (Guinness 2000: 88) due to the advancement of extended metropolitanization; and that while the approach adopted by external 'big powers' (e.g., the World Bank) 'to posit no clear domination and call for no clear opposition' (Hall 1993: 242) increases the invisibility of the colonial stratum, deconstruction of the colonial appears to be progressing through restructuring of the city center and suburban development.

Now we come to consider the direction the aforementioned over-urbanization and symbiotic relationship between urban development and Kampungs will take. At the megacity stage, the city has clearly left the colonial stratum in which a concatenation of development-industrialization and urbanization takes place at the initiative of a small privileged class without a substantial new middle class. The progress of this post-overurbanization entails the appearance of a landscape peculiar to postmodern cities as well as the construction of certain types of infrastructure such as highways and large-scale new towns and shopping centers, as mentioned earlier. However, this shift from the colonial to the postcolonial stratum is a process of recomposition (i.e., colonial deconstruction–reconstruction) as well as transformation of the colonial. At the base of megaurbanization, there is still an undercurrent of the elitist thinking pattern deeply rooted in the colonial which tries to reconstruct a symbolic capital city using the system of prestige and dignity. In other words, the landscape of the capital city continues to be represented by categories and symbols from the colonial era under the hegemony of the elite who received education heavily tinged with colonialism. Of course, it still exists as a de-integrative emblem under the postcolonial system and does not directly represent national integration.

At the same time, with reference to KIP (Kampung Improvement Planning),[9] for example, which is considered to have prepared the ground for megaurbanization, what is embedded in the symbiotic relationship between urban development and Kampungs is not unequivocal challenge or resistance but a localization trend to live with KIP and reinterpret it and the diversity of 'experience' of internal forces lurking behind it. Details aside, we can see the process of 'rereading' imposed cultural and economic systems by 'indigenous' people, as well as the mechanism of coexistence and reproduction of 'the old' and 'the new' (this is not a simple repetition mechanism). However, such 'rereading'/'activeness' are losing their direction with the transition from the post-Orde Baru (New Order) Era to the Reformation Era. Or more precisely, they are transforming into the pseudo-'emergent' as a kind of communitarian reaction to globalization intensifies.[10]

The topology of 'socio-cultural structure'

Asian megacities are facing a dilemma of the modern, at least evident in the case of Jakarta. They are grafted to the colonial stratum but presenting with extreme limitations/deformations. Multitiered and diverse disparities and differences are increasing inside these megacities and at the same time various subjects are entangled in multiple layers at the life-world level. Here various aspects of the life-world with 'life which is very flexible due to lack of a fixed form, social structures which have no centrality due to their ambiguity, and individual ties which are non-exclusive and free due to their looseness' (Ishizawa 1989: 79) become apparent.

Since these aspects still take some forms of expression in the local community dimension, however, we need to identify the mode of existence and configuration of the people, things and events anchored in the local community and examine them by returning to the question of how the colonial 'socio-cultural structure' at the overurbanization stage is 'disembedded' and 'reembedded' in the post-developmental local community. To take a slight detour, I shall start this examination by mentioning factors in the formation of Kampung and *gotong royong* (mutual aid)/'*rukun*' (harmony). On this point, I shall begin by citing my previous discussion on the history of the colonial city of Jakarta as a plural society.

> During the seventeenth century when Jakarta was historically formed as a plural society it is said that what was peculiar to the colonial city and its external form had been mostly completed by 1740. That is to say that various ethnic groups which had arrived from other regions were forced to shift outside of the walled city of Batavia with a small number of exceptions (the Chinese and slaves). The Netherlands settled each ethnic group in the land outside of the walls in segregation and allocated miscellaneous jobs, including the development of

surrounding areas/hinterland. It formed the foundation of Kampung by ethnic group/native place. Batavia was subsequently called the "queen of the Orient" and enjoyed prosperity for a period before experiencing a decline in its inner city population and a rapid rise in its peripheral/ hinterland population. As the Europeans eventually shifted to live in the hinterland, the decline of old Batavia became a certainty. At the same time, the central functions of colonial rule were also moved to the hinterland. Walls and canals which had segregated Batavia from the outside were destroyed and filled and the old city of Batavia became the "graveyard of the Orient."

The wave of the Industrial Revolution eventually reached Batavia, accelerating the construction of infrastructure such as railways, ports, roads, sewers and dwellings as well as the expansion of the municipal area. However, these were essentially carried out for the Europeans and Kampungs were left untouched. To the native Indonesian population, Kampungs became the sites where they carried out their self-contained daily living for better or worse. This plural social structure consisting of the colonial city and Kampungs continued until the postwar (post-independence) era. (Yoshihara 2005c: 329–330)

As we can see (Figure 6.1), the colonial city of Jakarta had exhibited a form of spatial occupation associated with its historical dual structure/ plural society since its Batavian origins.

From the beginning, Kampungs were not subjected to direct colonial administration. Consequently, their communal nature based on *adat* (local customary law) remained and the neighbor relationships of Javanese farmers—extended application of reciprocal exchange and asymmetrical relationships between equals among relatives characterized by 'proximity of residence'—was embedded in the plural city. According to Maotani, the former (reciprocal exchange) means 'an exchange in which an equal amount of labor is returned by half-day work,' and 'many forms of mutual cooperation between neighbors (so-called *gotong royong*) fall in this category' (1983: 146). The latter (asymmetrical relationships) is represented in the example of 'the custom of giving neighbors trays of food during the last ten days of Ramadan' (Maotani 1983: 146). What is considered important in these neighbor relationships is not cooperative activity or labor exchange at the visible level but facilitation of social linkage through exchange of goods and services. For this reason, 'harmony' between neighbors in order to promote social linkage, which is called '*rukun*,'[11] has been emphasized and *rukun* itself has emerged as an expression of cohesive

Figure 6.1: Jakarta at around 1885: historical dual structure

Source: Kidokoro (1998: 222).

force in actual neighbor relationships. Also, 'the relationship between the wealthy and the poor [in the *desa* (village)]... is transformed and absorbed into the patron-client relation and one mimicking the senior-junior relation among relatives' (Maotani 1983: 287) through *rukun*.

Incidentally, the concepts of *gotong royong/rukun* have a political flavor evident from their history of having been captured into the state policy of Pancasila democracy and compulsorily introduced from above in the form of *tonarigumi* (neighborhood group). Especially during the period of the developmental despotism system, the institutional 'top-down' injection and impregnation of *gotong royong/rukun* were carried out with the momentum of pre-modern compulsion. In fact, there was very limited dynamism for involvement in the development process and enjoyment of benefits from it. At the same time, such 'capture and absorption' from above were possible precisely because *gotong royong/rukun* were functioning properly in Kampungs. It is possible to suppose that the multitieredness of Kampung's complex and diverse land systems/relative rights, which were the product of colonial rule, combined with their 'ambiguous' constellation and promotion of 'shared poverty,' had a positive effect on the maintenance of the autonomy of neighbor relations in Kampungs.

If we look at this situation from the viewpoint of 'the ruled,' it may be possible to say that the process of strengthening their framework for 'cooperation in life' as they receive and capture development as a resource provided by the outside and enhancing individuals' communal life skills through it has been embedded in the realities of local community represented by RT (neighborhood group)/RW (neighborhood association).[12] This has occurred under the nation-state system as a given condition, of course.

Globalization, post-overurbanization/-development and locality

To summarize the above discussion on the colonial-postcolonial stratum again, the main points are as follows: that overurbanization has enabled the continuation of 'development' by shouldering and reducing the cost of top-down organization through 'cooperation in life'/'shared poverty' and that, in turn, the key to the continuation of 'development' was the 'mechanism of organizational experience accumulation' (O'uchi and Yogo 1985) over a long period of time such as RT/RW and other local resident organizations. There is no point in arguing over the merits and demerits of 'top-down' and 'bottom-up' perspectives here because the former is more or less obsessed and captured by the 'modern West,' which in itself is a 'fiction,' and the latter by an illusion called 'traditional non-West,' both of which are stereotypes of orientalism.

What we should rather pay attention to is the spreading of mega-urbanization to the entire urban society as the further advancement of globalization has loosened control 'from above.' In particular, structural adjustment programs undertaken by the '"Wall Street-Treasury-IMF" complex' after the Currency Crisis and full-scale restructuring of urban space based on them at once pushed Jakarta to the post-overurbanization/post-development phase. The forcible implementation of structural adjustment programs 'from outside' caused serious damage to the entire accumulation system promoted under the developmental despotism system and also caused the decline of many Kampung communities adjoining the CBD in particular which were swallowed up by expanding transitional zones and the hollowing-out of export-oriented industrial estates in the outskirts amid an overseas re-transfer boom of the manufacturing industry (during the developmental despotism period, the functional differentiation system was already established and under which the central city (DKI Jakarta, especially the Golden Triangle) acted as the base for a 'new international division of labor' and Botabek (Bogor, Tangerang and Bekasi) carried out the preparation and siting of export-oriented industrial estates and the development of new towns (for the new middle class)). In these areas, it has become impossible to maintain the counterbalancing power of local community arising from local interactions of individuals based on 'proximity of residence,' and the cohesive force of neighbor relationships has decreased dramatically. This situation is being accelerated by the presence of a great number of urban underclass,[13] the growth in the number of people who are not absorbed into the traditional practice of 'cooperation in life'/ 'shared poverty,' and the spread of serious human disorganization problems (drug dependency, etc.).

At the same time, the socio-cultural structure = locality which had always constituted the base stratum of Kampung/local community from the colonial to the postcolonial period is not necessarily identified with the national (Pancasila nationalism which has been used as a means for the formation of Indonesian national identity) in the process of the shift from the 'development era' to the post-development/Reformation Era as well as the fall of the nation-state from the position of the ultimate goal of modern history (Wong et al. 2001). Conversely, amid this increasing community disorganization due to globalization, the role of 'socio-cultural structure' = locality as a 'defensive safety net' is attracting attention. The activity of the latter with its inherent communitarian reaction, together with its orientation towards the pseudo 'emergent,' runs the risk of sympathizing with neonationalism and easily leading to the restoration of the authoritarian state. In order to avoid this pitfall, I would like to reinterpret the substance of the aforementioned 'socio-cultural structure' = locality as an internal resource possessing sociological particularities (Hosaka 2005: 144), so to speak, not as a 're'-enclosure of a resource by the state and not identifying with natural market commodification, and consider its possibilities. Let us discuss this below as much as space permits.

Considering the current state of Jakarta in which megaurbanization is progressing outside of the nation-state mechanism, the first thing we need to think of in our inquiry into the possibility of 'socio-cultural structure' = locality is the changing manner of external involvement and the state of post-development as a decisive factor. We need to clarify here that, as the perception that external involvement under the developmental despotism system = 'mobilization-type development' did not work efficiently becomes dominant while the stability and unity of the nation-state are becoming increasingly shaky in the current post-development era, there is an increasing need to search 'from outside' for an internal logic arising from 'the ruled' and for a 'rediscovery' 'from above' of local communality that does not necessarily sympathizes with development.

The next point to be clarified is that, against the backdrop of this orientation, a wide range of strategies for living (the re-hanging of safety nets) which are devised by people at the very limits are about to be implemented in a manner where 'people on the scene generate various solutions, which change and create a new consensus, and policies change accordingly, relationships between people change, and problem structures change' (Satō 2005: 130). Of course, such strategies for living are unfurled on collaborative relations with the state administration and the decentralization system while having their roots in local communality nurtured under *gotong royong/ rukun*. The substance of local communality, which is the cornerstone of strategies for living, draws our attention here. Although it is based on 'being at the scene,' it does not necessarily converge with local completeness; it is underpinned by the diversity and amorphism of Kampung and subjected to interactions between multiple agents. For this very reason, the most important issue is to extract the local activities of people which have accumulated upon 'plural institutional identities' of privies themselves.

In any case, in this post-development era, 'socio-cultural structure' = locality as an internal resource has no choice but to rely on 'emergence' arising from interactions/networks of multiple agents based on the utilization of internal and external resources while it exists on postcolonial synchronic 'cooperation in life.' Of course, in this case, the biggest decisive factor is globalization. Judging from the current state of 'production of space' in Jakarta, the interactions/

network formation which lead to the aforementioned 'emergence' have only just begun.

A new horizon of Asian cities

We have so far discussed the topology of Asian cities from the perspective of the colonial-postcolonial stratum which has been rather overlooked in preceding discussions, and I must say that the enormity of the impact of globalization on Asian societies is truly striking. More than anything else, globalization has brought an end to the authoritarian political system that permeated Asian countries for a long time and the developmental despotism system under industrialization supremacist economic development policies. It then forced a reexamination of the understanding that 'modern' Asian societies were created by 'top-down nationalism,' that is, 'official nationalism' suggested by Benedict Anderson (Yoshihara 2006a: 327). In terms of urban theory, megaurbanization which progressed in conjunction with globalization has resulted in the loss of the substantive foundation of overurbanization theory and strongly prompted megacity theory to come to the foreground of society. Although only secondary, it helped highlight the basis of the perception that Asia was the underdeveloped 'world in the dark.'

At the same time, globalization prompted a regressive move toward the national as a counter proposition to itself, and as far as cities are concerned, it created a flow to shift the interpretation of 'sociocultural structure' embedded in urban space from 'backwardness'/'peculiarity' to 'uniqueness.' As urban restructuring, tallying with the advancement of globalization, increases homology[14] between the landscapes of the megacity and the global city, and as it increases the accumulation of people who have no means to feed themselves at the bottom stratum of urban space, more interest is drawn to this 'uniqueness' as something containing 'emergence.' Now that the split between state and society/divergence between national integration and social integration is a certainty, it is difficult to imagine that such 'uniqueness' will immediately shrink into a 'national narrative' which conforms with the interpretive system of 'official nationalism.' However, it is impossible to say that there is no risk of this anticipated 'emergence' easily transforming into the pseudo 'emergent.'

Therefore, if we are to find a phase of 'socio-cultural structure'/locality containing 'uniqueness,' we must discuss it in relation to another phase of Asian societies appropriately exposed by the advance of globalization, namely, multiphase and polyphyleticness,[15] and ascertain the implications of the real nature of 'socio-cultural structure'/locality which is very ambiguous and mobile. In the meantime, social organizations, social groups and networks and sociations originating from them which appeared to have retreated into the background under national integration during the period of developmental despotism are reemerging as something which connects people and people and societies who have been divided and forced to be isolated by the advancement of globalization. I believe that what is required more than anything else now is to not only identify the difficulty and helplessness of Asian megacities but also the strength and broadness inherent in them with the aforementioned movement in mind. This is an unavoidable task for the very reason that they contain the dilemma of modernity which has persisted both in primate cities and Asian megacities.

7 The Gated Community and the Slum

The Near North Side is an area of high light and shadow, of vivid contrasts—contrasts not only between the old and the new, between the native and the foreign, but between wealth and poverty, vice and respectability, the conventional and the bohemian, luxury and toil. (Zorbaugh 1929: 4)

Introduction

Discussions on the issue of Indonesia's multitiered hierarchical structure and inequality in the post-development system in recent years often refer to the polarized spatial form of 'the gated community and the slum' which figures prominently in Jakarta—captain of the Asian megacities. In sociology and geography, this spatial form is called a 'dual city' or 'divided city' and is often considered to be a structural feature of the postindustrial city. It is notable that the archetype of this 'divided' urban topography has often been related to Zorbaugh's *The Gold Coast and the Slum* (1929), which treated Chicago from the turn of the century to the 1920s as a laboratory.

According to Zorbaugh, the Near North Side, where the Gold Coast emitting 'effulgent rays' and the 'slum' sinking deep in 'poverty' and 'hardship' formed 'vivid contrasts,' was in the midst of the natural history of the 'shock city' (Mellor) of Chicago, and the 'area shook by instability and change' ('zone in transition') steeped in the mechanics of *laissez faire* (Zorbaugh 1929). For this reason, the spatial form described as 'vivid contrasts' came to lead the narrative of assimilation to America in which various migrants to the city moved upwardly through social filtering to acquire the sense of 'We Americans.'[1] In other words, 'the gold coast and the slum' was positioned as a 'transient phenomenon' which would end in, or which was expected to end in, 'the entire city under the rule of the middle and upper classes' rather than an example of a polarized spatial form (Schwendinger 1974: 485).

If that is the case, 'the gold coast and the slum' observed by Zorbaugh and 'the gated community and the slum' discussed in this chapter are clearly different in context and topography, even though they appear to exhibit a similarly 'divided' cityscape. Above all, the former exists as a constellation of natural areas in which the *laissez faire* mechanism projects/is projected directly whereas the latter takes the form of spatial fragmentation which is brought about by the cycles of disintegration-innovation and dislocation-counterturn of the community prompted by urban restructuring tallying with the advancement of globalization and which deeply sympathizes with the instinctual drive of neoliberal capital. This 'divided' aspect is thus absorbed by and identified with the metabolism = pulse of the *'laissez faire* city' on one hand and the multitiered and segmented hierarchical structure and spatial inequality of the Asian megacity on the other. In the case of the latter, the aforementioned multitieredness and segmentation are entangled with the colonial/postcolonial stratum peculiar to the Asian megacity and give the polarized pattern of 'the gated community and the slum' contents that cannot be dissolved into a perfunctory 'tale of two cities.'

This chapter will describe the contents in relation to the overall theme of this thesis and, through it, examine the 'standpoint' = 'the present' of Asian megacity Jakarta in the global world.

The slum in a scrap-and-build process

As I mentioned in the previous chapter, Jakarta received a vast number of migrants from various regions within the country while its urban infrastructure was underdeveloped at the primate city stage. Most of these migrants entered the urban miscellaneous services sector/informal sector and settled on public domain lands, including those from the colonial period, with uncertain (and therefore loosely managed) land titles by way of semi-legal occupation. Shanty towns, or slums, which created 'subhuman' living conditions for these squatters spread to various parts of the city. Earlier migrants from other regions had got together with those from the same native land and formed densely populated Kampungs, but many of them became slum-like because they were located in lowlands with poor drainage.

These slums were left alone for a long time throughout the colonial and postcolonial periods. Although social development led by the U.N. took place in Asian countries from the 1960s, it mainly targeted the formal sector. In this type of social development, the slums tended to be regarded as agglomerations of 'subcultures of poverty' and slum residents were seen as culturally and mentally backward, lacking a capacity for rational action and unequipped with sufficient skills or modern values to develop careers in the city.

The slums became the subject of public policies in some way or other under the KIP (Kampung Improvement Program). Under the KIP, the development of the minimum physical infrastructure of Kampungs, including footbridges, water supply, sewerage and waste disposal facilities, was undertaken as a stop-gap measure. However, housing itself was left to the residents themselves and excluded from the program. KIP was formally launched in Jakarta in 1969. It was initially implemented at the local government level and later adopted and undertaken as a national policy measure under the Second Five-Year Plan. This policy measure became known internationally and even received funding from the World Bank.

It is said that the KIP method achieved significant results and became the first of the slum improvement programs in developing countries (Funo 1991). The most notable among the results was the introduction of a community organization process into Jakarta through the incorporation of what Geertz calls 'shared poverty,'[2] which is a type of mutual aid practice for living, into KIP by way of RT/RW (neighborhood group/association), *arisan* (rotating credit associations), and PKK (Family Welfare Association) etc. This is significant because it supported the development regime based on an authoritarian political system and industrialization supremacism from the grass roots level and played a part in preparing the ground for subsequent urban restructuring (to be discussed later) coinciding with the advance of globalization. Although KIP was widely reported as a successful example of a slum improvement plan domestically and internationally, in the end the slums remained because the complicated issue of entangled titles and rights was not resolved under KIP.

In the 1990s the Indonesian government and the City of Jakarta began to implement post-KIP slum improvement measures in full swing. These measures effectively took the form of forced slum clearance. During the 1990s, squatter households that accounted for forty percent of Jakarta's total households daily faced the danger of losing their 'lives and living' as the forced clearance progressed. The clearance was enforced under the internal security law which even permitted the burning down of slums in the daytime, and people were banned from resettling in the cleared area or organizing with the intention of gaining legal permission to settle. Although a plan for low-cost housing provision was devised[3] as the forced clearance progressed, only those who were in regular employment (nineteen percent of Jakarta's total population) could enjoy this benefit.

In 1994, about 600 soldiers raided Bendungan Hilir in central Jakarta and evicted 300 residents from their homes at dawn. This community was turned into Jakarta's most expensive and prestigious shopping district. The evicted residents were given no compensation and their protests were met by firearms and teargas attacks from the government. In 1995, homes in Kedoya Utara and Kebon Jeruk in West Jakarta were bulldozed and hundreds of people were evicted. The official reason for the forced clearance was illegal occupation of the riverbank but the real reason was to secure the safety of the adjoining housing estate for the wealthy. In 1996, thousands of residents in the fishing community of Dadap were forcibly removed. An international aviation show scheduled to be held near the International Airport in June was the reason for the clearance (COHRE 1998).

In any case, the violent clearance of the slums was enforced by the government and the city in order to create a major city that is sanitary, orderly and attractive to investors and to implement urban renewal to construct high-value houses and buildings. Many persons left behind in the development were abandoned on the street. This is why the forced clearance of the slums resulted in their relocation rather than eradication. In fact, the slums continued to increase and spread to all parts of Jakarta City (metropolitan area). Table 7.1 is a list of slums targeted by NGOs carrying out slum improvement projects. They are all located on public land but it is clear from the table that slums are scattered all over the metropolitan area with the exception of South Jakarta district.

This trend of slum diffusion intensified as the currency crisis of mid-1997 increased the number of poor residents dramatically (from 378,000 in 1996 to 861,000 in 1998). Today, slums consisting of very poor living conditions are appearing everywhere as reported by one science writer. The following observation was made in Kampung Kandang in North Jakarta:

> Kampung Kandang is typical of the illegal squatter settlements that line rivers and railway tracks... To the rear of the settlement, I watch a chicken in the swamp, scratching on an undulating surface of garbage... The communal water tap opens into a bucket that hangs right above the swamp water that residents use as a latrine... an elderly woman wades in the water, collecting swamp plants to sell for wicker... The public toilet in Kampung Kandang costs up to US$0.10 to use—no small sum for a family living on about US$2.50 a day, "So people

Table 7.1: Distribution of slums in DKI Jakarta, 1998–2002

	Kampung No.	Area (ha)[a]	Number of households/population[a]
I. Jakarta			
Central Jakarta	1	20	*
	2	10	
	3	40	1,620/70,000
	4	10	800/
	5	10	700/
	6		60/
	7	500	2,000/5,000
	8	4	
West Jakarta	9	9.5	1,230/
	10		
	11		417/2,085
	12		
	13	1.5	190/
	14	4	187/
North Jakarta	15	40	1,081/5,345
	16	2.75	357/1,175
	17	0.3	66/313
	18	5.6	2,000/
	19	4	200/
	20	10	300/
	21	6	100
	22	5	220/
	23		4,000/
	24	4	50/
East Jakarta	25		12/
	26	20	500/
	27	11	300/
II. Bogor	28		470/1,714
III. Tangerang	29		
	30		
	31		100/
	32		35/
	33		75/
	34	10	800/
	35		3,000/

Note: a = Blanks denote unknown/unavailable data.

Source: Based on internal materials of the Department of Social Welfare, DKI Jakarta and Urban Poor Consortium (UPC) (2005), Kampung Masalarh.

Photo 7.1: Kampung Kandang

Source: Marshall (2005: 314).

just do it everywhere"...Water pressure from the tap is low,... so the villagers rely on water vendors, who sell 60 litres of water for about US$0.20—several times what wealthy Jakartans pay for water from a utility company. (Marshall 2005: 313)

Slums have not only sprung up along the rivers and railways but are also squeezed into the space under raised motorways in the city. Social safety-net plans have been implemented since 1999 as poverty reduction measures for slum residents struggling in the wake of the economic crisis. More specifically, the community-based action program to respond to the economic crisis (CBEC) was carried out in fifteen slums in extreme poverty and the urban poverty reduction program (P2KP) was implemented in 201 slums. These social safety-net plans have not produced any visible results so far. In fact, a considerable number of slums are in such a degenerate state that the traditional safety-net of 'shared poverty' can hardly continue to function.[4]

Segmentation of the lower class and polarization of the middle class

The previous section provided an overview of the scrap-and-build condition that the slums have existed in as Jakarta metamorphosed from a primate city into an Asian megacity. I also pointed out, more than anything else, that this condition has been exacerbated by the aforementioned structural adjustment program led by the '"Wall Street-Treasury Department-IMF" complex' since the currency crisis and the full urban space restructuring undertaken based on said program. Now, I would like to turn my attention to changes in the urban lower and middle classes during this period, because these changes are closely related to (DKI) Jakarta's built environment, namely, the formation of the landscape containing the functional division of the central city and suburbs and the progression of the aforementioned scrap-and-build process of the slums.

Let us begin with the urban lower class. As we have already seen, the size of the poor class increased by 2.27 times in just two years between 1996 and 1998. An income-based class composition in around 2000 shows that about thirty percent of Jakarta's population were high to middle income earners, forty percent middle to low income earners and thirty percent were people in poverty (Kitano et al. 2001: 95). I shall focus my argument on workers in the urban miscellaneous service industry/informal sector in the urban lower class in relation to the preceding discussion but, unfortunately, there is no statistical information on changes in the number of these workers in Jakarta as far as I know. In Indonesia as a whole, however, the employment sector ratios for people aged fifteen and over (informal sector/formal sector) were 58.8/31.5 percent in 2000, 55.8/35.0 percent in 2001, 57.9/33.6 percent in 2002, 60.0/32.7 percent in 2003, 59.2/34.5 percent in 2004, and 60.6/34.3 percent in 2005 (*Kompas* 15 April 2006), clearly showing a gradually increasing trend. This trend is expected to be found in Jakarta as well and it is estimated to be even stronger due to the expansion of the producer and consumer services sectors as a result of its transformation to a megacity triggered by globalization.

Nevertheless, here we are more concerned with the spatial configuration of the informal sector workers rather than their numerical shift. I have already mentioned that the informal sector acted as the main receptacle of overurbanization at the primate city stage and constituted a driving factor in the formation and expansion of slums. I would like to point out further that Jakarta's transformation to a megacity has not only increased the size of the informal sector but also promoted its multilayering and segmentation; this has also become a factor in transforming the spatial configuration of the slum. For example, the following findings from Dwianto's study of *pedagang keliling* (street hawkers) in Menteng Atas suggest that this is occurring in a highly complex form.

According to Dwianto, 'while typical characteristics of the informal work force such as "impermanence of residence," "reflux-flow type" and "guest laborer type" are still observable among *pedagang keliling* in Menteng Atas, those who do not fall in the guest laborer category or the seasonal inhabitant category are increasing in number' (2005: 189). It is clear from the study's findings that a large number of *pedagang keliling* are 'maintaining their connection with their hometowns through provincial fellowship in employment (a tendency for migrants from the same rural area to engage in the same informal sector activity) or societies for countrymen' (Dwianto 2005: 189) and that these provincial networks are functioning as safety-nets in the slums or slum-like Kampungs where they live. It is also undeniable that this is promoting the reproduction of the traditional slums for which 'shared poverty' is an essential pre-requisite.

Conversely, *pedagang keliling* who operate in the residential districts for the urban middle class in the outskirts are similar to commuters and their lifestyle is not very different from that of formal sector workers. Consequently, they have brought non-traditional divides into the slums and Kampungs in which they live. In any case, these changes in informal sector labor demographics are considered to have brought specificity as well as mobility/variability into the spatial configuration of the slum itself in addition to causing a planar expansion of the slum. It goes without saying that these changes basically coincide with the segmentation and multitieredness caused by the functional division of metropolitan space.

By the way, Jakarta has been conducting the 'cities without slums' ('clean cities,' so to speak) campaign since the summer (August) of

2001 and has taken strong measures to banish or screen informal sector workers trading on the street as well as conducting the aforementioned forceful clearance of slums. According to Dwianto, the Jakarta city authorities apply a double standard to the informal sector. They divide informal sector workers into those who are eligible for social welfare and those who are not[5] and enforce oppressive clearance policies on the former while leaving the latter unregulated with the expectation that they will become a major tourism resource for Jakarta (2006: 86–87). As a result, it is undeniable that this discriminatory regulatory measure by the administration in relation to the informal sector is reinforcing the abovementioned specificity of the slum itself.

Combined with these changes in the urban lower class, the following changes in the urban middle class are deeply impacting on the progression of the scrap-and-build process of the slums discussed in the previous section and the expansion/spreading of gated communities along expressways crisscrossing the metropolitan region. We are again constrained by lack of data, but the process of urban middle class formation in Indonesia has already been described aptly by Hiroaki Konno based on Robison's (1992) and Pinches' ((ed.) 1999) discussions outlining changes in the urban middle class in Southeast Asia as a whole and the class composition calculated from population censuses and labor force statistics. According to Konno, the new middle class of non-manual type was formed and expanded by employment growth mainly in the government sector from the 1970s to the first half of the 1980s and employment expansion in the private sector amid industrialization prompted by a rapid rise in foreign direct investment from the second half of the 1980s. The non-manual new middle class grew further as the Indonesian economy deepened its links with the global economy through a series of deregulatory moves and liberalization policies (Konno 2006).

While the urban middle class is a 'child' of the development economy, Jakarta 'has a mechanism by which children of the new middle class in regional cities reproduce the middle class and there appears to be no mobility from the laboring class to the new middle class at all; it has a rigid structure in terms of interclass mobility' and, conversely, it appears to have another structural characteristic stemming from the 'relatively slow development of its industrial sector compared with its neighboring countries' in that it 'maintains the structure in which the incoming population continues to remain in the old middle class (which mostly means small to medium business people and the self-employed)' (Konno 2006). Setting aside the question of whether this perception of Indonesia's 'relatively slow' industrialization is correct or not, the observation that Indonesia's urban middle class is built on the coexistence/stratification of the new and old middle class is notable because this fact is casting a complex shadow over the landscape of 'the gated community and the slum' in Jakarta.

Incidentally, the abovementioned growth/expansion of the non-manual new middle class highlights the habitat preference pattern of the urban middle class carved into the urban space and their lifestyles and values that are important decisive factors for this pattern. Firstly, the habitat pattern shows that a majority of the urban middle class live in residential estates in the central city and new residential areas in suburbs. Figure 7.1 is a map of locations of major residential developments and industrial estates and zones in DKI Jakarta around 1996 and clearly shows that large-scale residential estates were extending along expressways. The new middle class living in these large residential estates, especially those who are called the new rich whose numbers have risen rapidly from the second half of the 1980s, purchase cars that are beyond the reach of ordinary people, frequent malls and shopping centers, and drive the expansion of consumer finance. They are completely accustomed to individualistic consumers' ways of life gripped by extravagant object-supremacism and their consumption cycles are far shorter than those of the urban middle class up to the mid-1980s, signifying more wasteful spending habits.[6]

In addition to their consumerist lifestyles, the urban middle class has often been discussed as the key player in 'democratization.' These days, however, their 'conservative nature/aspect' rather than their 'progressive nature/aspect' is highlighted, as noted below.

> In terms of the role or social position of the middle class, its "progressive nature/aspect" has been emphasized in the past. In particular, intellectuals critical of Orde Baru (the New Order administration) tended to see homology between the rises in student activism, NGO activity and criticism by the media and artists and the rise of the middle class. Some actually identified the middle class with a societal group (or grouping) consisting of intellectuals, newspaper editors, the new business class, lawyers and various other professionals. Even those who considered that the middle class was comprised of mid-level bureaucrats, middle managers of large corporations and small company owners tended to think that the middle class was the main support base of the PDI (*Partai Demokrasi Indonesia*: Indonesian Democratic Party). In any case, a

Figure 7.1: Location pattern in Jabotabek, DKI Jakarta

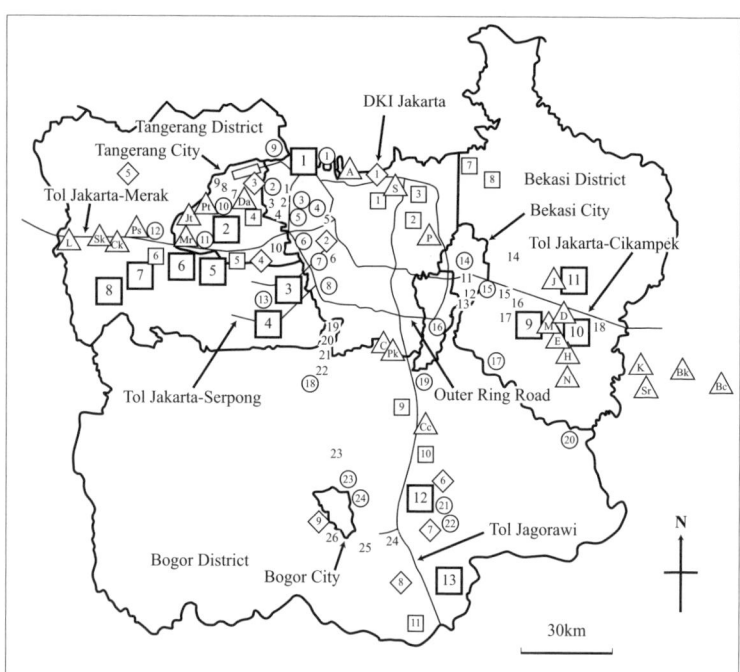

Source: Konagaya (1999: 102–103).

Notes:

(1) Major residential development sites (partially from Procon)

☐ 1000ha>: 1. Pantai Indah Kapuk, 2. Modern Land, 3. Bintaro Jaya, 4. BSD, 5. Gading Serpong, 6. Lippo Karawaci, 7. Citra Raya Tangerang, 8. Kota Tiga Raksa, 9. Kota Legenda, 10. Lippo City (Cikarang), 11. Cikarang Baru, 12. Royal Sentul Highlands, 13. Lido Lake Resort.

☐ 500–1000ha: 1. Sentul Agung Podomoro, 2. Kelapa Gading, 3. Gading Kirana, 4. Banjar Wijaya, 5. Alam Sutra, 6. Villa Permata, 7. Pantai Modern, 8. Harapan Indah, 9. Emerald One, 10. Sentul Hill, 11. Dutara Country Estate.

◇ 250–500ha: 1. Taman Impian Estate, 2. Taman Kebon Jeruk, 3. Citra Garden, 4. Kebayoran Regency, 5. Villa Tangerang Regency, 6. Hanbalang, 7. Gunung Geulis, 8. Ranca Maya, 9. Taruma Resort.

◯ 100–250ha: 1. Pantai Mutiara, 2. Taman Surya, 3. Taman Permata Bhuana, 4. Green Garden, 5. Puri Indah, 6. Taman Mulya Hilir, 7. Permata Hijau Regency, 8. Pondok Indah, 9. Villa Taman Bandara, 10. Royal Green Garden, 11. Palma Spring Village, 12. Kedaton, 13. Villa Melati Mas, 14. Jaka Mulya, 15. Kemang Pratama, 16. Cikunir Ring Road Park, 17. Cileungsi Country Wood, 18. Pamulang Villa, 19. Raffles Village, 20. Kreo Country Ranch, 21. Rainbow Hills, 22. Bell Air, 23. Bilabong Park View, 24. Jasmin Garden.

Figure 7.1: continued

Numerals only: 50–100ha: 1. Taman Kencana, 2. Palm View Garden, 3. Kosambi Baru, 4. Taman Semanan Indah, 5. Green Build, 6. Taman Alfa Indah, 7. Duta Garden, 8. Duta Taman Bandara, 9. Cipondoh Makmur, 10. Metro Permata, 11. Taman Galaksi Indah, 12. Pondok Pekayan Indah, 13. Jatai Bening Estate, 14. Bumi Anggrek, 15. Pondok Hijau Permai, 16. Jati Mulya Jaya, 17. Taman Nargon Indah, 18. Sentosa Garden, 19. Puri Cinere, 20. Villa Cinere Mas, 21. Bukit Cinere, 22. Pamulang Estate, 23. Villa Pertiwi, 24. Bogor Lake Side, 25. Villa Duta, 26. Bogor Country Estate.

(2) Major industrial estates/industrial zones

⚠ Jakarta: A: Ancol, S: Sentul, P: Pulo Gadung, C: Ciracas, Pk: Pekayan.

Tangerang: Da: Daan Mogok, Pt: Pabuaran Tumpeng, Jt: Jatake, Mn: Manis, Ps: Pasar Kemis, Ck: Cikupa, Sk: Sukanagara, L: Liman.

Bekasi: M: MM2100, E: EJIP, D: Delta Silikon, H: Hyundai, N: Newton, J: Jababeka.

Karawang Purwakarta: K: KIIC, Sr: Surya Cipta, Bk: Bukit Indah Karawang, Bc: Bukit Indah Cikampek.

Bogor: Cc: Cibinong Center.

tendency to speak of the middle class as "the catalyst of change" taking a gradualist position was predominant.

However, many members of the middle class lost their jobs in the economic crisis from 1997 or fell into relative poverty due to hyperinflation and a rapid depreciation of the rupiah caused by the deepening of the economic crisis. This situation gradually exposed their "conservative nature." The middle class was originally a "godsend" of Orde Baru and a major "beneficiary" or "recipient" of economic growth under development despotism. This side came to the surface suddenly as destabilization of, and threat to, social order from systematic upheavals became a reality. In other words, "the other nature" of the middle class hiding behind its "progressive nature" surfaced when the basis of its existence was shaken during the transition to the post-Orde Baru period. (Yoshihara 2006b: 142–143)

Here, we must not overlook the fact that the urban middle class is polarizing. Especially after the Asian economic crisis, many people dropped out of the urban middle class and the class distinction between them and the urban lower class became less clear. They have come to exhibit an ambiguous nature in that they live in Kampungs and maintain consumerist lifestyles while becoming involved with Islamic moral values (Konno 2006: 205–205). Nevertheless, the upper and middle strata of the urban middle class are expanding steadily and making the aforementioned 'conservative nature' more evident. This is most symbolically embodied by the gated community. Gated communities may partially erode or overwhelm Kampungs but they are primarily spreading to suburbs/outskirts.

The growth of gated communities

As mentioned above, the ambiguous nature of the urban middle class has surfaced due to the economic crisis and manifested in the gated community in a spatially deformed manner. Its most conspicuous feature is the deliberate establishment of a border between itself and the outside world, be it an artificial fence or a natural barrier such as a river or mound. The gated community creates a 'private' homogeneous space constantly protected by security guards and surveillance cameras. However, it was only relatively recently that such gated communities appeared as a 'new phenomenon.'

The growth of gated communities is directly related to land development associated with globalization. A spate of land development projects began when this process came under the jurisdiction of the 1981 Jabotabek Metropolitan Development Plan[7] in its 'haphazard urbanization' (Goldblum and Wong 2000). From that point, land development became a big business. Overseas Chinese-affiliated conglomerates became involved in land development and created new demand for housing. These developers initially bought up large tracts of land cheaply and let them lie idle as dormant land (*tanah tidur*) (Firman 2000). Over a period of just two years (1991–1993), about 58,000 hectares of farmland were converted to residential land. By the mid 1990s, Jakarta had twenty-five large-scale subdivision plans ranging from 500 to 30,000 hectares and hundreds of small-scale subdivision plans of up to 500 hectares in the metropolitan area (Firman 1997). Thus, thousands of communities packed with houses for sale were marked on the street maps of Jakarta/Jabotabek. In particular, luxurious exclusive housing estates = gated communities that were developed jointly by those conglomerates and foreign investors sprang up in the outskirts/suburbs such as Tangerang. The oligopoly of conglomerates in the housing market escalated following the Asian economic crisis.

Let us look at Lippo Karawaci (hereinafter called 'Karawaci') in Tangerang as an example of burgeoning gated communities. The development of Karawaci began in 1992. The initial development included 500 hectares for the central district and 2800 hectares of

Photo 7.2: The gate at Lippo Karawaci

Source: Leisch (2002: 345).

housing sites, followed by 1300 hectares. By 1999, a total of 6000 hectares of land was developed. The new town has a residential district at its center. The district is surrounded by walls and is accessible only through one main street, which is a public road. The entrance has a gate but it is always open. Guards are stationed at the gate and monitor or check people coming and going (Photo 7.2). This residential district is called the free protective zone (TPZ). It has a golf course at the center and the houses built in and around it are said to be the most expensive and safest. Every house in the TPZ is surrounded by low walls or fences (Photo 7.3). Conducting business and the entry of minibuses (public transport) in the district are prohibited for safety reasons. Hospitals, shopping malls, cinemas, bowling centers, sports and golf clubs, restaurants, schools and universities are located around the residential district, making Karawaci literally a 'self-sustained' community.

According to an interview survey of 754 Karawaci residents by Leisch, these facilities are too expensive for a majority of residents to use on a daily basis, but the use of these facilities in itself represents their preferred lifestyle (American way of life) and living in a town with such facilities enhances their prestige. These reasons rank higher than safety in decisions to move to the new town. While residents can be considered homogeneous in that many of them have been

Photo 7.3: A streetscape at Lippo Karawaci

Source: Leisch (2002: 345).

educated abroad and most live in nuclear families, residents in the same neighborhood do not often mix or associate. For this reason, developers organize activities such as 'neighborhood watch' in an effort to create a sense of community. In any case, the town represents 'a mixture of societal needs, modern design ideas and capitalist imperatives,' carrying symbolic connotations (Leisch 2002: 341).

The gated community as a highly 'privatistic' space as discussed earlier does not appear to have emerged here. A peculiar tendency of residents of the gated community to identify themselves with their own community more strongly as they grow cooler and more indifferent to the outside world does not appear to have manifested clearly either.[8] However, it appears to have already reached the prototypical stage of the gated community which attempts to establish itself according to its own discretion and responsibility rather than relying completely on the 'public.' It is interesting to find a harmonious blend of the 'progressive nature' and 'conservative nature' of the urban middle class here. This trend has been attracting interest in global dimensions in recent years. It is impossible to readily determine whether Karawaci will develop a closed, homogeneous nature as a community. Nevertheless, it is true that the community rearing its head is one in which the gate defining its border with the outside world promotes not only physical segregation (isolation) but also social seclusion.

A noteworthy question is whether the growth of gated communities such as Karawaci will lead to the situation occurring in the U.S. where excessive privatization has effectively resulted in the denial of the 'public' and increased tensions between gated communities and the outside world that has no choice but to rely on the 'public.' (See Chapter Four for details.) This point is better examined through a field study of gated communities in the central city that are directly encroaching on or overwhelming Kampungs rather than a new suburban town such as Karawaci. In any case, it is easy to imagine that the expression of divides which essentially did not exist in the megacity Jakarta in the past, or were contained in the world of Kampung where it existed, will become a major issue in the future.

Conclusion

Let us return to the problematics raised at the start of this chapter. One involves the question of how spatial fragmentation induced by the instinctual drive of neoliberal capital is expressed in the form of 'the gated community and the slum' as a result of urban restructuring aligned with the advance of globalization. When its origin is traced, it certainly appears to resonate with the natural area-based pattern of 'the gold coast and the slum' which was frequently addressed by the early Chicago School. As has become clear from our discussion so far, however, the pattern of 'the gated community and the slum' itself is based on spatial inequality and the multitiered and segmented structure of Asian megacities. The question is whether the multitiered and segmented nature should be explained in the context of globalization in general or examined at the level of socio-cultural structure inherent in Jakarta. This chapter is an attempt to look at this multitieredness and segmentation closely from the latter viewpoint. This leads us to another issue, which is the question of how the colonial/postcolonial strata peculiar to Asian megacities intertwines with the polarized pattern of 'the gated community and the slum.'

With these two questions in mind, I have attempted in this chapter to interpret the scrap-and-build process and the rise of the gated community as the 'superfecundation' of urban restructuring and explain them from the perspective of the dynamics of disintegration and innovation and turn and counterturn of these communities.

Consequently, I have strongly indicated the need to examine the original structure of 'the gated community and the slum' from the standpoint of the colonial/postcolonial strata and provided some orientation, but I have yet to carry out this task.

One thing I would like to reiterate here is that the sight of intelligent buildings and Kampungs or shopping malls and *kaki lima* (portable stalls) standing side by side found everywhere in the central city and the landscape of the gated community thoroughly pervaded with imitative lifestyle, practices, tastes, fashions and consumerism promoted by the McDonaldization and Madonnaization of the world are peculiarly postcolonial yet deeply anchored in various extant factors in society. This complex relationship truly represents the dislocation of 'the local' captivated by globalization but it is also true that the realities of the globality of megacity Jakarta are visible through this displacement.

In any case, the conclusion of this chapter for the time being is that the Asian megacity of Jakarta exists not on a plane of coexistence and confrontation between the slum and the gated community, but rather on a concentrate consisting of multiple layers of both.

8 Islam in Bali

> Like a continual under-sea ballet, the pulse of life in Bali moves with a measured rhythm reminiscent of the sway of marine plants and the flowing motion of octopus and jellyfish under the sweep of a submarine current. (Covarrubias 1937: 11)

Introduction

On October 12, 2002 and again on October 1, 2005, terrorist bombs blasted Kuta, Bali's downtown area in the southern part of the island. The bombs deeply shook Bali, 'island of the gods,' renowned as a tourist destination. Needless to say, the number of victims claimed by the bombs shocked the world. More importantly, the incident highlighted to the world that Bali is no longer untouched by the contradictions brought about by globalization. In fact, the substratum of Balinese society has been hit by seismic changes since these two events—changes that are continuing to have an impact today. For example, walking down the streets of Denpasar, the capital, one cannot help but notice the brand new mosques, both large and small, that are being erected everywhere as if to eclipse the pura or Hindu temples that represent Bali. Indeed, when entering the bookshop located in central Denpasar, one can also spot crowds forming in front of shelves stacked with Koran-related books. I have been conducting fieldwork in Bali for over ten years now, and up until recently this was unthinkable.

Interestingly, these trends have been overlooked by the world. Based on my observations, I argue that the silent progression of Islamization occurring in Bali at present is intimately related to the development of global tourism. Incidentally, as of 2004 the number of Japanese tourists visiting Bali stands at over 325,000 annually, far surpassing the number of overseas visitors from any other country (BPS 2005). This situation remained the same in 2007. The vast numbers of Japanese tourists headed for Bali on a daily basis are contributing to the development of global tourism on the island. Nevertheless, most Japanese visiting Bali continue to cling to fixed images of the island from the past, and seem completely disinterested in the Islamization that is occurring, despite the fact that the Japanese are, in effect, contributing to Balinese Islamization through their role in promoting global tourism.

Undoubtedly, Muslims living in Bali are a minority when we consider their number. However, it is a fact that the Islamization of Bali, as described below, has started to cause disintegration in some parts of the cosmological order prescribed by Balinese Hindu *adat* (customary law).[1] In other words, Balinese Hindu, the traditional thematic construction premised on a homogenous race, can no longer stand.

Based on information gathered during my recent fieldwork, this chapter elucidates how Islamization is actually taking place in Bali, and examines the impact this process is having on Balinese society.

Development of global tourism in Bali

First, let us briefly examine how tourism developed in Bali. According to Scholte (1996), the origins of tourism in Bali can be traced back to 1908 when the Dutch colonial government succeeded in forcing the Klungkung kingdom, which was stubbornly resisting its rule, to capitulate. At this time, the Dutch army's massacre of locals (so-called *puputan*) was widely reported throughout the world. A policy for preserving Balinese culture was then adopted to evade mounting criticism. As part of this move, a tourism office endorsed by the colonial government was established in Batavia (now Jakarta), and the catchphrase 'Gem of the Lesser Sunda Isles' was used to promote Bali's allure. Later, in the 1920s, the colonial government deployed a policy known as Balinization, which urged Balinese youth to embrace their cultural heritage. The result drew outside interest to Bali. Incidentally, Bali became a household name after Balinese dance was displayed at the Colonial Exhibition held in Paris in 1931.

In line with this development, regular ocean crossings connecting Surabaya, Semarang, Batavia, Singapore and Bali were established between the late 1920s and the mid-1930s. In addition, the number of visitors to Bali gradually increased after the establishment of hotels such as the Bali Hotel (Denpasar), Kuta Beach Hotel and Suara Segara ('Sound of the Sea'), among others. Official records of the aforementioned tourism office show that the number of travelers visiting Bali increased rapidly from 213 in 1924 to 1428 in 1929, and to approximately 3000 in 1939 (Picard 1996). Bali thus experienced a tourism boom mainly through the workings of external agencies during the colonial period. However, this was just the beginning. Locals were not yet actively involved in the tourism industry.

It was only after the arrival of Suharto's Orde Baru (New Order) that the wave of tourism swept through Bali. Suharto, the hero of the independence movement and Indonesia's first president, showed a sustained interest in Bali, partly because his mother was Balinese. However, the presence of foreign travelers was not very noticeable during his rule (1945–66) (Pringle 2004). Bali's development as a focal point of international tourism was formed after the establishment of the Bali Beach Hotel in 1966 (with war compensation funds provided by Japan) and the opening of Ngurah Rai Airport in 1969.[2] Indeed, the number of overseas tourists visiting Bali increased at an exponential rate from 86,000 in 1969, to 313,000 in 1974, and to 642,000 in 1982. Furthermore, foreign currency earnings gained from tourism also increased rapidly from US$10.8 million in 1969 to US$359 million in 1982 (Erawan 1994; Bali Government Tourism Office 1997).

The crucial factor in the development of tourism was the successive establishment of Nusa Dua Beach Hotel managed by the state-run Garuda Indonesia, and various world-class hotels (such as Club Med, Hilton, Hyatt, Sol, Sheraton, Shangrila, Ramada and the Hard Rock Hotel) after the opportunity presented itself with the opening of the Bali Beach Hotel and the airport.

We cannot overlook how, in line with this development, Garuda Indonesia and other airlines (such as KLM, Lufthansa, UTA/Air France, Lauda Air, JAL, ANA, Singapore Airlines, Cathay Pacific, Malaysia Air Service, Air New Zealand, Thai Airways, Qantas, Ansett Australia and Continental Micronesia) competed with each other in establishing regular flights to Bali. The first five-year development plan under Orde Baru (1969–74) acted as the underlying driving force. Tourism was incorporated into this five-year plan and the development of Bali's tourist industry was pursued as part of national policy. In 1983 the move to allow tourists in without visas, for example, was implemented as part of this policy.[3] Subsequently, business tycoons who joined hands with Suharto's family maneuvered behind the scenes, causing tourism to expand across Bali from the 1980s to the mid-1990s. The erratic development was not limited to the uncoordinated building of hotels, but extended to the establishment of resorts and land reclamation for golf courses.

Such relentless expansion of tourism was part of a process that strengthened the notion that Bali was actually a 'colony of Jakarta' (Hitchcock and Putra 2007: 22). It was believed that the slump in tourism across the nation following the 1997 Asian financial crisis and the ensuing collapse of Orde Baru would also have a great impact on Bali. However, Bali did not experience such a downturn. The reason behind this was that Japanese and Australian tourists, who enjoyed

Table 8.1: Shifts in overseas tourist numbers, 2001–05 (Unit: person)

	2001	2002	2003	2004	2005
Asia/Oceania	764,508	726,289	524,213	920,590	816,454
	(9.55)	(–5.00)	(–27.82)	(75.61)	(–11.31)
Australia	238,857	183,389	107,386	267,338	249,520
Japan	296,282	301,452	228,013	325,849	310,139
Europe	430,214	392,262	295,340	316,419	396,964
	(–2.42)	(–8.82)	(–24.71)	(7.14)	(25.46)
United States	97,828	76,064	54,489	67,566	76,903
	(–15.53)	(–22.25)	(–28.36)	(24.00)	(13.82)
ASEAN	54,664	70,146	97,432	128,450	114,823
	(69.55)	(28.32)	(38.90)	(31.84)	(–10.61)
Middle East	322	3,770	3,925	9,572	2,543
	(–86.52)	(1,070.81)	(4.11)	(143.87)	(–73.43)
Others	1,791	11,156	13,180	23,915	5,043
	(–96.09)	(522.89)	(18.14)	(81.45)	(–78.91)
Total	1,356,700	1,285,642	993,185	1,472,191	1,419,269
	(0.07)	(–5.24)	(–22.75)	(48.23)	(–3.59)

Note: Figures in brackets indicate percent shifts from the previous year.
Source: Based on BPS (1996, 2001, 2006).

the benefits of a strong yen and Australian dollar against the rupiah, continued to arrive on the shores of Bali. The maelstrom surrounding East Timor's independence in the post-Orde Baru era and the Bali riots that occurred due to the opposition in the Indonesian Democratic Party of Struggle to the appointment of Abdurrahman Wahid (also known as Gus Dur) as president did little to stop the flow of tourists to Bali. It was the Bali bombings, carried out by terrorists in downtown Kuta on October 12, 2002, that saw the number of tourists sink to record low levels (see Table 8.1). The number of overseas tourists fell by 22.75 percent in one year from 2002 to 2003. Moreover, most of this fall was in the numbers of tourists from Australia and various European countries. In 2004 there was a shift towards an underlying upward trend, but once again it took a sudden turn for the worse when the second terrorist bombings occurred on October 1, 2005 in Jimbaran and Kuta.

While tourism in Bali developed under highly dubious circumstances when seen in this light, it has been, at least until recently, closely linked to globalization. It is evident that the establishment of air routes between Denpasar and major international cities, as well as the setting up of numerous hotel chains, acted as a driving force. Furthermore, it is also clear that the development of tourism brought about a domino effect, which encouraged the growth of restaurants and other industries, particularly art, handicraft and clothing, which cater for foreign tourists and visitors (Hitchcock and Putra 2007: 23). Today, however, Bali represents even more than that. Bali is an international brand in its own right. It has turned into a base for exporting products made in central and eastern Java, as well as Indonesia's eastern islands (namely Lombok), to the world. Naturally, multinational corporations have gathered in Bali to cooperate in the pursuit of profit; the momentum of which is transforming it into a city of conventions.

Indeed, it is not the intent of this chapter to further elaborate on this point. The aim here is to show that the development of the aforementioned global tourism has destroyed, and indeed is still destroying, the ecosystem that Bali inherited from time immemorial; it is also drastically unsettling Bali's agriculture, which has served as its economic mainstay, as well as the closely linked Hindu-based society. For example, mangrove forests are being cut down and replaced with artificial cultivation ponds to keep up with the massive volumes of shrimps consumed by tourists. Coral reefs are being destroyed to fulfill the rising demand for lime in connection with the rush to build hotels. Mountain forests and wilderness are being flattened to create nature reserves to protect wild animals from tourist treks. In relation to this, the aim of this chapter is to elucidate the impact of Islamization as a global phenomenon on Balinese society.

Influx and settling of Muslims in Bali

In examining the effect of global tourism on Bali's existing society through the study of Islamization, it is clear that it can be understood most plainly in terms of two phenomena. First, the extraordinary growth of hotels and restaurants means that indigenous Balinese, particularly young people, are being employed by the business sector in droves. As a result, more and more young people leave the agricultural sector, thus causing a situation in which there is an acute scarcity of agricultural workers. Incidentally, a comparison of the workforce in the different industries between 1980 and 2004 (as shown in Table

Table 8.2: Changes in Bali's workforce by industry, 1970–2004 (Unit: person; '( )' indicates % distribution ratio)

Year	A	B	C	D	E	F	G	H	Total
1970[a]	(66.7)	(5.8)	(2.5)	(10.5)	(1.2)	(0.2)	(8.3)	(4.9)	(100.0)
1980[a]	(50.7)	(9.8)	(4.8)	(14.5)	(2.2)	(0.5)	(15.3)	(2.0)	(100.0)
2000	552,248	252,420	134,285	412,014	82,188	37,632	227,539	11,626	1,709,952
	(32.4)	(14.7)	(7.8)	(24.1)	(4.8)	(2.2)	(12.6)	(0.7)	(100)
2004	681,320	190,420	104,595	489,750	86,245	21,215	234,725	26,895	1,835,165
	(35.3)	(14.2)	(7.2)	(23.0)	(4.0)	(2.0)	(13.4)	(0.9)	(100.0)

Notes:
A = Agriculture, forestry and fisheries[b]
B = Manufacturing
C = Construction
D = Business, restaurant, hotel
E = Transportation, storage, communications
F = Finance, public health
G = Services[c]
H = Others[d]
a = Actual figures for 1970 and 1980 are unknown.
b = Includes farm workers.
c = Includes public services.
d = Others include mining and quarrying, as well as electricity and gas supply.
Source: Nagano (2007).

8.2) reveals that while the distribution ratio of agricultural workers decreased from 50.7 to 35.3 percent, that of business, restaurant and hotel employees showed a gradual increase from 14.5 to 23.0 percent. Second, the expansion of tourism goes hand in hand with the birth of various related industries. In particular, the development of Bali as a brand saw the rise in demand for clothing and handicrafts, namely batik (fabric on which wax is applied to create a pattern after dyeing). Consequently, rows of batik factories were set up in the suburban area in South Denpasar, where many semi-skilled laborers were hired. Figure 8.1 shows how the batik factories are located in groups, mainly in *Desa* Pemogan in the South Denpasar subdistrict of Denpasar city. The number of factories peaked around the year 2000.

In relation to the first phenomenon, agricultural land surrounding Denpasar is being destroyed bit by bit, either to be turned into housing areas or to be used partly for building inexpensive accommodation called *losmen* to service low-paid workers (Hitchcock and Putra 2007: 23). What is most interesting, however, is the fact that many of the

Figure 8.1: Location of batik factories

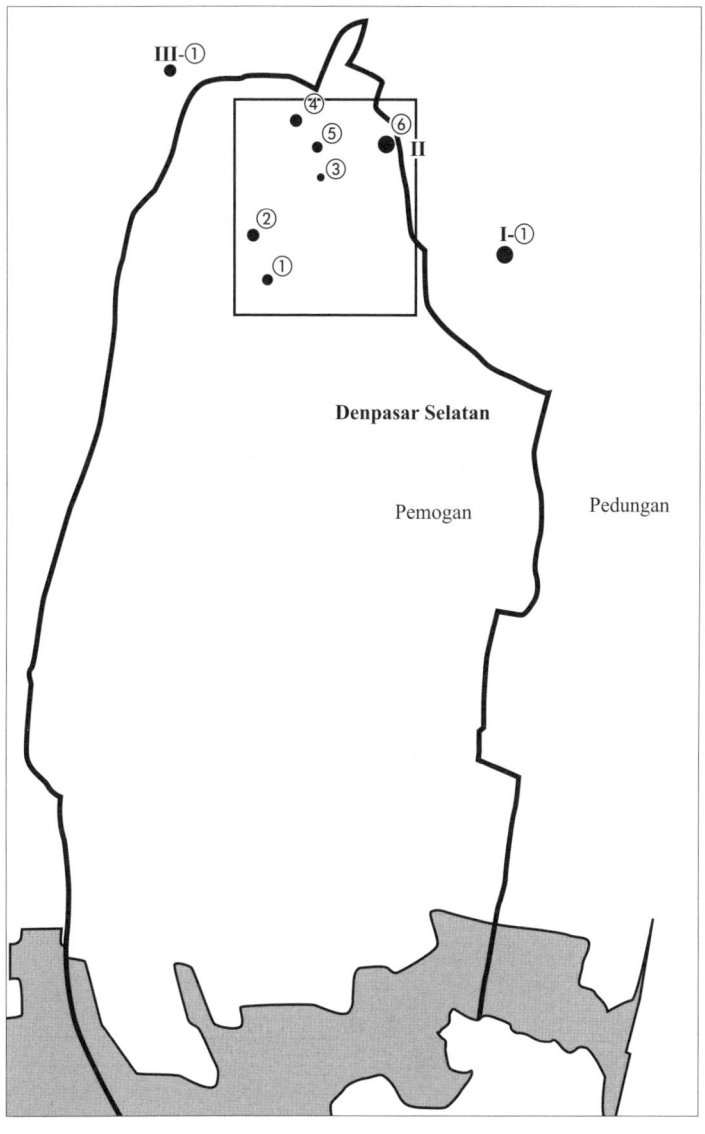

I Pendungan
① Three locations (1985)

II Pemogan
① Three locations (1991–96)
② Four locations (2001–06)
③ One location (1995)
④ Three locations (1985–2001)
⑤ Six locations (2006)
⑥ Fifteen locations (1998–2002)

III Pemecutan Kelod
① Three locations (2000–06)

Photo 8.1: Tents inhabited by KIPEM (taken by author)

farmlands abandoned by the young people are being farmed by temporary residents from Java. They are generally farmers who have come from eastern Java as immigrant workers using their networks of relatives or acquaintances from the same hometowns. They rent farmland from the Balinese, and do everything from rice planting to harvesting by hand. Once they finish, they move on to the next location.

Similar to the so-called seasonal immigrant workers, they send the money earned to their families back home, and sleep and eat (they do their own cooking) in tents set up either on vacant land they have rented or on the roadside (Photo 8.1).

Now let us shift our attention to the second phenomenon. The batik factories themselves are mostly run by Javanese immigrants who have already registered as residents. The semi-skilled workers employed by these batik factories are also mainly Javanese from either central or eastern Java (there are virtually no Balinese involved). They are basically temporary residents working in jobs under dirty, hard and dangerous conditions. They are similar to the previously mentioned immigrant farmers in that they have come seeking jobs because they are no longer able to sustain themselves in their own hometowns. Also, most of them find their jobs through their networks of acquaintances from their hometowns and relatives. Their workplaces are 'sweatshops' in every sense of the word—no ventilation, extremely hot and humid. They lodge in places that look like shacks next to the factories (see Photos 8.2 and 8.3). Furthermore, in addition to the waste disposal issue, the batik factory effluent is also a major issue and recently involved neighboring residents when it polluted the irrigation canals of the *subak* (irrigation association) and rice paddies (see Nagano 2007).[4]

Photo 8.2: Batik factory worksite (taken by author)

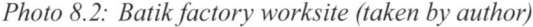

What further warrants our attention is that not only do the temporary residents from Java, as outlined above, support the progress of global tourism from below, but, together with manual laborers (mainly in tile factories) from Lombok called the *buruh* Lombok, they are also in the process of constructing a lower-class society in Bali. They are mostly Muslims, and are doubtless a minority group in the Hindu-dominated Balinese society. At present, this minority group, which is

Photo 8.3: Shack-like housing inhabited by batik factory workers (taken by author)

made up of temporary residents, is increasing in conjunction with the development of global tourism. The influx and settling of this minority group is resulting in the creation of shanty towns, and the number of *ruko* (*rumah* = house, plus *toko* = shop) being erected as a result of this trend is immense. Although they may return to their home towns in Java due to the temporary closures of the batik factories (as a result of the effect of the two terrorist bombing incidents, or the shadow cast by the entrance of the late bloomer China into the market), as long as Bali offers a place where people can avoid starvation, they will inevitably return.[5] Either way, while Balinese want to avoid dirty, hard and dangerous jobs, and absolute poverty persists in the hometowns of the temporary residents from Java, then the influx and settling of the latter group in Bali is inevitable.

Needless to say, it is difficult to accurately trace the changes in the population of such temporary residents from Java due to their high mobility and migratory nature. Table 8.3 shows that since 1996 the growth of the Muslim population in Denpasar seems to outrival that of the Hindu population. However, the figures here only include Muslims who have been registered as residents, and do not include temporary residents. Consequently, the actual number of Muslims living in Bali, especially Denpasar, is estimated to be a few times the number shown in Table 8.3. In fact, the inclination of the local community to label the temporary residents as illegal residents and expel them has had the adverse effect of 'sheltering' or hiding their existence, and thus allowed their numbers to grow. This point is further elaborated in the next section.

Top-down population control and the community's response

Bali's provincial government and the authorities in Denpasar city have, up until now, labeled the temporary residents from Java as KIPEM, and basically adopted a policy of curbing their influx. KIPEM (Kartu Penduduk Musiman, or seasonal resident's identity card) originally signified an identification card. In Bali, however, the word KIPEM also refers to people who hold this form of identification—in many cases, immigrant workers. In this chapter, KIPEM refers to people. In 1998 KIPEM were divided into temporary residents, seasonal residents and visitors based on the 'Provincial regulations on population management in Bali,' and were differentiated from residents who have settled there. Under the existing rules, they were required to either submit a change of address form or report to their administrative authority at the lowest level, such as the *desa* or *kelurahan* (non-autonomous village). Furthermore, the provincial governor's declaration, 'Policy on the execution of population registration in Bali,' dated February 27, 2002, which was dispatched to the head of each district and city, stated that 'it has become increasingly necessary to carry out population control through population registration as the influx of KIPEM is causing the

Table 8.3: Population shift by religion, 1996–2006 (Unit: person)

Year	Muslim	Hindu	Buddhist	Protestant	Catholic	Total
1996						
Bali	163,259	2,672,151	16,054	10,454	12,157	2,874,075
	(5.7)	(93.0)	(0.5)	(0.4)	(0.4)	(100.0)
Denpasar	43,119	312,667	6,743	2,497	6,388	371,414
	(11.6)	(84.2)	(1.8)	(0.7)	(1.7)	(100.0)
2001						
Bali	183,977	2,823,173	18,844	21,255	15,782	3,063,031
	(6.0)	(92.2)	(0.6)	(0.7)	(0.5)	(100.0)
Denpasar	44,626	357,684	7,653	8,295	7,755	426,013
	(10.5)	(84.0)	(1.8)	(2.0)	(1.8)	(100.0)
2006						
Bali	198,933	2,956,875	20,925	48,799	22,258	3,247,790
	(6.1)	(91.1)	(0.6)	(1.5)	(0.7)	(100.0)
Denpasar	68,705	342,629	9,329	32,350	10,902	463,915
	(14.8)	(73.9)	(2.0)	(7.0)	(2.3)	(100.0)

Note: Figures in brackets indicate percent changes compared with the previous year.
Source: BPS (1996, 2001, 2006).

population in Bali to grow.' With this in mind, the declaration outlined the registration conditions for KIPEM, and enumerated the general principles (standards) such as, among others, the issuance of the certificate of immigration/change of address, creation of a register for immigrants, obligation of the (housing) tenant to report to the *banjar* (hamlet), and obligation for the employer of a KIPEM to report to the *desa* or *kelurahan*. However, up until this point the provincial authorities were overwhelmed in their attempt to gain an understanding of the trend in KIPEM influx, and the instructions relating to the general principles more or less failed to go beyond a mere afterthought.

The terrorist bombings on October 12, 2002 drastically changed this situation. The 'Policy relating to the population registration of immigrants' issued by the governor on November 14, about one month after the bombings, to the head of each district and city emphasized the 'restoration of social order.' It specifically pointed out that this should be achieved through the complete registration of the immigrant population. Detailed regulations, such as the requisites (a registration fee was first mentioned at this time), forms and procedures concerning the general regulations were now determined. Yet, the response of the *desa* and *kelurahan* towards this policy was varied. For example, the registration fee they collected was not uniform. Conversely, a move to expel the KIPEM strengthened at the community level. Incidentally, the Kompas newspaper reported on January 7, 2003 that indigenous vigilantes called *pecalang* were frequently forcing their way into houses in the middle of the night in Denpasar and demanding that residents show their temporary identification cards (referred to as KIPP). In the midst of all this, the central government ordered the adoption of a more systematic and effective population control measure/policy to curb KIPEM. Subsequently, on February 10 the governor issued Declaration Number 153 of 2003, entitled 'Agreement between the Bali provincial governor and the heads of all districts and cities on the implementation method of population control in Bali.'

The agreement detailed everything from the definition of population registration to matters regarding guarantors, procedures, administrative fees (registration fees) and others. In particular, it made the guarantors bear joint responsibility for the registration of KIPEM and their period of stay (valid for three months and only permitted to be extended once). It also included the fine details, such as prescribing a uniform administrative fee of 50,000 rupiah for the issuance of temporary identification cards (re-issuance of temporary identification cards in the case of extensions also incurs an administrative fee of 50,000 rupiah) as a measure to avoid confusion regarding the onsite population control system and regulations regarding the treatment of KIPEM. It was evident that this was an effort to force the burden upon both the KIPEM and those accepting the KIPEM. It also shows that there exists a thinly veiled intent to curb the influx of KIPEM. At the same time, we can also grasp the administrator's logic of trying to reorganize the population control system (which was made chaotic by the influx of KIPEM) in a top-down fashion by clarifying who is responsible and unifying the administrative procedures. Incidentally, the governor issued Declaration Number 3 of 2005 on January 20, entitled 'Regarding the information system relating to Bali's population control,' which instructed each level of administration from the head of the village/town/ward/city to that of the district to put together a report on a daily basis containing information on population control and submit it to the higher authorities.

Now let us examine how the lowest levels of administration and the *banjar* actually handled the situation in the midst of the tightening population control from above, particularly the regulation of KIPEM. First of all, the registration fee is usually paid to the *desa* via the *kelian* (head of *banjar*). In the case of the abovementioned *Desa* Pemogan, the fee is 100,000 rupiah. Of the fee paid, the *desa* takes 50,000 rupiah, while the *banjar dinas* (the hamlet under the local government) and *banjar adat* (the hamlet under local customary law) each take 20,000 rupiah.[6] The remaining 10,000 rupiah is used to cover fees to maintain village security and running costs of teams assigned to collect unpaid identification administrative fees. Meanwhile, the registration fee for extending an identification for three months is 30,000 rupiah. Of the fee paid, the *desa* takes 15,000 rupiah, the *banjar dinas* and *banjar adat* take 6000 rupiah each, and 3000 rupiah is used to cover the running costs of teams assigned to collect unpaid KIPEM administrative fees. Regardless of the amount, the point is that as far as these administrative fees are concerned they generally fall within the framework determined from above.

Let us now refocus our attention on the form taken by the abovementioned teams that collect unpaid administrative fees from the point of view of the community's response. These teams were clearly formed at each *banjar* in response to requests received from above. At the *banjar* (a *banjar* under Desa Pemogan) where I conducted my fieldwork, the team would visit the temporary residence of the KIPEM in the *banjar* once a week on a Sunday to check each KIPEM's period of stay. The results were reported to the *desa*. The *desa* would conduct a *sidak* (spot check), and prosecute and fine those who had not paid or had overstayed. However, the team concerned never took any punitive measures. Instead, it would reduce the administrative fee, allow for payment in installments, or even provide loans to pay the fines if the KIPEM were having difficulties finding work or struggling with low pay.[7] In other words, the community is not responding to calls from above for tighter regulation as in the abovementioned newspaper article. Rather, the community tends to contribute by forming and rebuilding the safety net for KIPEM.

It goes without saying that this community response is just one example. However, we cannot overlook it as merely one example when we consider how it reveals that the top-down suppression of KIPEM is not affecting the community in a uniform manner. At any rate, as long as global tourism continues to develop and the community response to the top-down intervention and regulation of KIPEM is varied and flexible, the influx and settling of Muslims within Balinese society will continue.

The *ajeg Bali* undercurrent

At the same time, it is also important to point out that the influx and settling of Muslims within Balinese society is becoming a fresh point of tension in Bali. Of particular interest in relation to this is the *ajeg Bali* ('sustainable and strong Bali') movement, which was started by the *Bali Post* in April 2002 and called for the preservation of Balinese traditions. After going through some twists and turns, the movement later found sympathy among groups that responded negatively to the influx and settling of Muslims within Balinese society. While *ajeg Bali* has more than one origin, it is obvious that all members share the same spirit of post-Orde Baru decentralization. Decentralization introduced a new move in Indonesian society that aims to review the centralized system (prevalent up until then under Orde Baru) and establish local identity. In Bali the *Bali Post* group started the *ajeg Bali* movement when it called for the promotion of local culture as part of the move to establish identity (Hitchcock and Putra 2007: 173). However, for most Balinese the call made by *ajeg Bali* was not a novel idea, nor did it seem like a meaningful expression of culture.[8]

It was only after the terrorist bombings of October 2002 that *ajeg Bali* went beyond the simple promotion of an outdated tradition. The incident transformed *ajeg Bali* from a mere expression of culture into a social and political slogan. It began to clearly demand that the island be protected from terrorism. In other words, safety and security came to be prioritized above culture, and it was through this that the movement was linked to the development of tourism. But tourism can bring about negative impacts in that it acts as an external agent that destroys the environment and increases the gap in living standards. Consequently, expelling such 'evils' and protecting and maintaining Bali became the main purpose of *ajeg Bali* as a movement. Incidentally, those who cry out for *ajeg Bali* perceive the 'evils' that have been pointed out and KIPEM as one and the same thing. This is why KIPEM have become an object of suppression and expulsion.[9]

Ajeg Bali, indeed, is not a monolith. As the term *ajeg Bali* floods Balinese society, various viewpoints that intersect in a complicated manner with one another have started to manifest themselves. Some see it as cultural propaganda, or as a political movement, while others see it as a market strategy adopted by media groups. Furthermore, it is not unusual for *ajeg Bali* to become a point of contention at the national government level. Some are starting to see *ajeg Bali* through an analogical perspective of 'unity in diversity' at the nation level. Yet, regardless of how broad the issue becomes, it still does nothing to stop the undercurrent that is running through *ajeg Bali*, and neither does it help ease the tension created with the influx of Muslims into Balinese society. At any rate, while the *ajeg Bali* movement began by calling for the protection of Bali and preservation of Balinese tradition from outside influences, which have been brought on by the development of global tourism, it is now spreading in an ominous fashion by turning into a practical movement that is at one with the community in seeking to expel 'foreign elements' as a means to increase Bali's security.

The events reported by the *Bali Post* amidst this situation on June 4 and 6, 2007, as described below, cannot in anyway then be seen as a mere coincidence. According to the *Bali Post*, a group of Muslim youths from Kampong Islam Kepaon was trying to pass through the neighboring Bali Hindu *banjar* of Jaba Jati on their bicycles in the early morning hours before dawn (3 am) on June 3 when they got into a fight with youths from Jaba Jati. The youths of Jaba Jati hastily hit the *kulkul* (wooden signal drum) when they realized they were about to lose, and awakened the whole *banjar* in an attempt to rally support. As a result, the residents of Jaba Jati rushed to the site en masse. Meanwhile, the youths in Kampong Islam Kepaon who heard this, especially the women, panicked and were overcome by fear that the residents of Jaba Jati were going to descend on them. While the incident itself is simply something that arose from a quarrel between two groups of youths living in neighboring areas, it is evident that there is a subtle link between its underlying cause and the call for *ajeg Bali*, or the social trend that operates by the same principles.

Conclusion

Bali, the 'island of the gods,' hitherto maintained a unique social construction in which the whole island was whitewashed with Balinese Hindus under Indonesia's principle of 'unity in diversity.' Ironically, this played an important part in the nation-building endeavor of 'imagined communities' (Anderson 1983). However, the fall of Orde Baru and the development of global tourism, which piggybacked on it, undermined the very foundation of social construction that exists, or is believed to exist, only in Bali. Most significantly, the development of global tourism is forcing Bali to accept Islam, which represents an element that the traditional and dominant Bali has found difficult to accept. Bali is today facing the prospect of being engulfed by the wave of Islamization that is sweeping across the globe. Needless to say, this is precisely the reason why traditional Bali or conservative Bali is popping its head out of the ground in a frantic attempt to protect itself from this gigantic wave. These trends seem to take a stance of suppressing or expelling foreign elements, and carry with them an inherent inclination towards locality by adopting a 'closed protectionist' principle. In other words, there is a force that is working to contain Muslims living in Bali, regardless of their residential status, as a minority group. However, it does not take much to know that such reactions have already been anticipated by the trend of globalization.

In this chapter we took a brief look at the present state of Bali, which is struggling to come to terms with its exposure to the global phenomenon of Islamization. Even if the struggle between two different elements supposedly causes the 'emergent'[10] to arise from within Balinese society in the future, it will probably be a considerably long time before it happens. With regard to this matter, we can only continue to pay close attention. However, I would like to finally touch upon the significance that the Islamization of Bali, as described above, has for the Japanese.

As mentioned in the beginning, the Japanese play the greatest role in assisting Bali's global tourism. Despite this, however, the Japanese are ridiculously ignorant of the Islamization of Bali that is progressing hand in hand with the advance of global tourism. A majority of them just accept as 'existent' the thematic construction of a homogenous race based on the image of Balinese Hindu that they have been presented with, and merely act as its consumers. To these people, Islamization is virtually non-existent. Furthermore, Japanese tourists cannot get past this notion because in their minds the Muslim presence in Bali will remain an absolute minority. Naturally, since Bali is, for them, merely a 'different group of people' who exist only to be gazed upon, it is probably impossible for them to even conceive of the idea of Islamization. However, the 'existent' is starting to fade away from Bali's reality. Conversely, that which was labeled as 'non-existent' is starting to take over as 'existent.' Consequently, it is imperative that the Japanese gain a deeper awareness of this matter, together with a sense that their own experience as tourists is, in fact, spurring on Islamization.

A deepening of such sense/awareness could, in a way, relativize the way the Japanese presently perceive things in Japan. It may allow them to go beyond their conception of 'existent' (a homogenous society that has been tacitly solicited by the nation-state) to look at the social realities, and to be more critical of the way they blindly reject new trends that do not fit with their conception, especially the way they reject as 'non-existent' the emergence of 'ethnoscape' (Appadurai 1996), or the scape created by people who move around the globe. At present, here lies my main interest; that is, the potential that the Islamization of Bali offers the Japanese.

9 Bali and the Japanese

...most people are not settled at or near the top or center but at some region lower down, further out—whatever the image should be. (Geertz 1984: 158)

Globalization and 'people who cross borders'

With the advancement of globalization, territories and borders which used to define the nation-state or national society have become highly fluid and the borderless flow (movement) of people, objects and money is dramatically changing people's life-worlds. The existence of 'societies beyond society' is becoming a hot topic. Regarding the flow of people, it is gradually becoming hard to maintain a strong tie with nationality. It is becoming difficult to distinguish between travel and migration, and the distinction between the everyday world and the non-everyday world is blurring. Rather, living in a 'gap' between states, societies and nations is becoming the 'form' of living for the new mobile subject. In this sense, what Cohen calls 'global diasporas' which try to circumvent modern nation-states undoubtedly represent an early manifestation of this form (1992). Diasporas and nomads[1] as 'ambiguous being[s] that do[..] not belong to any territory' are about to come to the foreground of society for the first time in history (Iyotani 1998: 239).

Conversely, the borderless flow of people re-territorializes as well as de-territorializes enclaves in the host country. At the same time, various sociations are being formed through this process.[2] These sociations are emerging through 'open' involvement in local society rather than identification with 'closed' community. What is evident here is not the 'ethnoscape' (Apadurai) formed around 'a set of basic support systems for daily living centering on overseas Japanese companies, including real-estate companies, retailers, the service industry, schools and preschools, clubs etc.' (Iwasaki 2003: 4), but that characterized by 'de-company.' Again, the nimble 'people who cross borders' who traverse national boundaries and differentiate niches at their will are the key players here.

The Japanese who are the subject of discussion in this chapter are essentially part of this trend; or, if anything, they are actively creating this trend. Bali has positioned itself at the leading-edge of global tourism[3] by turning its image as a somewhat nostalgic 'home of healing' into an ultimate tourism center and is already attracting a flow of overseas visitors making a 'pilgrimage to Bali' who are enchanted by this image. At the same time, the orientation to de-nationality of migrants who have crossed the border for clearly different purposes than for those tied to overseas corporations is having new impacts on Bali's Japanese society. The 'attachment to homogeneity' of many Japanese communities abroad which are comfortably closed is not found here. However, it is true that 'people who cross borders' are deeply anchored in 'the present' of Japan while moving back and forth between travel and migration.

Let us now highlight 'the present' of the Japanese people in Bali by addressing several cases based on a hearing survey conducted in August 2007.

From 'corporate emigrants' to 'lifestyle emigrants'

The Japanese presence in Bali became rather conspicuous during the 1990s. It is said that the commencement of JAL flights in 1994 in particular triggered a Bali boom and a flood of Japanese tourists. According to statistics (*Bali Dalam Angka*), Japan overtook the perennial leader, Australia, as the source of tourists to Bali in 1999 (299,233 Japanese to 228,568 Australians) and since that time has always maintained its top position. The terrorist bombing incidents in 2002 and 2005 certainly threw cold water on Japanese tourism in Bali. The number of Japanese tourists dropped by 38.4 percent from 2002 to 2003 and 17.5 percent from 2005 to 2006 (Bali Government Tourism Office archive). Yet, this upward trend continued.

As the number of Japanese visitors to Bali increased, the number of Japanese residents also rose steadily. Table 9.1 shows the rise in number of Japanese residents in Bali from 1997 to 2006. Since these are the figures for Japanese residents registered with the consulate-general, the actual numbers are considered to be much higher. Table 9.2 shows the number of Japanese residents by area, revealing that 96.7 percent of them were staying in the leading global tourism districts (Denpasar City, Kabupaten Badung and Kabupaten Gianyar) and just under sixty percent of all Japanese residents were female. This is perhaps related to a marriage boom between Japanese women and Balinese men which started in the 1990s[4] and continues to this day

Table 9.1: Changes in the number of Japanese residents in Bali

Year	1997	1998	1999	2000	2001	2002	2003	2004	2005	2006
Number	737	841	921	1,005	1,226	1,330	1,372	1,453	1,568	1,657
Change (%)	10	14	10	9	22	8	3	6	8	5

Source: Compiled from archival material of the Consulate-General of Japan in Denpasar.

Table 9.2: Numbers of Japanese residents by area, 2006 (%)

	Male	Female	Total
Denpasar City (Denpasar, Sanur)	253 (37/43)	334 (35/57)	587 (35/100)
Kabupaten Badung (Kuta, Seminyak, Jimbaran, Nusa Dua)	306 (44/42)	416 (43/58)	722 (44/100)
Kabupaten Gianyar (Ubud)	109 (16/37)	184 (19/63)	293 (18/100)
Kabupaten Buleleng	10 (1/50)	10 (1/50)	20 (1/100)
Kabupaten Tabanan	4 (1/36)	7 (1/64)	11 (1/100)
Kabupaten Karangasem	4 (1/31)	9 (1/69)	13 (1/100)
Kabupaten Jembrana	4 (1/67)	2 (0/33)	6 (0/100)
Kabupaten Bangli	1 (0/25)	3 (0/75)	4 (0/100)
Kabupaten Klungkung	0 (0/0)	1 (0/100)	1 (0/100)
Total	691 (100/42)	966 (100/58)	1,657 (100/100)

Source: Compiled from archive material of the Consulate-General of Japan in Denpasar.

Note: For the numbers in brackets, the number on the left denotes the percentage for the city/*kabupaten* and the number on the right denotes the male-female ratio.

(an average of three Japanese-Balinese marriages per week these days according to the Japanese consulate) and a substantial increase in the number of long-stay people such as retirees[5] in recent years.

What is notable in the case of the Japanese in Bali is that the mainstream emigrants are 'lifestyle emigrants' such as middle-aged and older women and age-based retirees. As noted by Shinji Yamashita and others, 'corporate emigrants' directly associated with the overseas expansion of Japanese corporations are more commonly observed in other countries and regions (Yamashita 2007; Shimamura 2007). For example, the Japanese population in Jakarta consists mainly of 'expatriate employees of Japanese companies and their full-time housewives.' They are said to form a relatively closed and homogeneous community—a highly hierarchical expatriate Japanese society in which one's title exercises great influence, so to speak.

As we will see below, the Japanese in Bali tend to switch between travel and migration and become involved in Balinese society *on their own terms*. Consequently, their 'form' of living is somewhat indeterminate and fluid unlike the traditional settlers and immigrants. This tendency itself resonates with the de-bordering/mobilization of life/the living associated with the advancement of globalization. What is the actual form of existence of this expatriate Japanese society defined by de-integration and mobility? To what extent does it function as a safety net in a sociocultural context that is different from 'the image of Japanese society'? Let us begin with a description of the Japan Club in Bali, which is considered to be its keystone.

The foundation of the Japan Club in Bali

The Japan Club in Bali (Photo 9.1; hereinafter called the 'Japan Club') was founded in 1991. It was formed as a representative organization for the purpose of negotiating with the Ministry of Foreign Affairs and other authorities for the establishment of a Japanese Language Continuation School (hereinafter called the 'Japanese school') that opened with eleven pupils. The Japan Club has two membership categories—corporate and individual membership—and fifty-two member companies with 154 people (including sixteen family members) and 271 individual members as at the end of July 2007. JAL, HIS, JTB and their related companies are the main corporate members. Among individual members, only sixteen families have two Japanese parents and the rest have one Japanese and one Indonesian (Balinese) parent. They must join the Japan Club in order to enroll their children at the Japanese School. Its preschool branch (three years) currently has eighty-eight children and its elementary and junior high school branch teaches 115 pupils. The preschool has nine teachers and the elementary and junior high school has eight, only two of whom are employed as full-time teachers, the others volunteering their services.

Figure 9.1 shows the organizational structure of the Japan Club. There are seven sections along with the Ubud section at the same level,

Photo 9.1: Japan Club in Bali (taken by author)

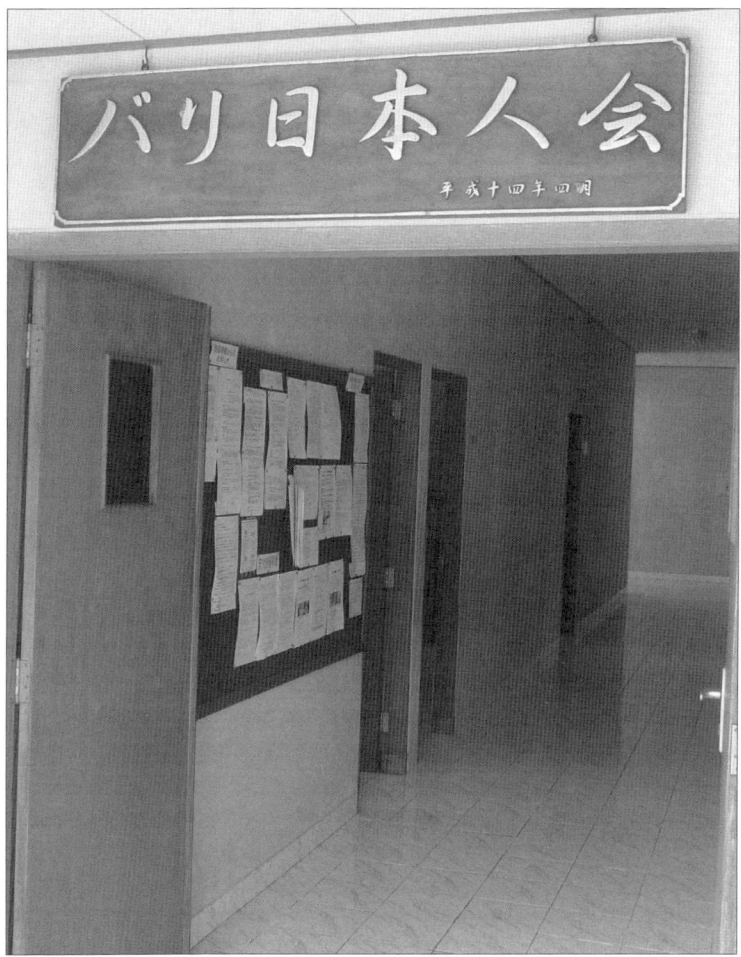

below the positions of president and vice-president. The operating committee consisting of section chiefs and deputy chiefs from all sections meets on the third Thursday of each month convened by the president and discusses matters such as each section's operation policy and the appointment of officers. It is in effect the executive organ of the Japan Club. The annual general meeting is held in March, but the submission of the financial report is the only agenda item and the attendance rate has been at around ten percent in recent times. Major events of the Japan Club include *bon-odori* (Japanese traditional

Figure 9.1: Organizational structure of the Japan Club in Bali

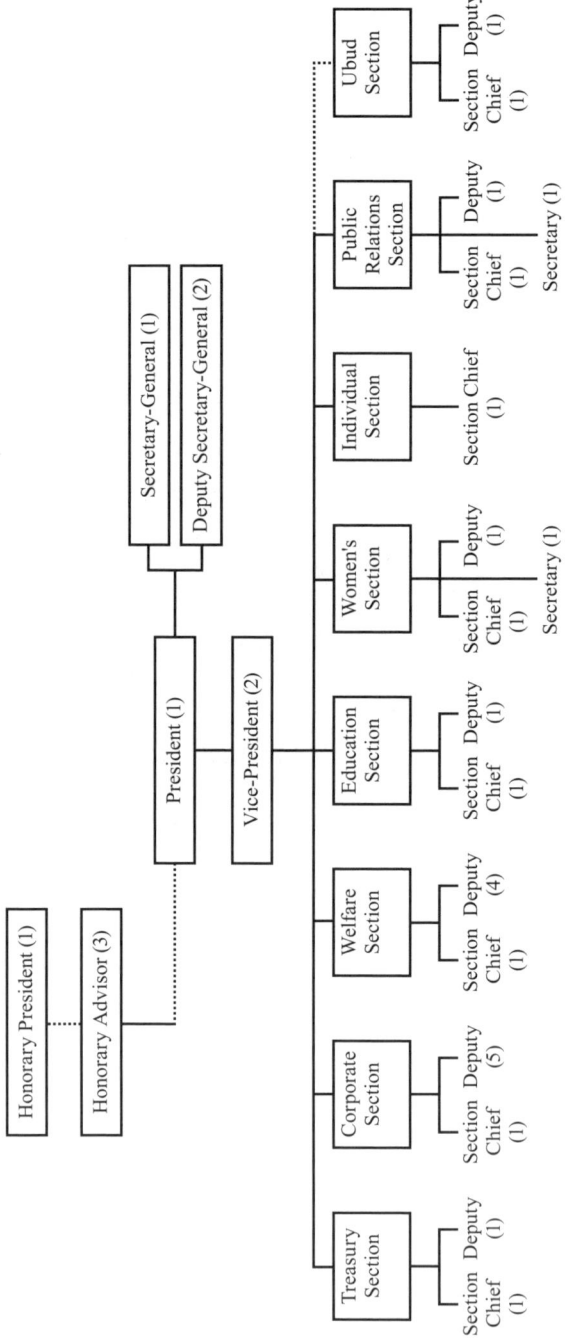

Source: Compiled from material supplied by the Secretariat and gathered in the hearing survey.
Note: The number in brackets denotes the number of people in the position.

dance), a field day and three-city (Jakarta, Surabaya and Bali) sports days in addition to the end-of-year party. Each section conducts various club activities. The costs of operation (including labor costs) and various activities/events are covered by membership fees. The secretariat has only one paid staff member and the rest are volunteers. The operation cost of the Japanese School is covered by monthly tuition fees, subsidies from the Ministry of Foreign Affairs/Japanese consulate and other revenues from bazaars and other activities.

To an outsider, reasons for the existence of the Japan Club for the Japanese in Bali are not necessarily clear except the perfunctory reason of 'amity,' so to speak. Still, it is undeniable that at least all sorts of information are exchanged via the Japan Club and some opportunities to form loose sociations within the Japanese community are arising. It goes without saying that the club newsletter (*Tile Book Print Kecak*[6] (Photo 9.2)) published by the public relations section four times a year and the club website play a major part in this. Another notable point is the high proportion of retirees and women who chose an 'alternative way of living' and crossed the border at one point in their lives among the key operational staff of the club. It is likely that the Japan Club has not become a highly cohesive body for the Japanese in Bali because it strongly reflects their 'orientation to lifestyle' without the center point in one sense. This form of existence of the Japan Club in fact represents the state of being of the Japanese in Bali quite accurately. In any case, it is possible to read some kind of 'form' of the Japanese in Bali through the Japan Club.

Let us describe this 'form' more concretely based on several case studies in the next section.

Japanese people living in Bali

At the end of the journey: from America to Ubud

First is the case of N. N is a forty-seven year old man, born in T city, S prefecture. His father managed a seafood processing company and his mother was a full-time housewife. He is the youngest of their three sons. He went to public elementary and junior high schools in T city, then a private senior high school in Tokyo, and studied politics and economics at a private university. After graduating, he worked in casual jobs to save travel money, then went to the U.S. to learn English for three months. Upon returning to Japan, he gained readmission as an undergraduate to the British and American Studies Department of

Photo 9.2: Tile Book Print Kecak *(taken by author)*

a national university (part-time) due to his 'obsession with English.' Upon graduating, he worked at a photography company in Tokyo for two years, then found a job at a publisher of in-flight magazines. The main motivation for the career change was a chance to go on overseas assignments. During his five years at this publisher, he traveled overseas (mostly to the U.S. and Europe) a half-dozen times every year. He went to work for another publisher for a year, then joined a new company to produce in-flight magazines for Garuda Airlines which was set up by a friend of his from the first publisher. He visited Bali for the first time in October 1995 when he accompanied this friend on a trip to gather materials for the magazine.

N stayed in Bali for three weeks. He initially stayed at a Nusa Dua hotel and once this assignment finished, he visited Ubud as a backpacker. He was not impressed by the main street where tourists hang out. He hired a bicycle and came to a *desa* where he now has his home. He stayed in the only inn in the village. A sweeping view of terraced paddy fields in front of the inn took his breath away. He returned to Japan and went back to the same *desa* two weeks later and stayed for one month. He met his current wife at this time. During his month-long stay, he was very moved, even though he did not understand the language, to see many people from the whole *banjar* gather at one place (*bale banjar*[7] or hamlet pavilion) for a chat every night. He came to think that he might be able to spend the rest of his life in this *desa*. Meeting his future wife was of course a major factor. He was thirty-four and his future wife was twenty-four at the time. After that, he traveled between Japan and Bali several times and finally married her in April 1997. He bought a piece of land and had a new home built on it. He now has two daughters and one son. The family speak Japanese at home as a rule. All children go to the Japanese School.

N earns his living mostly from inn management (for long-stay). Business has been rather quiet and he has been reaching into his savings from his old days as a salaried worker. He occasionally works as a guide for Japanese tourists to supplement his income. While he intends to continue living in Ubud, he tells his children to maintain their ties with Japan.

N actively participates in the various activities of his *banjar* and has the feelings of awe and respect for the world of *adat* (local customary law). However, he is highly aware of the fact that part of the work of the *banjar* is contracted out to external operators these days and those who are working in the paddy fields are mostly elderly people, and that ornamental articles that used to be feted as objects of art and craft are no longer selling as a result of overproduction/overcompetition. N is no longer an 'enthusiastic youth' with regard to the life of Ubud. He is witnessing with his dispassionate eyes the way Ubud is being transformed rapidly by huge waves of global tourism.

Giving up role expectation

H is a forty-six year old woman, born in A city in the Tokai region. She is one year younger than N. Her father was a public servant (now retired) and her mother was a full-time housewife (now working part-time). She has a younger sister and brother. She went to local public elementary and junior high schools and a public senior high school in A city. After graduating from a women's university in Tokyo, she worked as a copy writer at a Tokyo advertising production company for four years. She then worked at a film distribution company for two years. After working as a writer at a magazine production company, she became a freelance writer. She visited Bali once during this period.

H came to Bali alone in the year she turned thirty. Without a set itinerary, she traveled around Thailand, Malaysia and Indonesia (from Medan to Bali) for two weeks. She met a few Japanese people in Ubud. As she talked with those who actually lived there, she came to think about the option of living in Ubud. She was vaguely attracted to the 'nature, relaxed rural landscape and friendly people of Ubud.' Yet, she could not make up her mind then. She decided to return to Japan and sort out her thoughts. She needed one year to make up her mind. She worked as a freelancer during that period in order to take time out for herself. She rented a flat and lived alone. In the end, she turned her back on a choice between a career and a marriage and decided to go to Bali. In other words, she gave up her own role expectation and chose Bali.

She arrived in Bali at the age of thirty-one. She soon found a property to open a clothes shop, which she continues to manage to this day. She initially did the designing and cutting by herself. At one stage, she went to a class in N city to master tie-dyeing A skill and incorporated it into her dressmaking. The introduction of this tie-dyeing technique was beneficial for her business. She currently employs ten people and has a shop in the main street of Ubud, Jalan M.

At the age of thirty-three, she married her current husband who was introduced to her by a friend. After dropping out of university in Medan, he had several different jobs before taking up painting. He is also a devout Muslim. They have one son and two daughters who all go to the Japanese School. H has become a Muslim but she does not attend *pengajian* (Muslim prayer meeting) or the mosque. She pays her fee to the *banjar* but she does not participate in *gotong royong* (mutual aid). The center of her interest lies in Japanese society through her work and her children. A majority of her products are made to order for Japanese clientele. While she sometimes sells to wholesalers, her client base is expanding by word of mouth through buyers from Japan.

The selling point of her products is that they look Balinese to the Japanese eye and Japanese to the Balinese eye because of a combination of tie-dyeing A and Balinese design and colors. On the other hand, her contacts with Japanese society are steadily increasing through her children. She does not socialize with the Japanese residents who are totally immersed in Ubud but she is actively involved in various women's networks through the Japanese School.

H lives in Ubud as a 'foreigner.' She keeps her distance from both Hindu rituals and Islam as her husband's family lives far away. She intends to live in Bali for the time being but she wishes to send her children to university in Japan once they finish high school. This is why she sends her children to learn the Japanese language and they have admiration for Japan. Since her parents are getting old, it is an appealing idea to send her children to university from her parents' home in Japan. She feels that her children can decide by themselves in the future how they wish to involve themselves in religion.

Fascinated by the beauty of the Indonesian language

T is a thirty-eight year old woman, born in Y city, S prefecture. Her father used to work for H metal company and her mother is a full-time housewife. She has one brother who is four years older. After finishing public schools in Y city, she went to a women's junior college in Kyoto.

After graduating at the age of twenty, she found a job in a sales department of a major clothing company. She relocated to Tokyo when her father was transferred in 1997 and she was on unemployment benefits for six months. She then found a part-time job at S travel company.

T visited Bali for the first time in September 1997 while she was unemployed. She was inspired to travel abroad after reading novels by Banana Yoshimoto and other authors. She was initially interested in Italy and was preparing to travel there with her former workmates at the clothing company. One of them had to cancel the trip at short notice and the remaining two women chose Bali as an alternative destination. They stayed at the Hilton Hotel in Nusa Dua for three nights and she was immediately captivated by the Indonesian language. After a meal in Kintamani, she was very excited when her '*terima kasih* (thank you)' elicited a reply of '*sama sama* (you are welcome).' She began to learn Indonesian seriously when she returned to Japan.

After studying at a language school, she went to a night course at T university to master the Indonesian language. She began to attend social meetings with Indonesian students.

She and a friend visited Bali again in March 1998 while she was still working at S travel company. After spending ten days at a Kuta bungalow, she had to fly back alone for various reasons. At the airport, she went to the check-in counter to ask about her boarding gate and the person who attended to her was her current husband. They chatted for a while and she was shown his KTP (identification card) and got to know that he was a younger son and unmarried. They exchanged their addresses and took a photo together at the gate. She sent him the photo from Japan and began to communicate by email. She was not thinking about marriage to start with. She traveled to Bali with her family during the May holiday season in the same year. She saw him again and felt very close to him. After that, she traveled to Indonesia every four months or so. She stayed in Bali for one month on the pretext of attending an Indonesian language seminar for foreigners under Professor R of the University of Udayana and began to think about living in Bali. She married in October 2000. Although she was shocked by the strenuous objection of her parents, she was not worried about the marriage. She had a strong desire to live her life with her husband in Bali. They currently have one daughter.

T has kept her Japanese citizenship after marriage, although her child has Indonesian nationality. She intends to keep it while her parents are alive. Japanese citizenship is advantageous with regard to insurance and immigration and provides better protection if the political situation becomes unstable (which is a major reason stopping her from becoming a naturalized Indonesian). Conversely, lack of Indonesian citizenship is a disadvantage in obtaining a driver's license, visa and land ownership.[8] T will reconsider naturalization when her parents pass away.

T avoids contact with the Japanese community. She says, 'Bali is a small place and living in an even smaller community would be bothersome.' She is not a member of the Japan Club and she does not send her daughter to the Japanese School. She can obtain necessary information about Japan through the Internet and other information through her old friends from the Indonesian language school. The clientele of the dental clinic where she works part-time is predominantly Japanese and she gains information from them too. Her Japanese parents visit Bali every year.

T suspects that in the future her daughter may have the identity problem of being neither Indonesian nor Japanese but thinks she should choose her own path in the end. She keenly realizes that Japanese society is highly efficient. This is the very reason that she did not feel 'alive' there. When she was living in Japan, she always wondered to herself, 'Is it right for me to continue to live here like this?.' In Bali, the feelings of 'creating every day' and 'living every moment with passion' well up in her. To her, it is her love of Bali rather than her love for her husband that keeps her there.

Rising from the depths of malaise

I is a forty-eight year old woman from S town in G prefecture. Her father is a dairy farmer and her mother is a full-time housewife. She has a brother who is six years older and a sister two years older. After finishing local public schools, she studied arts at university, majoring in clothing design. She did one year of postgraduate study at a design research center in Tokyo. She found a job in a design company listed in the second division of the Tokyo Stock Exchange. She became an assistant designer, then a chief designer for a new brand. After five years there, she was headhunted by F group. She was appointed chief designer but she had to leave the job after two years due to illness. Her illness was clearly a 'setback' for her life but she says it was an opportunity to 'reset life.' After taking a year off, she worked as a contract employee of K company. She got married while she was working there.

She had often traveled to Italy and Paris on business but she had never been to Bali. While she was working at K company, she had a colleague who knew Bali very well and introduced her to her current husband. Her husband's family runs a hotel in Sanur. After finishing high school, he went to Australia for six months, then went to Japan to study. He studied at a private university near Tokyo and worked at the Tokyo office of an Indonesian company after graduation. The marriage was opposed by not only I's father but also her husband's parents. They moved to Jakarta soon after their marriage (according to her husband's wishes). She secured a space when S department store opened in Blok M and started up a made-to-order clothing shop. She employed ten seamstresses who worked on the second floor of her home. Her husband ran a trading business from home. She disliked dealing with snobbish Indonesians and Japanese people. Her husband's business was not doing as well as he hoped. When riots broke out in 1997, they left Jakarta, stayed in Japan for one month and headed for Bali. After managing villas and bungalows together, they joined her husband's family in hotel management. She opened a shop selling clothes and muse bags in 2004.

They have three children who attend a local elementary school as well as the Japanese School. Her husband wants them to study at universities in different countries as did he and his brothers[9] but the children wish to go to Japan. Like her husband, she thinks that her children should go to various countries, not limited to Japan, to broaden their perspective, but she will respect their wishes in principle.

She limits her involvement with the local Japanese community to the tasks assigned by the Japanese School. Her dealings with long-term guests at her family's hotel take up more of her time. Naturally, she socializes with the Japanese people who gather at the hotel to use tennis courts or play a game of *shōgi*. She maintains regular contact with her siblings and keeps in touch with her friends from university (she travels to Japan at least once a year). She attends her local *banjar* events (*ngaben* (cremation ceremony), for example) and always participates in the rituals and ceremonies of her family and relatives. In her view, the Japanese residents who socialize only with other Japanese residents do not do well and those who learn the language and actively participate in Balinese society flourish.

In search of work/life balance

Both Mr. and Mrs. W were born in K prefecture. He is forty-three years old and his wife is thirty-seven years old. Mr. W went to local public schools before attending a language school (where he met his future wife) and went on to study management at N university of technology in the U.S. at the age of twenty-four, graduating at the age of twenty-seven. Mrs. W migrated to Jakarta with her parents when she was in the third-grade. She finished lower secondary education at a Japanese school in Jakarta, and returned to Japan to go to O high school, which was a full-boarding school. After finishing high school, she went to a language school (where she met her future husband) to prepare for her overseas study. She enrolled at N university in New York at the age of eighteen (the department of environment and health) and graduated three years later. They returned to Japan together. Soon afterwards, they moved to Jakarta to work for a seafood export company owned by Mrs. W's parents. However, they felt uncomfortable with work-centered and profit-oriented business life and started their own business (in the same industry) in 1996.

Mr. W was thirty-two and his wife was twenty-six when they married. They have two sons and two daughters. They migrated to Bali just before their second child was born and tried to develop the same business there. They closed the business after two years and moved on to establish a new company selling natural cosmetics. The venture was based on what Mrs. W studied at university (environment and health). They currently have a head office in Bali (with eight employees) and a branch in Jakarta (with four employees). Mrs. W is concentrating on raising their children. The idea for their business stemmed from their concerns for the environment and health for children but it now has the future of Balinese society in its perspective. They naturally question the way development is taking place in Balinese society. Since they are considered *tamu* (guests) in their local *banjar*, they rarely participate in *banjar* activities. However, they encourage their employees to get involved in their *banjar* and also put a lot of effort into child rearing. In other words, they would like their workers to value their own lives more than the company. According to them, 'that is the foundation of our business and we left our parents' business because we questioned the work-centered way of life.'

They socialize with members of the Japan Club to some degree. Mr. W is member of a baseball team and a soccer team through the Japan Club but he confines these relations to the sports ground. Mrs. W has acquaintances through her children's Japanese School which have expanded to contacts with Balinese society (as a natural consequence of one of the parents being Balinese in many cases). Conversely, they consciously avoid 'contacts which stick tight and drag on' among the Japanese. They have noticed lately that there is an emergent willingness in Balinese society to accept the Japanese people as they are due to an increase in the number of new forms of inter-marriage. They think that the mode of assimilation of the Japanese residents into Balinese society may diversify in the future. Alternatively, they are concerned lately that the Japanese women they see in Bali all have the same *noh* mask expression on their faces. 'In relation to our business, we suspect that they only eat food from convenience stores and fast food outlets and do not pay enough attention to their own health.' Mrs. W says that her younger sister is also living in a Southeast Asian city due to her husband's overseas posting but she notices a 'gap' between her attitude towards the society of her host country and her view of her husband's work.

A 'de-Japanese' long-stay

Mr. and Mrs. K are both from T city in S prefecture. He is sixty-six and his wife is sixty-four. They are more than two decades older than Mr. and Mrs. W discussed in the previous section. Mr. K was the second son of a shrine carpenter who went to work for a textile sales company after finishing junior high school. He married at the age of twenty-seven. He left the company in 1974 to work in a building materials sales company set up by his wife's brother (who later became a prefectural assembly member and a city mayor). He stayed there until 2002 (his final two years as a non-regular staff member). Mrs. K finished local public schools and worked in her family business (men's clothing sales) until she married at the age of twenty-four. She became a full-time housewife. They have one son.

Mrs. K migrated to Bali three months before her husband's age retirement. Since she had been to Bali many times with her niece, she had no reluctance or hesitation about the move. She found their current home, which was under construction at the time, and decided to rent it. Mr. K had promised her earlier that she could do anything she wanted once he had retired because their life had revolved around his work for a long time. This is why Mrs. K went to Bali first. Still, Mr. K was initially worried about the language and food. Once he arrived, however, he had few problems with food. With the language, he decided to 'take it as it comes.'

Since they arrived, they have actively socialized with their next-door neighbor who is the owner of their rented house and participated in the ceremonies of various families whom they got to know through their neighbor. While they have expanded their contacts with their neighbors, they refrain from becoming involved in the Japanese community. They are not members of the Japan Club. When they lived in Japan, they were always dragged into the election campaign of the wife's brother (presently the mayor of T city) and became very tired of the strong 'constraints' imposed on people by Japanese society. They certainly had a latent desire to shed such 'constraints' by moving to Bali. In their eyes, the Japan Club is still dragging such 'constraints.' They are more interested in *gamelan* (instrumental percussion music) practice. Mrs. K in particular loves festivals and used to act as an MC for the lion dance at night festivals. She has enjoyed playing *gamelan* since she arrived in Bali. They are making new Balinese friends through their *gamelan* practice.

Life in Bali poses few financial problems for Mr. and Mrs. K. His employee pension and her national pension[10] together with some rental income in Japan are enough for them to live on. It has been agreed that the lease of the house shall be renewed every three years. They are considering making Bali their final habitat. At the same time, the recent appearance of some Japanese people in Bali who defraud the middle-aged and older Japanese residents or introduce 'host country wives' to business bachelors from Japan makes them feel that 'the Japanese never learn' more than embarrasses them.

Living like a traveler

Finally, Y is a thirty-six year old man, born in Y city, K prefecture. He is the youngest among the people mentioned here and unmarried. He finished public elementary and junior high schools in M city in suburban Tokyo and dropped out of a private senior high school in his second year. 'I increasingly wondered whether it was right for me to continue my schooling, then I found myself dropping out.' He worked in various construction sites and found a diving job at the age of twenty-three. He went to the Nishiomote Islands, the Ogasawara Islands and the Amami Islands, then finally Bali. He was twenty-eight years old. He did not have any special interest in Bali before this time. He vaguely wanted to go abroad and his destination happened to be Bali. Once he arrived in Bali, however, he felt that the place suited him.

Soon after arriving in Bali, Y found a job at a diving service company where he is still employed. The company is owned by a Japanese resident in Bali and acts as the sole agent of a Japanese tour company. Y has been the general manager since 2003. He has twenty employees under him. Only one of them is Japanese and the rest are locals. The main clientele are couples in their late thirties and women (mostly office workers) who are experienced divers. Y has been living in Bali for eight years and has returned to Japan only twice during that period. He is unsure whether he will stay in Bali but he wishes to continue his current diving work.

Y lives alone in a single detached house in Sanur. He is not involved in *banjar* but he often attends events such as *ngaben* and *upacara potong gigi* (teeth cutting ceremony) with his Balinese friends. They are very kind to him and he values their friendship. He socializes with his next-door neighbor who is the owner of his house. He often attends ceremonies for his neighbor's grandchildren, for example. As the owner's relatives are living in the neighborhood, Y has day-to-day contact with them as well. He now identifies with Bali more than Japan. He encounters some problems with the Balinese at work such as their unpunctuality and their habit of eating, chatting or disappearing during work hours but he feels that that is the way they are. He tries not to be judgmental about things that may appear unacceptable by Japanese standards. However, he tries to get them to understand the ways of Japanese society since a majority of their customers are Japanese. He says that balancing these two sides is a very important issue for him.

Y does not try to get involved in the Japanese community but he has a lot of business contacts with the Japanese people working for tour companies and in hotels. He sometimes has meals with them outside of his work. He became involved in the diving business not as an extension of his hobby but out of his desire to escape from the rigidity of Japanese society. He says that he feels 'encouraged' now that he has found out he is not the only person who feels this way from his contacts with other Japanese people through his work.

The hidden side of 'lifestyle emigrants'

Overseas migration and migrants from Japan and the Japanese communities abroad were dragging their nationality along in some ways for a long time regardless of whether they or their communities were aware of it. Although this tendency is still evident among 'corporate emigrants' who are sent abroad by their employers and the Japanese communities dominated by them, the advancement of globalization has undermined its foundation and spawned various forms of overseas migration and migrants. In particular, the overseas migration of Japanese people in mixed marriage situations is clearly different from the preexisting types of migration containing some kind of orientalism.[11] Setting aside the question of whether this group can be bundled into the category of 'lifestyle emigrant,' we must take note of the emergence of new modes and styles of migration that are not constrained by territories and borders and at the same time the incipience of Japanese communities characterized by such terms as mobility and de-integration. It may be an exaggeration to state that this trend is manifesting intensely in the Japanese people and community in Bali discussed in this chapter. However, it is also true that its beginning or early signs are observable.

I believe that a more penetrating study will be required in order to identify the structural factors that define the abovementioned change. Most of all, we must take the current state of de-bordered immigration policies and global citizenship under globalization into consideration of the decisive factors underlying this trend. In that case, it is essential to account for the transformation of the historical inter-state system in Asia. At the same time, the inclusion of this viewpoint will require consideration of the ethnoscape created by the flow of 'people who cross borders.' While it is expected to be an imaginary transnational landscape founded on a multitiered safety net rather than a unitary information network, this point will require an exhaustive study.

Nevertheless, the 'form' of 'de-Japanese' migration is situated on a horizon where so many vectors intersect that it is unlikely to fit easily into a stereotype. Moreover, while it appears to be standing in a 'gap' between Japan and Bali, it is deeply anchored to the pressing issues—the aging population problem, for instance—facing 'the present' of Japan. This is making the aforementioned 'form' of migration extremely complicated. I doubt that I am the only person who is bothered by the magnitude of the latent contradiction (symbolically expressed as a gap) as more emphasis is placed on the lightness of footwork of these migrants. In my view, 'lifestyle emigrants' with their nimbleness carry the aspect of forced migration and drag along much of the internal 'darkness' of Japanese society.

Postscript

This chapter is based on the results of fieldwork (hearing survey). The fieldwork itself was carried out in collaboration with I Made Sendra and I Made Budiana of Udayana University. However, this chapter was written by the author alone with their consent. This chapter is part of the outcome of research of a Grant-in-Aid for Scientific Research (A) (from 2004 to 2008) awarded by the Japan Society for the Promotion of Science, the title of which is 'Comparative and historical study of neighborhood associations in the post-occupational period.'

10 Coordinate Axes of the Post-Global City: Urban Spatial Turns in Contemporary Asia

Like the spider whose entire world is enclosed in the web it spins out of its own abdomen, the sole support which strangers-in-meeting may count on must be woven from the thin and loose yarn of their looks, words and gestures. (Bauman 2000: 95)

Introduction: Multilayered regions and invisible cities

The advancement of globalization has put regions of various spatial scales on the agenda. At least, the region identified/equated with the nation-state is no longer absolute. The formation of global, regional, national, national-regional and local regions as well as those formed via the corporeity of various individuals is said to be taking place (Iwanaga 2008). Needless to say, these multilayered regions have appeared as a result of 'shrinkage of distance,' which is the most significant feature of globalization and have an inherent tendency toward integration and division into new regional communities.[1] This tendency is already stirring up debate in East Asia (including Southeast Asia) in the form of the East Asian Community and the Asia-Pacific Region (and ASEAN plus 3, more recently) transgressing it (i.e., the advancing reorganization of the concept of region).

In addition to the activity surrounding the formation of these new regions, the homogeneous landscapes on the surface of cities and the so-called intercity competition across national borders are also generating debate. It has been considered that both were brought about by 'shrinkage of distance,' both physical and social. I once made the following comment on the former.

> Today, a forest of towering skyscrapers is a ubiquitous landscape not only in large cities in developed countries but also in those in developing countries. At the same time, it is no longer unusual for someone who used to live in New York for many years, for example, to experience a similar sense of time in a faraway megacity in Asia. It appears that dense time found in individual cities which used to fascinate all visitors has been frozen completely. The only thing left is a borderless feeling

that is felt by the body. Old architecture and sculptural styles of the city were tools of the "sacred emblem" of power, which ruled the rural area outside of the city and ensured its own survival, and, in that sense, they had a mythical nature. What do cities use in order to express themselves these days? Are they creating any mythical systems or illusions to protect themselves? (Yoshihara 2002: 255)

I have pointed out that 'coordinate axes of the city are becoming extremely obscure' in describing these de-nationalized landscapes which seem homogeneous across borders, and have discovered the mechanism of globalization and 'shrinkage of distance' behind them. While these landscapes underlie both the global city Tokyo and Asian megacities, it has been my other argument that, as far as Tokyo is concerned, its landscape has not totally been disconnected from the nation-state. I shall briefly explain this point again in the next section. I shall also touch on intercity competition. I have not been able to elaborate this point fully in the abovementioned argument because its roots are embedded in a situation that is unmistakably different from the global city, namely the situation of the post-global city, even though it is founded in 'shrinkage of distance' as is the global city Tokyo.

As we shall see below, Tokyo appears to be far removed from the city which once existed as a 'frontier of change' or a 'watchtower of society' in the age when bureaucracy and collective consumption were subattributes of the nation-state.[2] It was not until the 1990s, however that it clearly broke away from the lineage of 'the city of the empire' and 'the capital of the nation-state.' This is the stage when 'spaces of flow' mediated by multiple aerial and electronic networks appear as they intermingle with the escalating instinctual drive of capital, and competition between cities, including a series of Asian megacities, intensifies across national borders under the gregarious growth of these 'spaces of flow' (Castells). This gives rise to new global cities (post-global cities). Interestingly, this intercity competition forms a ridgeline, so to speak, between the aforementioned integration and division into regional communities and acts to stimulate a transition into post-global cities.

Accordingly, we shall first explore the topography of global city Tokyo. Then, we shall consider the meaning of its transformation in terms of its interface with Asian megacities from the viewpoint of these cities. This chapter mainly aims to summarize the discussions of Part II and preface the Epilogue.

World city Tokyo

Urban social theory began to evolve in its own way during the twentieth century after being heavily influenced by various perceptions of the city held by Marx, Weber, Smith, Simmel and others. In the field of sociology, Chicago School sociology swept through the twentieth century, followed by 'new urban sociology.' As is commonly known, these two schools contrasted sharply on the question of whether to see the city as an independent or a dependent variable, or in other words, whether to treat external forces to the city as decisive factors, in very simple terms.[3] In hindsight, however, this point of contention stemmed from a very superficial interpretation of their ideas and it would in fact be appropriate to say that they were standing on common ground in the sense that they were firmly founded upon the context of capitalist modernity (Savage and Warde 1993). The concept of 'spatial turn,' which was proposed against not only Chicago School sociology but also 'new urban sociology,' provided a good opportunity to recognize this reflexively. After this 'spatial turn,' urban social theory confronted a series of world city theories from the late-1980s to the 1990s. Just like its response to the 'spatial turn' concept, the reaction of sociology to this was again very muted and 'introverted,' except for a small segment of the discipline. It certainly maintained distance from political-economical arguments, and it was not in a position to take the initiative.[4]

World city theories, which were vocally proposed on the back of Friedmann's world city hypothesis, Sassen's global city theory and Fujita's 'flexible specialization' etc., were essentially analyses of the dynamics of megalopolis in the advanced nations in the context of multitiered structure, mediated by the nation-state. Certainly, their common focus was 'world city' as a phenomenon that monopolized people, money and information and opened up to transnational channels, and their theoretical scope included the concentration of headquarters of multinational corporations and the establishment of global financial centers which were to more or less accelerate the development of integration and control functions on a world scale. Yet, the phenomenon of 'world city' referred to here was still the political and economic center of the advanced nation within the framework of the Keynesian welfare state/interventionist state and symbolically represented a 'national capital' which acquires/possesses globality (internationality) in its boundless expansion. It was therefore merely an expression of one *standpoint*, so to speak, in the changing organizational pattern of political and economic centers in conjunction with the transition of the world's hegemonic states, and moreover the progression of internationalization and 'transnationalization' based on the premise of national economy.

Let us examine a detailed monograph on the world city of Tokyo by Takashi Machimura (1994). It vividly describes the spatial constellation of world city Tokyo, which effectively stood alongside the 'factory of the world' (London) and the 'military police of the liberalist world' (New York). It realistically portrays the mechanism by which Tokyo was penetrated by the vertical division of labor in the world market led by multinational corporations while acquiring centrality within the nation-state of Japan which spilled outward. The world city of Tokyo portrayed by Machimura therefore did not completely shake off the narrative of nation-state identity which it had embedded in itself through its transition from 'imperial city' to 'national capital.' Of course, it is true that frequent questioning of its national identity took place during the process of its development from 'imperial city' to 'national capital' and also during the process of change in zonal composition from three major metropolitan areas to unipolar concentration in Tokyo alone. Nevertheless, it is undeniable that the globality exhibited by world city Tokyo rested on the privileged central origin (based on the 'center-periphery' pattern) that had been nurtured by the nation-state since the prewar era. However, this privileged central origin inherited from the 'imperial city' and the 'national capital' underwent a dramatic transformation during the 1990s. It was in a sense destroyed from without and torn up from within. A post-global city came to the forefront of society in full view. What was involved, and what kind of action or counteraction was concerned, in the appearance of a totally different dimension of globality?

The establishment of a new globality

With regard to conditions for the appearance of a new globality, it is notable firstly that mobility and hybridity brought about by globalization must add new planes to the city, as I mentioned in Chapter Two. They nurture globality by which the city itself is de-contextualized and superspatialized through the expansion of the 'space of flow' based on multiple aerial and electronic networks, and at the same time distance and territoriality are dissolved by 'the instantaneous.'[5] What becomes important here is the contents of 'shrinkage of distance' represented/substituted by 'the instantaneous.'

Drawing on Sugiura's argument (2003), Toshio Tasaka states in relation to this point that there is a move to overcome 'friction of distance' in terms of both 'physical distance' and 'social and institutional distance' stemming from 'border measures such as customs and trade/investment restrictions as well as differences between economic systems and domestic standards or cultural differences such as language and lifestyle differences,' and effectively identifies it with globalization (2005b: 11). According to Tasaka, 'physical distance' has shrunk dramatically due to innovation in transport and information technologies and 'social and institutional distance' has been greatly compressed by the formation of a borderless and homogeneous economic space permeated with universal economic norms.[6]

Tasaka pays close attention to the fact that the 'permeability of national borders' infinitely increases as 'friction of distance' is reduced (what I refer to as 'shrinkage of distance'). The principle of this reduction of 'friction of distance' is what Harvey calls 'time-space compression.' According to Harvey, this 'time-space compression' by which 'space appears to shrink to a "global village" of telecommunications and a "spaceship earth" of economic and ecological interdependencies and time horizons shorten to the point where the present is all there' (1989: 240) constitutes a pivotal point for a conversion from Fordism to flexible accumulation in post-Fordism. Its prominent feature is that it accompanies the acceleration of turnover time in production. In any case, it can be said that the globality accompanying the reduction of 'friction of distance' or 'shrinkage of distance' has appeared as a result of change to the meaning of the world's space caused by the speed of capital turnover far exceeding that of spatial transformation.

However, such globality is neither smooth nor fixed. Once it has come into existence, it separates from the global plane of capital and drifts about in a state of constant motion. It no longer drags along the remnants of origins of the 'imperial city' and the 'national capital.' In other words, the globality referred to here is not something that starts from the city as 'earth' and comes into being as its oscillation spreads in a network-like manner; it is rather brought about by various constantly moving and intricately interwoven networks which spread as global flows. Borrowing Poster's expression, its main theme would be '"rhizomic" nomads who daily wander at will across the globe' rather than '"arboreal" being, rooted in time and space' (Poster 1990: 15). In the case of Tokyo, this globality cannot be portrayed by copying the 'pattern' of the aforementioned world city Tokyo nor explained by simply painting over it. Quoting Ryūzo Uchida, it is very interesting that Shunya Yoshimi and Kan Sang-jung propose the 'paradox of global cities' as follows:

> Tokyo began to experience "a sense of anxiety about the bottom surface to which it is stuck" at around the time of the start of the bubble period. It was brought on by the aimless mobilization of Tokyo rather than its endless expansion. Therefore, "Tokyo's expansion to new suburban spaces and the waterfront was an expression of winding and denial of the order of by-gone Tokyo by the new sociality which Tokyo gave birth to inside itself, and a problem of self-differentiation rather than the disappearance of borders or strained relationships between Tokyo and the outside." In other words, Tokyo did not expand outwardly by simply evolving into a world city. Rather, Tokyo has allowed the appearance of another self that denies its own identity as Tokyo internal to it under globalization, and this autotemmous pattern has been deepening gradually. (2001: 102–103)

This situation, described as the 'counterturn of globality of global cities,' indicates the mode of existence of the post-world city which doubtlessly stands as a 'view' rather than an 'earth.' This is precisely the manifestation of another aspect of world city Tokyo as a global city, or the 'paradox/ambiguity of global cities.' Our attention is drawn to the hybrid networks of various sizes completely accustomed to the global sense of distance[7] which crisscross the city in the form of flow based on the 'counterturn of globality' = 'paradox of global cities,' and various sections of so-called polarization/ division that are appearing on the back of it. While this antinomious composition has complex and diverse elements, it can be said in broad terms that it is compatible with a somewhat modernistic way of understanding in relation to a positive on one hand and a negative on the other. In fact, the networks which constantly multiply, move, construct and destroy borders and divides and the five oppressive relationships—exploitation, marginalization, powerlessness, cultural imperialism and violence—that are considered by Young (1990) to be an acute expression of polarization/division have a certain functional relationship. It is valid to explain this analogically according to the relationship between a positive and a negative to that extent. However, this understanding does not quite hit the mark in view of the current situation in which the endless multiplication of information has expanded the base of the mediascape at once and even dissolved what

Harvey calls the built environment as a space of capital into a screen devoid of spatial expanse and depth of place.

What is more important here is that the latter condition of polarization/division is manifesting in the form of issues such as the secondary citizen problem[8] that is spreading beyond national borders rather than a 'class problem' within the nation-state. This problem is widespread and mainly involves women, 'ethnic' people, political minorities, culture (based on homosexuality and regionality in particular), residents with foreign nationality and various disability groups (Iwanaga 2008). In reality, it is often debated as part of problematics such as the issue of the city and social exclusion. However, the point of debate is clearly beyond the level/dimension of the establishment of rights within the nation-state and deeply rooted in the substrata of the former, which are hybrid networks.

For this reason, it is necessary to discuss the fluctuation of the nation-state (interventionist state) or the diminishing role that underlies both and is deeply connected to the aforementioned 'counterturn of globality' and is in fact increasing the 'permeability of national borders.' Through the organization of labor and the civilization ideology, which have acted to create a closed 'center-peripheral' cyclic structure in each nation, the modern nation-state has contained the buds of polarization/division within certain regions and blocked the eruption of transborder and mutilayered networks. It thus played the role of an interventionist state. Now, what Hirsch calls 'competitive states'[9] have emerged with the mission of providing the optimum conditions for systematic rationalization in preparation for competition in the global market and eased or abolished various regulations and systems (1996). As a result, the 'permeability of national borders' has increased further and polarization/division is exhibiting more 'tubularity.' These entities have given rise to various networks that are spreading in all directions beyond territorial boundaries.

Nevertheless, it will be inadequate to focus our discussion on world city Tokyo alone if we are to explain the establishment of new globality. It seems more appropriate to try to prove this globality by looking at how world city Tokyo is transforming into global city Tokyo at a series of interfaces with Asian megacities and in turn at the counteractions it has on these Asian megacities. With these points in mind, let us explore the substance of new globality more deeply with a focus on various phenomena/aspects that are appearing *significantly* in Asian megacities and other cities that are intricately intertwined with them.

Globality in Asian megacities

We shall firstly look at the state of what is called the East Asian urban cloister and the intercity competition taking place around it in order to examine the substance of globality of Asian megacities at their interfaces with global city Tokyo. The East Asian urban cloister is the term usually used to describe cities which belong to the IMS-GT (Indonesia Malaysia Singapore-Growth Triangle) and the Huang Hai Rim Economic Region. The former refers to the triangle formed by Japan, Singapore and ASEAN2 (Malaysia and Indonesia) and the latter by Japan, Taiwan and China. The following argument shall focus on this East Asian urban cloister based on our earlier discussion from Chapter Six to Chapter Nine.

The first thing to point out is that the East Asian urban cloister has always exhibited a highly hierarchical nature in that Singapore, Hong Kong, Taipei and Seoul were positioned as cities having a regional-base function around global city Tokyo as the core. Especially notable is the fact that this hierarchical nature was essentially based on an intercity system by the articulation of individual cities built on individual nation-state-based territorial foundations. Come to think of it, a deep sympathy between the aforementioned centrality of Tokyo at the apex and the formation of primate cities in the quasi-periphery as outlined in Chapter Six only became possible subject to such an intercity system. The rules of the market inherent in each state exerted stronger effects than did the articulation between individual cities and in a way acted as national borders.

The East Asian urban cloister was therefore a relatively 'minor' intercity network beyond the state, at least up to a certain point in time. It was fundamentally comprised of ties and connections with a regionally partitioned hierarchy of 'industrial accumulation of satellite type' (Markusen). So what is the current situation? Certainly, the East Asian urban cloister has been maintained continuously to date through the regional-base function of the aforementioned cities, especially Singapore. However, the situation in which the East Asian urban cloister has become the main arena for intercity competition through this function is clearly different from the previous state of affairs. It heavily overlaps with the 'de-nationalization of the state,' the transformation of world city Tokyo into a post-global city and the transformation of primate cities into megacities. Intercity competition has intensified on the horizon where these cities converge, and the aforementioned new globality has suddenly appeared with newfound reality.

The East Asian urban cloister appears to have taken on a different quality since the Asian financial crisis. While it is basically an intercity junction with an inherent hierarchy, it has become an arena for fierce competition as intercity governance has developed beyond the state level. The advancement of globalization originally gave rise to the flow of people, objects and money along multiple networks between cities: the flow has grown further since the financial crisis in a manner that accentuates intercity differences = advantages-disadvantages even more. In relation to the aforementioned point, cities turn into 'competitive agents' which contend with one another in order to overcome 'friction of distance' and/or achieve 'shrinkage of distance' and develop a comprehensive accumulative environment[10] as a powerful incentive to attract corporations, especially transnational ones. Consequently, the gap between cities with a competitive advantage and those that are forced into an inferior position becomes evident. Tasaka's argument below is very lucid on this point.

> During the post-Fordism period [...] intercity relations rose to the surface [...] the nodes of time-space convergence = hub cities draw an influx of information and hence an inflow of investment. Cities emerge as "competitive agents" and enter a "knockout competition over place" in order to secure the nodes of the flow. [...] the "knockout competition over place" creates regions (cities) with competitive advantage and disadvantaged regions. In defeated regions, an outflow and loss of jobs continue and the desolation of regions and industries is aggravated." (2005a: vi)

Rather than displaying individual positions, or a constellation for positional change in the hierarchy within the East Asian urban cloister, the cities mark their respective standpoints in the middle of the 'division between "regions (cities) that acquired place" and "excluded regions (cities)"' (Tasaka 2005a: iii). By the way, it is worth noting that competition and division are also taking place within each of the cities with competitive advantage as well as other cities in concurrence with the progression of intercity competition and division. So-called gentrification and informalization have become the features of every urban space. While this can be regarded as a clear expression of 'self-differentiation' = 'self-denial'[11] (by cities themselves) amid global integration in the context discussed earlier, this situation has in fact been brought about by a series of spatial restructuring moves of 'competitive states' in order to become preferred locations for corporations.

For this very reason, it is necessary to examine the contents of administrative intervention implemented by 'competitive states' in order to gain locational advantage in sync with the advancement of globalization and the specifics of spatial restructuring arising from it. The former basically requires 'all matters from social policy to cultural policy, including education, science promotion and environmental protection policies, to submit to a supreme command for the "securing of location points," or in other words, a supreme command to create a "frame condition" which brings profits to globally active capital (i.e., structural reform)' (Tasaka 2005b: 7). Details aside, cities enter intercity competition as 'competitive agents' on the premise of this pursuit for the 'securing of location points' by 'competitive states.' They become part of an ambivalent mechanism peculiar to globalization that involves integration and division, subsumption and exclusion and so on.

The latter spatial restructuring, as far as we can see in Asian megacity Jakarta, is parallel to that of post-global city Tokyo. At least, an analogue for globality found in global city Tokyo (a counterturn of globality) can be found to a considerable extent. As discussed in Chapter Six, the two-layer constitution such as the phenomenon of gentrification and informalization spreading in the metropolitan region of Jakarta, and its acute spatial expression in the gated community and the slum (see Chapter Seven), for example, is manifesting in both Tokyo and Denpasar to some degree.[12] In a sense that it is turning into a pressing problematic with the new connotation of internalization of self-denial under globalization, Tokyo, Jakarta and Denpasar are about to stand on an almost common ground.

'Washington Consensus' and the homogeneous landscape

Globality found in Jakarta and Denpasar as discussed in Part II, however, is not exactly the same globality observed in global city Tokyo. There are at least some topographical differences between them. The spatial composition in both Jakarta and Denpasar bears the marks of colonial experiences[13] and post-colonial developmental despotism and the deep shadow of archival records of place as the primate city. Moreover, the accumulation of functions specific to the Extended Metropolitan Region (EMR) (Tasaka 1998) carved in the space highlights differences rather than similarities between them and Tokyo. It is in itself a projection of the snaking state of intercity competition developing between the cities within the East Asian urban cloister.

I have already mentioned that Singapore has consistently maintained its intermediary position within the East Asian urban cloister. Together with this fact, I must point out that Jakarta and Denpasar emerged late as 'competitive agents.' They lagged behind in the intercity competition. After the financial crisis, they were rapidly catching up with the others in the East Asian urban cloister (but were not quite abreast). There are many possible reasons for this, but the main factor was the acceptance of the Washington Consensus (a collective term for the Washington Economic Consensus and the Washington Security Agenda, or the 'Wall Street-Treasury Department-IMF' complex (Harvey 1989: ch. 17)) by these states.[14] Held describes the Washington Consensus as follows:

> The both (Washington Economic Consensus and Washington Security Agenda) have now linked to the inherent form of driving force of globalization. They together assert that the government should not actively get involved in the central area of social economy ranging from market regulation to disaster management planning and that the provision of international coordination and regulatory measures inhibits freedom, puts the brakes on growth and development and restricts profits. They do not necessarily explain the structure of the current globalization but they are at the center of the political environment of globalization. (2007: 86–87)

The financial crisis and the resultant economic collapse provided momentum to the implementation of structural reform based on the Washington Consensus (it was effectively the enforcement of 'global standardization' through the IMF and World Bank) and the resultant spatial restructuring and consequently allowed Jakarta and Denpasar to secure firm footholds in the East Asian urban cloister. It also meant that the East Asian urban cloister itself had been subsumed by the Washington Consensus. My suggestion in the first part of this chapter that the apparent homogeneity of the city landscape and the so-called intercity competition across national borders are one and the same thing is more easily understandable in this context.

In any case, it has become clear that globality found in Tokyo, Jakarta and Denpasar is now changing its direction from high differentiation to uniformity through 'self-denial.' While globality is considered to have contained momenta for differentiation and uniformity from the beginning, the move toward the latter has clearly become dominant since the forced adoption of the Washington Consensus. As it becomes more dominant, of course, uniformity will give rise to new differences = divides in each city. The condition of inequality or disparity is one example. However, it is exhibiting extremely diverse and articulated forms as an expansion of the 'space of flow' increases borderless mobility and hybridity of people, objects and money. I would like to elaborate on this point in closing my discussion in this chapter.

Conclusion: Out of interchangeability and emergence

The 'space of flow' that defies national borders is making an unbridled advance, ironically aided by the administrative intervention of 'competitive states' according to the supreme command of market fundamentalism. This unrestrained expansion of 'space of flow' promoted by administrative intervention is certainly increasing the maturity of the take-off conditions for post-global cities. The reality of new globality growing in them can be explained by the mode of operation of the informational city and its underlying 'paradox.' Again, the informational city is not merely a nodal point of information. The outstanding characteristic of the informational city is that it acts as a field to articulate and manage the flow of people, objects, information and money, that is, as a regulator, rather than as a field of accumulation of people, objects, information and money, that is, as a container (Yoshihara 2002). 'The present' of the informational city exists, containing varying degrees of progress of decentralization and governance at the national level and boundaries between various forms of axes of conflict appearing at that same level. The cities discussed in this chapter that are conjugated with the East Asian urban cloister and posses the aforementioned globality as their own in some way exactly overlap with such informational cities.

For this reason, there is a need to make various invisible boundaries and divides apparent and clarify how they are connected to the aforementioned globality or how they constitute a 'counterturn of globality.' By doing so, we can highlight the irregular appearance or shape of globality projected on urban space. The difficulty in this case is, however, that the axes of conflict underlying these boundaries and divides cannot be explained easily within a framework centering on 'one-on-one concatenation,' so to speak. The aforementioned 'paradox' = 'counterturn of globality' becomes visible only when one stands on the level where various axes of conflict form a complex of networks.

For example, various difficulties facing Muslims coming to Denpasar as described in Chapter Eight are similar to those facing the extreme poverty level and the weakest layer of society that are expanding in Tokyo and Jakarta. The orientation of Japanese lifestyle emigrants towards mobility as discussed in Chapter Nine undoubtedly stems from the de-nationality of space and in this sense resonates with the mentality of relative indifference to nationality found among some sections of the middle class in Jakarta.[15] However, the abovementioned 'one-on-one concatenation' can only provide an explanation up to this point. It is not necessarily clear how they impact on the aforementioned intercity competition or in what forms they exist in the base stratum of intercity competition. They may have been derived from a heightened state of mobility or hybridity prompted by the advancement of globalization, but it is unclear what positions they are occupying in relation to intercity competition. The only thing I can point to here is that they fundamentally represent one of many outcomes of intercity competition carried on by 'competitive states' according to the Washington Consensus which is an acute expression of social segmentation.

Globality that is deeply penetrated by structural multitieredness may be understood as a dichotomy between integration and division or subsumption and exclusion at the levels of individual events in question that are found there. However, on the horizon where these phenomena intermingle and interact beyond national borders, globality is deeply characterized by a mechanism featuring the interchangeability and emergence arising from its operation itself to allow various elements to collide and articulate with one another. Incidentally, when we again consider this mechanism of interchangeability and emergence in the context of the East Asian urban cloister, we can see that it not only underlies individual cities but also reaches far into the base of intercity competition.

Lastly, I would like to comment on the manifestation configuration of locality in the field of the formation of globality in which the aforementioned mechanism of interchangeability and emergence is in operation. Once again, it does not seem easy to find an answer to this question but we must take note that the type of local reaction that may lead to re-impregnation of nationality as discussed in Chapter Nine is no longer *exceptional* nor *peripheral*. Such a move has appeared more or less in every urban space and now constitutes a major momentum for urban spatial turns. Of course, differences in cultural and religious configuration and tradition structures of individual cities certainly infuse such reactions with a particular type of individuality. However, such difference = individuality does not negate the similarity between individual reactions.

On the point of local reactions constituting a momentum for urban spatial turns, we should also pay attention to the appearance of a series of attempts to create civil society on the back of the aforementioned reactions. They are something that seldom appeared in the foreground of society in Asian cities in the past but they constitute a noteworthy activity in that it also has its feet deep inside the aforementioned mechanism of interchangeability and emergence. Details aside, this activity is an indication that social segmentation and disparity are not the only outcomes of intercity competition. Of course, such an activity is constantly at risk of falling into the trap of governance from above by 'competitive states.'

In any case, the condition of post-global city contained within new globality is extremely winding and chaotic. The paradox found here exists on various vectors struggling with one another and does not easily find a focus. However, there is no doubt that difference in uniformity and uniformity in differentiation are circuitous but penetrating metaphors of this paradox.

The next question is the reality and direction of place for which the aforementioned globality engages in fierce maneuvering.[16] Since I have run out of space here, I shall discuss this topic in the Epilogue.

Epilogue: The Question of Place

> How to organize human life in a machine society is a question that confronts us anew. (Polanyi 1968: 59)

From cultural plurality to place

The advancement of globalization has given rise to the widespread appearance of 'a space in which entire populations subject to the law of the market come into contact physically and symbolically' (Balibar and Wallerstein 1990). Scenes of the intermingling of a diverse group of people sharing a social space are unfolding all over the place. At the same time, the slogan/hollow words of multicultural coexistence based on the premise of cultural plurality has been hanging over our world as if it were a 'specter.' In reality, however, it is a longing for unitary local culture irreconcilable with diversity that permeates deep and wide.[1] This longing resonates with what Saitō and Iwanaga call 'racism based on difference theory.'

> It (racism based on difference theory)... is asserted by turning anthropological cultural theory to its advantage. Structuralist anthropology represented by Levi-Strauss valued cultural diversity and equality and emphasized impossible reduction of difference. New racism founds its argument on this cultural anthropological view. Mixing cultures and extinguishing cultural distance entail a disassembling of the human intellect. It is none other than a breakdown of control which guaranteed the survival and development of humankind. We must therefore preserve our group identity by preserving cultural traditions. The "right to difference" of cultures once advocated by anti-racism should be recognized with regard to French culture as well. This is how it justifies a move to protect cultural traditions being adulterated due to "invasion" by immigrants and drive out foreign cultures. It brings forth racism which mainly focuses on the danger of extinguishment of boundaries and differences without the postulate of superiority to other groups. (1996: 249–250)

Interestingly, this 'racism based on difference theory' forms the substratum of a series of political paradigms which stirs up political activity today. According to Rapport and Overing, culture and difference have actually become a strategy in various nation-states and play a part in keeping cultural identity within a local region under the centralized government system (Rapport and Overing 2000). Kiyoshi Nakamura astutely points out that 'locally fixed cultural identity' is almost the same as 'the creation of unitary local culture which excludes diversity'[2] in the following comment, using contemporary Indonesia as an example.

> The motto of multiracial Indonesia, "unity in diversity," (the exhibits at) theme parks such as Mini Indonesiam Park TMII which visually demonstrate racial diversity, or the (then) Department of Education and Culture project for cataloging local cultures which collected folktales, folk utensils and customs show the presence of multiple ethnic cultures within the "Indonesian nation (*bangsa Indonesia*)" and assign them to local areas. At the same time, cultures in these areas are standardized. When a "community" of a virtual race called the Indonesian nation ("*bangsa*") was created, ethnic races ("*suku*") were not extinguished; they too were newly created as its constituents. (Nakamura 2009)

In the case of Bali, '"standardized" Balinese culture for the province of Bali (a culture which has never existed anywhere in Bali in the past) has been "imagined/created" as if it has existed everywhere in Bali' (Nakamura 2009). It is difficult to deny that the Balinese culture conceived by *ajeg Bali* discussed in Chapter Eight has been 'imagined/created' this way *to a certain extent*. However, I shall not go into details here on this point. I would rather turn my attention to the fact that the fear of 'extinguishing boundaries and differences' underpinning this trend is manifesting itself as a yearning for place which (supposedly) supports stability and problem-free identity and has shared history and collective memories of people embedded in it, to borrow Massey's phrase discussed in Chapter Four. This is because it conceals a mechanism by which place as a fiction strongly connected to the past is presented as a 'genuine place' through culture and difference.

In this case, the 'form' of exteriorized people, nature or objects is read out from a differential landscape condensed in a place. Some (Massey, for example) superimpose Heidegger's 'dwelling'[3] on this 'form.' How does this 'form' relate to things that are (supposedly) inherent in place? And how does it relate to practical/active possession of space mentioned in Chapter Four?

Space and place

The aforementioned longing for unitary local culture which is the reversal of cultural plurality = multicultural coexistence may be, in a way, an acute 'expression' of the situation that is erupting in the form of the global-local paradox, which was explained briefly in Chapter One. As I have mentioned several times, Castells (1989) argues that the 'flow of space' appears in the foreground (of society) as the 'space of place' recedes into the background amid the advancement of globalization. The implication here is, if interpreted literally, that placeness = locality is denied and the world is overwhelmed by the 'space of flow.' However, it has another implication as pointed out by Saitō and Iwanaga: 'new localization is sought through rivalry between the power of multinational corporations and supranational institutions (the "power of placeless flow") and the social movement based on placeness ("place without power")' (1996: 280).

The 'form' of this rivalry is discussed by Saitō and Iwanaga at a more fundamental and basic level as 'a rivalry between the rule of absolute space and the restoration of placeness by way of abstraction of it' (1996: 280) in relation to the aesthetics of modernity. I have also discussed this point in Chapter One and a previously published book (Yoshihara 2000). Saitō and Iwanaga firstly consider a struggle between two opposing forms hiding in sociological aesthetics by quoting Simmel.

> The first aesthetic form is a rational form called symmetry. This aesthetic form aims to integrate various elements as parts of the whole and construct a mathematically compact and balanced system. [...] according to Simmel, however, this symmetrical beauty rejects connection with the outside and suppresses individual freedom within society. This breeds an aesthetic motive to countervail symmetrical beauty. It is romantic aesthetics of the rivalry and isolation of the individual against the whole. Here, individual freedom is the greatest aesthetic concern and aesthetic individuality which cannot be reduced to a symmetrical and harmonious whole is emphasized. (1996: 280)

With further différance of this axis of conflict of aesthetic forms highlighted here, Saitō and Iwanaga propose another axis of conflict, namely, 'a rivalry between the aesthetic form of abstract space of flow and the aesthetic form of concrete sense of place.' They position 'heterotopy/differentiated space' pointed out by Lefebvre on the line extended from this conflict axis. It exists as an antagonist which an abstract space conceives inside itself at the end of its rule (Saitō and Iwanaga 1996: 280).[4] Thus the global-local paradox is examined at the root of modernity.

The question in that case is, while the aforementioned 'heterotopy' might exist as 'place without power,' to what extent does it guarantees the reality of placeness based on active/practical possession of space? As mentioned earlier, individuality or inherence of place rooted in the diversity of language, culture and race tends to be reclaimed by a fabricated unitary local culture that does not exist in reality. Therefore, 'heterotopy' exists as a manifestation of the condition in which two vectors—globalization and localization—are tearing up urban space as they drift away from one another.[5]

Incidentally, 'heterotopy,' or place, appears at first glance to be embedded in this torn urban space in opposition to abstract space. However, they are after all standing side by side in a pattern of shift 'from one end to the other.' In this sense, the denial of place by abstract space is also an unmistakable reality. Yet, this denial itself becomes possible only when it is founded on some particular place. In plain terms, the space makes the place empty and captures it. Conversely, the place asserts its individuality and inherence as it is submitted to the action of the space. Let us consider this dialectical relationship between space and place where unity and difference intermingle in a complementary way in the context of place.

'Taking root' and 'enclosing'

Lately, debate over place has been heating up. Heidegger's discourses are frequently quoted in such debate. For example, the following comment is widely quoted in relation to explanation of background factors in the place debate, which is enlivened by the advancement of globalization.

> Everything gets lumped together into uniform distancelessness. [...] What is it that unsettles and thus terrifies? It shows itself and hides itself in the *way* in which everything presences, namely, in the fact that despite all conquest of distances the nearness of things remains absent. (Heidegger 1971: 165; Iwanaga 2008: 196)

Borrowing Harvey's words, the fear of 'time-space compression' and the longing for propinquity, which is its reversed form, are the factors spurring the place debate. To Heidegger, the abovementioned propinquity can be acquired only by 'dwelling,' or in other words, attaining integrated cognitive mechanics in a 'gap' between man and object. Therefore, the feeling of 'taking root,' or '"I reside" or "dwell alongside" the world, as that which is familiar to me in such and such a way' (Heidegger 1929) is the key to 'dwelling' and, after all, construction of place. Nevertheless, the longing for propinquity and the sense of deprivation of roots in reality tend to push 'dwelling' in the direction of the construction of unitary and exclusive local cultures as discussed earlier, instead of broadening the possibilities which 'dwelling' nurtures between persons or person and object by physical occupation of space using five senses. This propensity is commonly found in the communitarian's understanding of place today.[6]

For this reason, the aforementioned 'taking root' makes a 'gap' to converge with a closed relationship which is complete within a defined area, or in other words, to specialize into 'enclosing,' under this propensity. This 'enclosing' is in reality manifesting from the phenomenon of individualization that is well under way in the home, school and community, and more than anything else, from the landscape[7] in which the individual and the market are directly facing one another due to the advancement of neoliberal globalization. Its symbolic expression is the gated community addressed in Chapter Seven as we all know. While it exists as a connotation of the aforementioned torn urban space, residents of the gated community as an enclave containing the middle class as well as the super wealthy class[8] are trying not only to drive out others who are different from themselves but also to annihilate publicness upon which the others must depend.

In any case, an attachment to propinquity/identification with 'enclosing' swirling around in gated communities is in itself an extreme form of the aforementioned individualization (self-choice/self-responsibility) as well as an antithesis of the complete severance of free association with others via human communications. In this sense, 'overextension of security'[9] (Takei 2007: 144) in gated communities can be considered an inevitable development. In my view, the mentality underlying the process from 'enclosing' to 'overextension of security' can be found in '"the selfish barbarity" to try to annihilate "the unpleasant"' (Abe 2006: 34; Yoshihara 2007: 24). It is based on the following comment by Shōzō Fujita.

> The mentality to wish for total elimination (annihilation) of the source of the unpleasant itself is a desire to do away with the chance to encounter the unpleasant itself instead of having to deal with individual pains and nuisances of various shapes and sizes properly on a case-by-case basis. To that end, it tries to eliminate the very things that evoke a biological reaction called displeasure. It not only lacks interactions with unpleasant situations but also entails the desire to annihilate all objects and natural phenomena associated with such situations. I would have to say that this is terribly selfish barbarousness. (Fujita 1995: 30–31)

The pathology of 'enclosing' stemming from the yearning for propinquity has brought about an 'overextension of security' especially in gated communities through 'selfish barbarousness,' which is an extreme form of individualization.

'Non-place' and '*trajectivité*'

Amid internal and external expansion of social relations and social processes against the aforementioned tendency toward the overlapping of 'taking root' and 'enclosing,' how is it possible to ensure the option of constituting 'dwelling' from a diverse range of experiences and understandings interlocking into multiple networks? This is fundamentally a question of the possibility of constructing a place based on what young Marx located at the core of *Gattungswesen*, that is, individuality that can be achieved by individuals only through *l'association* (association) with others. In order to ask such a question, however, we need to begin our discussion by going back to '(the action of) great civilization' brought on by globalization, or in other words, from the perspective of sociality engendered by the involvement of all people in globalization, or the fluid world. In relation to our earlier discussion, it presents as a problematic as to the supposition of the 'gap' between persons or person and object when a place asserts its individuality and inherence while being under the influence of an abstract space. Here, I shall consider the viability of the 'gap' between persons or person and object that is open to the outside by reference to two arguments, those of Auge and Berque, which are supposedly not necessarily anchored to 'taking root' = 'enclosing,' although they have their feet firmly in the 'dwelling' mentioned above. Firstly, let us hear what Auge says.

According to Auge:

...a place is defined as identitary, relational and historical. (A place is defined as) identitary, in the sense that a certain number of individuals recognize themselves in it and define themselves by means of it; relational, in the sense that the same individuals read within that space the relation that unites them with each other; and historical, in the sense that the occupants of the place find in it various traces of an old, former presence, the sign of filiation. (1994: 109–122)

Therefore, Auge argues that a place can be reinterpreted as 'the relation that each of its inhabitants has to him- or herself,' 'the relation that each of its inhabitants has to the other occupants,' and 'the relation that each of its inhabitants has to their common history.'

Conversely, a 'non-place' is 'a space where neither identity, relation, or history are symbolized.'[10] It means 'spaces where people coexist or cohabit without living together,' and according to Auge, proliferation of such 'non-places' 'is characteristic of the contemporary world.' While the situation of 'excessive proximity, the intrusive sharing and cruelties' or 'the "universe of recognition" effects produced by... the least amiable aspects of place' can arise in a place, 'individual freedom may be fully experienced, shelter from the "universe of recognition" effects' in a 'non-place' can occur (1994: 110). Ultimately, Auge contends, this freedom immanent in the 'non-place' will alleviate the overflow of the meaning assigned to the place and contribute to the construction of new placeness.

What Auge mentions as one of the things that have influenced his understanding of place (and 'non-place') is what Berque calls milieu (Auge 1994). It is very useful in explaining that a place as a 'gap' between persons or person and object is not necessarily premised on coexistence in a specific area. Berque considers a milieu 'as "*trajectivité*", that is, as "reciprocal becoming/*genèse réciproque*" (Piaget) between the constituents of a milieu, and "reversible traffic/ *cheminement réversible*" (Durand) from one constituent to another' (Berque 1986). A milieu is defined by the orientation/direction of society's involvement with its environment. This orientation/direction means a relationship (interaction) constructed between individuals through the medium of the environment in the form of 'beyond...' and 'across...' (Berque 1986).[11]

At the same time, Berque points out that this milieu = *trajectivité* is comprised of an 'intensional' tendency/intra-constitutive unity and an 'extensive' tendency/ex-constitutive universality, and that the 'non-similar (*non pareil*)' belong to one and the 'similar (*pareil*)' belong to the other (Berque 1986: 159). It is supposed that 'dwell/inhabit (*habiter*)' is an 'intensional' tendency/intra-constitutive unity and 'landscape (*payser*)' is an 'extensive' tendency/ex-constitutive universality. What is important here is that '*habiter*' and '*payser*' or '*non pareil*' and '*pareil*' are constantly summoning one another to forestall superfluity of either of them, and this is the main substance of '*trajet*' ('trajection'). It is this trajective union ('process') that nurtures placeness which does not head toward/close into internal centrality.

Seen in this light, it becomes obvious that the substance of placeness flowing through both Auge's 'non-place' and Berque's '*trajectivité*' and the substance of placeness derived from 'taking root'/'enclosing' discussed in the previous section belong to clearly different categories. Moreover, by closely reading 'non-place' and '*trajectivité*' to shed light on the sympathetic relationship between two opposing vectors, the *reactionary* nature of the longing for exclusive unitary local culture glanced at above becomes more apparent. Nevertheless, it does not elucidate the alternative 'gap' between persons or person and object. It only reveals a clue to the solution. Lastly, I shall attempt to discuss the form of existence of place that is not going to be reclaimed by 'taking root'/ 'enclosing' based on the preceding discussion and the findings explained in Part II.

Toward 'the emergent whole'

As the disparities and inequalities brought on by globalization are coming to light, the social climate clearly appears to favor anti-globalism. The tone of argument to extol locality, which is inseparable from territoriality, and the call for exclusive unitary local culture are gaining strength. In view of the need to reinterpret globalization in terms of the metaphor of fluid today, however, we are required to understand the 'gap' between persons or person and object as part of a process that arises and expands freely rather than a fixed area. Exploring the form of existence of this 'gap' on endlessly extending wings while based on 'taking root' is becoming central to the new *zeitgeist*.

However, explaining place as an aggregate of fluctuating processes is a rather difficult task. Place is certainly the embodiment of space construction (*chorésie*) in which the archival record of lives of people in the area is deeply embedded but, conversely, it is deeply involved in the *trajet* of becoming by which relations are continually created, destroyed and reformed. A string of interactionism theories represented by the phenomenology-based theory of living[12] certainly stood on the doorstep of this becoming. Yet, it appears that they did not consider interaction as something that forms an emergent order (the emergent whole) while maintaining de-territorial dynamic relationships between various actors. In other words, they did not appear to be very interested in its ontological formulation even though they were theorizing interaction.

In my view, the emergent whole is an aggregate of dynamic relationships 'having "openness on one hand and heterogeneity on the other hand" arising from multiple associations of people, objects and situations' in an environment marked by mobility (Yoshihara 2000: 250–251), and place is a de-integrative and de-centralized aggregation point of such an emergent whole/network. This position does not entail the founding of a territory from the outset of the formulation of place. Of course, 'dwelling' is the beginning in this case but the progression to the dynamic mechanism (of 'dwelling') cannot be achieved without the emergence cycle derived from the 'articulation' of various collective practices. This is where it is different from territory-vested spontaneous development.[13] While space of the commons, which develops from 'dwelling' and where many different people meet/mingle, has been attracting interest in recent years as something that guarantees a certain kind of placeness, it also requires the involvement of the emergence cycle.

Anyhow, it can be said that the boundary between 'dwelling' and 'taking root'/'enclosing' arises over the emergence of transboundary place. Today, people living in the complex world of mobility must either transcend the self and fling themselves into a transboundary place of continual polyphyletic connection or stay within a small partitioned space. Whichever they choose, they cannot escape the dialectical mechanism of the 'gap.' No matter who they are (even if they are living like travelers), those who are exposed to the waves of globalization cannot avoid facing collective practices based on the de-territorial and de-integrative emergence mechanism in some way.

Nevertheless, in the case of Asian megacities which have experienced colonialism over a very long period and whose institutional and non-institutional dynamics are totally different from Japan's, this emergent whole/mechanism is extremely difficult to find. Take for example the life-world assembled by slum residents and migrant laborers discussed earlier. It once emerged in various 'forms' at the interface with globalization but these forms are becoming even less visible in recent years. It appears that the narrative of the autonomous life-world mediated by the emergence cycle have been lost, at least to these people.[14] In some cases, they are no longer distinguishable from the narrative of spontaneous development.

It is of course possible to perceive spontaneous development as something that has 'become custom' and find in it a rich expression of interactive networks. Even in this case, however, it would be unavoidable to superpose spontaneous development on the emergent whole/mechanism and in order to do so, it would be necessary to re-postulate spontaneous development relationally and reposition it within the aforementioned *trajet* of becoming. This task also would be difficult because the *trajet* of becoming would have to be re-fluidized into the 'space of flow' coexisting with advancing globalization once the historical situation of colonial/postcolonial has been identified.

Urry's theory of globalization using the metaphor of fluid and Massey's alternative understanding of place have inspired me to embark on a journey on the interpretation of place. However, the journey has only just begun. Just as with the emergent whole, the journey to the understanding of place must be an eternal wandering. I wonder when the 'gap' between persons or person and object will be released from the 'state held by the earth.'[15]

Postscript

I inadvertently read Iyotani (2007) in first draft form. It is a very innovative work which examines the state of 'mobility and place' from the viewpoint of 'immigration as a method.' Although my book does not focus on immigration itself, it adopts a similar perspective on the issue. In any case, I will no doubt discuss his work on another occasion.

Notes

Prologue

1 Urry's writings during this period actively grappled with the question of 'mobility and locales' based on complexity and emergence theories (2000). However, in terms of the 'application to real-life situations' (Tuan 1990: 435) of complexity and emergence theories, they have many unrefined parts and aspects that have to be considered as preliminary discussion. This book is greatly indebted to Urry's argument and attempts to further develop immature points of argument concerning 'mobility and locales' in his writings based on the spatial turn in contemporary urban space, especially Asian urban space. At the same time, it is one of the aims of this book to demonstrate the importance of approaching the question of 'fluidity and place' from the perspective of Asian cities.

2 It is described as the process of the acceleration of the 'pace of life, while so overcoming spatial barriers that the world sometimes seems to collapse inwards upon us' (Harvey 1989: 240). Alternatively, Massey states that 'It (time-space compression) is a phenomenon which implies the geographical stretching-out of social relations (referred to by Giddens as time-space distanciation), and to our experience of all this' (Massey 1993: 59–60). Urry summarizes the new round of this 'time-space compression' as follows:

> [T]he accelerating turnover time in production; the increased pace of change and ephemerality of fashion; the greater availability of products almost everywhere; the increased temporariness of products, relationships and contracts; the heightened significance of short-termism and the decline of a "waiting culture"; the greater importance of advertising and rapidly changing media images to social life, the so-called "promotional culture"; the increased availability of techniques of simulation, including buildings and physical landscapes; and the extraordinary proliferation of new technologies of information and communication which transcend space instantaneously, at the speed of nanoseconds. (1995: 23)

3 According to Harvey, flexibility constitutes the basic value of what he calls 'flexible accumulation.' Flexible accumulation, by the way, corresponds with what is called 'post-Fordism' or 'flexible specialization' in the so-called Regulation Approach. It is considered to have appeared to replace Fordism following its crisis in 1973. Harvey has keen insight to address flexibility not only as a representation of the 'new experience of time and space' but also as some sort of cultural and social condition by looking to postmodern cultural practice and philosophical discourse. By the way, 'flexible accumulation' theory has been subjected to various comments (for example, being a takeoff of deterministic/reductionistic Marxism) but it is still extremely significant in that it provides a skeletal basis for the following discussion on mobility. See Yoshihara (2008a) on the trajectory of Harvey's theory.

4 Instantaneous time referred to here is a concept originally formulated by Urry (2000) as discussed below. Urry argues that it provides 'the paradigm case of ephemerality, disposability, temporariness, images and simulacra' (1995: 177) and that the future dissolves into the present under this instantaneous time. He asserts that it partially replaces clock-time. Please see chapter six, 'Globalization and the mechanism of instantaneous time' in Yoshihara (2004) for more details.

5 The shift from clock-time to short-lived and transient time appears to be positioned on a developmentalist thesis (and therefore a dichotomy) at first glance, but it exists as a manifestation of the ambiguity of modernity. On this point, Harvey pays close attention to the following passage written by Baudelaire. 'By "modernity" I mean the ephemeral, the fugitive, the contingent, the one half of art whose other half is the eternal and the immutable' (Baudelaire 1964: 12). Usually, the former aspect describes post-modernity but what is important here is that Harvey sees the principle of modernity in the preservation of these two sides that are repeatedly changing their state.

6 Bergson clearly distinguishes 'time (*temps*)' from what he calls *dureé*. According to him, *temps* is quantitative and spatially divisible, i.e., 'spatial time,' but it is not real time. *Dureé* is real time (Bergson 1889). By the way, Bachelard argues that the idea of qualitative, sensuous and livable space is at the center of Bergson's time as *dureé* (Bachelard 1957). In any case, Bergson's theoretical position to see *temps* as 'the time of becoming' connected to the physical pays close attention to the 'spatial time' inherent in human reality itself.

7 Discourses of globalization are analyzed in Chapter One and therefore not elaborated here. However, they are certainly not limited to the discourse based on annexation/domination of 'the small' by 'the large.' Rather, the general trend is leaning toward the interpenetration between the global (large) and the local (small). From there, discourses that advance their argument in the direction of '*différance* of the global to the local' or 'global development of the local' are gaining force (Yoshihara 2004: 180). Regardless of their arguments, these discourses are essentially similar in that they consider territoriality to be a priority.

8 The implications of spatial barriers certainly decrease under mobility coexisting with instantaneous time. This is the very reason why the sensitivity of capital to the variations of place/'quality' becomes stronger and the effect of incentives to attract capital becomes more powerful in the midst of the abstraction of space. Thus, competition among light-footed (meaning highly mobile) capitals for locales intensifies (Harvey 1989). In any case, battles are waged over locales with special qualities and access to low-cost resources, and due to these reasons, placeness is reinforced by capital.

9 This point is discussed in detail in Chapter Four. Massey places a 'progressive sense of place' on the opposite end of the spectrum to this interpretation. It is derived from Heidegger and features the notion that a place has its own innate identity, the notion that the identity of a place—a sense of place—is constructed from introverted history based on the exploration of the past in search of an internalized origin, and 'drawing

lines around a place' (Massey 1993: 64). Based on the aforementioned understanding of place, this 'progressive sense of place' clearly inherits the line of argument that holds placeness as the basis for identity but at the same time it resonates with the discourse that emphasizes 'the variations of place' for capital through 'propinquity.' This is where we can see the 'far, but near' relationship between the communitarian and the libertarian surrounding the understanding of place.

10 I once described the world of Park's human nature in relation to the underlying equilibrium theory of change as follows.

> Park's human ecology made an *a priori* assumption of the world of *laissez-faire* by a human nature. It was the world of *laissez-faire* submitted to the action of the so-called invisible hand of God. The argument found in that world which was inclined toward re-ordering through social Darwinist selection was in the end converged on equilibrium theory of change. Needless to say, the "world of a human nature" founded on it was analogical to the world envisioned by the Chicago School in which the logic of capital value proliferation acted as a direct and decisive factor. However, Park's human nature simultaneously guaranteed "human nature" and held "human potential" within it. Nevertheless, when we look at Park's human nature in the framework of the "man–nature relationship," we cannot deny that it lacks the perspective on dynamics between man and nature ("humanizing natures" and "naturalizing humans") through man's social labor and the stance of his ecological determinism is markedly leaning in the direction of spatial fetishism because of this. (Yoshihara 1993: 185)

I attempted to put forward a counter-proposition to the 'human nature' underlying Park's human nature from a Marxist perspective, but I completely omitted any discussion of the impacts of the built environment on human nature created by capitalism in the form of second nature from the turn of the century to the 1920s.

Chapter One

1 Criticisms of various discourses about postmodernity are extremely varied but, on balance, the liquidationist negativism without any reexamination of historical phases of the postmodern phenomenon is predominant. In this regard, the spatial turn discussed later is a fine product of critical ingestion of postmodern discourses.
2 The spatial turn is taking place, involving all fields of the humanities and social sciences today and making marked progress especially in geography, sociology and history. See Yoshihara (2002; 2004).
3 However, it is uncertain as to whether Giddens was truly free from these schemata. I shall briefly mention this point later.
4 The focus of the postmodernity debate rests on the question as to how to reproduce and represent 'the present' of modernity. In this regard, it is definitely different from those modernity arguments under the influence of Enlightenment 'knowledge' that criticized Japan for lagging behind and hoped to build a future through redressing the delay.

5 The statement below about the duality or ambiguity of Western European modernity is an edited and summarized version of part of chapter one of Yoshihara (2002).
6 A surprising number of arguments about postmodernity stress 'sensual transformation.' Harvey's argument (1989) is a typical example. However, he places 'postmodernity' on a contiguous line from modernity.
7 Put simply, Orientalism sees the history of Asia as 'something different' by reference to Western European modernity as 'something eternal and unvarying.' Criticism of Orientalism therefore tends more than anything else to be a denial of Eurocentricism and the narrative of Western European universality. And it attempts to extol Asian perceptions of time and space that are 'different' from those of Western European modernity framed/ enticed by Enlightenment 'knowledge,' as discussed later. Conversely, cultural studies set its sights on subcultures that are not 'genuine' cultures and therefore have been put aside because they have never been able to be the driver of cultural change from past to present. Microhistory study focuses on the *mentalité* of people that is not resolved into the 'collective consciousness' representing a certain age or society and attempts to highlight underlying differences between small villages.
8 The history of Enlightenment 'knowledge' in the humanities and social sciences reveals that its main concerns are the history of formation and development of the nation-state, its crisis (demise) and its prospects. In other words, the nation-state is a 'laboratory' to explain the condition of Enlightenment 'knowledge.'
9 The formation of modern Japanese society became possible through the uniform embedding of people in 'continuous space of geometry' and the invasion of their whole life-world by 'absolute time.' I have explained this through a content analysis of the Gleichschaltung (homogenization) that took place twice in and after early-modern times (Yoshihara 2004).
10 There are various social divides, including gender, ethnicity, class and generation. However, these were all consolidated into one 'nation' under the nation-state mechanism and there has been no integration through the full mobilization of the public sphere in civil society, so to speak. Needless to say, the basic position here is that all social orders surrounding the aforementioned classifications (races) have become shaky and the traditional problematic is losing effect.
11 The problem in this case is that the subject of perception is in a privileged or superior position over the object of perception and they are not on the same horizon on which they sympathize with one another as the same 'beings-outside-the-world' (i.e., ontological position). This problem also underlies the 'Western European perspective on the Orient' pointed out by critics of Orientalism. See Yoshihara (2006a) on this point.
12 Not all dichotomies identify with classical modernization theory but they without doubt serve to explain certain types of modernism in detail. Change is virtually replaced by disconnection in them.
13 It is possible to consider that Urry's mechanism of 'instantaneous time' is acting against streams of 'lived time' here. Regarding the mechanism of 'instantaneous time,' see Yoshihara (2004).

14 The global and the local do not have a relationship in which one dictates the other or the former is an independent variable and the latter a dependent one. They form a rather paradoxical relationship through which their action-reaction, defining-defined, and extension-intension need to be examined.
15 Harvey makes the following comment on this point.

> [T]he less important the spatial barriers, the greater the sensitivity of capital to variations of place within space, and the greater the incentive for places to be differentiated in ways attractive to capital. (1989: 295–296)

16 In this view, physical relationships are written/translated into it. It constitutes a typical example of spatial fetishism, which was placed within the scope of Soja's criticism of so-called 'bias to time without space.'
17 Although it may appear somewhat contradictory to Appadurai's words quoted above. Such a perspective is, however, never drawn into the 'death of something' type of narrative and the periodization that is developed and substantialized from it.
18 However, what is common to these views is that they place postmodernity on a contiguous line from modernity and hence do not necessarily provide convincing explanations about the momentum of modernity that disperses and reverses.
19 The 'tribe' is an 'imaginary' community ('community as metaphor') which retains primordial intimateness at its base while appearing to be founded on a postcolonial and diasporic identity.
20 In the class society that has emerged in front of us, association and solidarity are no longer keywords. If class struggle is to be portrayed around these notions, it will simply end up getting trapped in the schema of 'center and periphery.' Rather, it can be said that the *champ* (field) deeply concealing crevices (divisions and competition) created by fragmentation is the 'class' itself. In arguing thus, Bourdieu extracts something from 'class' that underlies habitus in a relational context.
21 However, I would like to stress here that the retrospective approach is not there to replace the successive approach or make up for its deficiencies. That would be no different from old-fashioned modernity theories. In the context of this chapter, it is important that they are mutually complementary.
22 By the way, if we are to explore the problematic of positionality in the context of narratology primarily concerned with the task of the restoration and reformulation of the lost subject, we must of course reexamine the role of intellectuals. It is certainly easy to declare that the intellectuals who preach 'enlightenment from above' and a 'meta-narrative of political liberation' are no longer realistic. However, it is not that simple a task to concretely portray the intellectuals who are supposed to be behind these arguments. For the time being, I would like to envisage 'mobile, cross-border intellectuals' who, rather than presenting their comprehensive perception of history, *measure the distance from others by questioning themselves and change their own positions in society by changing the distance* and therefore no longer limit themselves to speaking on behalf of others. Setting aside the details, these intellectuals are required to resist a siege mentality from the unbearable loss of 'master narratives' and proffer a clear vision to prevent them being sucked into the reorganization of 'master narratives.'

Chapter Two

1 According to Urry, the September 11 attacks are the most dramatic example of a new form of non-territorial network war or 'net war' caused by 'the multitude' which is very difficult for the hierarchy to grapple with (2003: 131).
2 Thinking that the global is an overwhelming *force majeure* and an integrated mechanics as a whole is in itself within the workings of modernity. The view that globalization is a pattern of modernity persists.
3 The notions of 'structure' and 'agency' were established based on structural determinism, that is, the argument that 'structure' exists as an order and is constantly reproduced, and that 'agency (actor)' is defined by this structure. However, structural determinism was overturned by Giddens' theory of structuration that suggested the 'duality of structure.' Giddens argues that 'structure' gives rise to action but is reinterpreted by countless resurgent actions of well-informed actors (1984). Although structuration theory has an epochal importance in the sense that it reveals a theoretical difficulty (reductionistic bias) with the determinist view concerning 'structure' and 'agency,' it has been pointed out in recent years that this position is itself within the fold of structural determinism. We have seen the appearance of views based on so-called complexity theory which attempt to explain the unpredictable and nonlinear relationship between 'structure' and 'agency' with recurrent, rather than resurgent, actions.
4 As notable as the debate about the transformation of the state is that on power. While Bauman has formulated what can be considered the key argument regarding the former, he has also proposed a highly polemic argument on the latter. According to Bauman, 'postpanoptic' power is detached from a particular territory or space; it rather exists as a flow itself. A fast, light, powerless power that races around various networks: it is a true embodiment of hybridity (Bauman 2000).
5 Castells' list of 'resistance identities' includes the Zapatistas of Mexico, American militias or rightwing groups of the so-called Patriot Movement, global terrorists, various environmental NGOs, women's movements that seek to protect women and children in developing countries from the impacts of market globalization, religious fundamentalist movements and so on (1997). They are more or less aiming for alternative globalization.
6 Take the development of the heritage industry coupled with global tourism for example. This phenomenon has emerged at places where folklore discoveries and 'consuming places' are connected but, curiously, it has been transmitted and developed globally. Virtual/imaginary communities organized on the Internet have played an important role here. People browse through web pages, arrive at iconic places and make them their own through imagination/creation. Thus, virtual travel promotes the branding of places and consequently contributes to the development of the cultural heritage industry.
7 Defining the position of culture in globalization is an extremely important challenge. Lash and Urry once pointed out that complex and nimble economies would spread on a global scale in an instant and that such economies would be comprised of signs and the people who operate in/escape from/are

surrounded by these signs (1994). Urry's comment that complex borders between the global and the local have been redrawn by these agile economies of signs (2003: iii) represents the possibility that a certain type of spatial semiotics may occupy a position in globalization theory.

8 The emergent referred to here is founded on the theory of complex systems. For this reason, I shall quote Langton, a complex systems researcher, here.

> [F]rom the interaction of the individual components [...] emerges some kind of property [...] something you couldn't have predicted from what you know of the component parts [...] And the global property, this emergent behavior feeds back to influence the behavior [...] of the individuals that produced it.
> (Cited in Urry 2003: 39–40)

This suggests that various elements within a system produce collective properties through voluntary and dynamic interactions between them.

9 By the way, Prigogine proposes the concept of a 'new pocket of order.' It involves an island of new order in the messy ocean of disorder, or a dissipative structure. According to him, this island of order maintains or enhances the state of order at the expense of the entropy or disorder of the whole. Thus, Prigogine describes how these pockets of order—they are actually highly organized turbulent flows of air or water—are adrift amid disorder (cited in Urry 2003: 101–102).

10 Although I am not able to discuss this issue specifically in this chapter, we must make a self-reflective inquiry into the fact that the globalization debate has been predominantly taking place on the side of developed countries. This debate has already spawned several strains of argument but we must not forget that they all originate from the side largely driving/promoting globalization. We hope that *the alternative globalization debate* will appear from the side that has been enveloped by the logic of globalization before we can truly grapple with this issue.

Chapter Three

1 With regard to globalization, the process of cultural homogenization used to attract greater interest in its early days but in recent years the fluid nature of globalization has become a stronger focal point of discussion. (See Chapter Two for details).

2 Negri and Hardt perceive such life-power as 'a form of power that regulates social life from its interior, following it, interpreting it, absorbing it, and rearticulating it' (2000: 23).

3 See also Yoshihara (2002: 83–87).

4 Unlike Suzuki's 'nodal institution' theory based on national society, Yazaki's view of a city as an 'integral institution' is applicable not only to 'cities within society/the state' but also 'cities beyond society' and noteworthy as a formula underlying both (1963).

5 Takeshi Haraguchi finds an example of 'cities within society/the state' in the concentric model formulated by the Early Chicago School, especially Burgess, and argues that the subsequent concentric urban development pattern is correlated with the system of capital accumulation which Harvey calls the 'Keynesian city.' Haraguchi states as follows:

> In a Keynesian city, the focus of capital accumulation was placed on the enhancement of labor quality and the stabilization of labor-capital relations through investment in the areas of reproduction such as transport, education and housing, and at the same time, the acceleration of capital turnover through expansion of consumption among the working class. Moreover, many social movements which went into full swing during the period of "urban crisis" in the 1960s successfully pushed the government to guarantee the area of social reproduction. A city was increasingly defined from the point of view of social reproduction and the residential area was expanded and aligned outwardly to suburbs. The concentric urban pattern became ubiquitous in this way. (2005: 145)

6 The scapes referred to here are things that are organized through complex and multilayered networks that are situated/exist within and between various societies (for example, finanscapes found between London, New York and Tokyo) (Urry 2000). See also Appadurai (1996).
7 See also Yoshihara (2005b) as it substantially overlaps with the following argument.
8 Super-high rise buildings are inorganic giant lumps produced by endless deregulation (privatization) that discards and writes off 'the public.'
9 According to Smith, it is almost meaningless to make 'a strict distinction between gentrification (which involved rehabilitation of existing stock) and redevelopment that involved wholly new construction' when we consider the gentrification from the 1990s (1996: 39). Certainly, the key to any consideration of the implications of the present (or at least from the 1990s) gentrification would be the deciphering of a catharsis embedded in it, or a paradox between destruction and creation. I shall mention this indirectly in the following discussion.
10 To be exact, new groups involved in gentrification include the new middle class gentrifiers represented by so-called 'yuppies' and the marginal ones represented by women participating in the high-wage labor market. Conversely, low-income earners, elderly people and minorities are deeply involved in gentrification as 'evictees' or 'the excluded.' The problem is that 'dropping-out' from the status quo among the marginal gentrifiers is becoming normal and 'the excluded' are becoming less visible.
11 This point perfectly resonates with Zukin's argument that urban space is comprised of capital investment and 'sensual attachment' (1996: 49). What is important is that these arguments are somewhat broadening spatial semiotics (Wright and Hutchinson 1997; Iwaki 2005).
12 *Nikkei Architecture* (No. 850, 11 June 2007) reports that the number of visitors to Tokyo Midtown exceeded four million one month from its opening and carries visitors' assessments that it 'emphasizes the path of flow to the inner section' and constitutes 'a contemporary psychedelic with a nod to absurdity.' It shows glimpses of the marketing culture strategy to separate/differentiate individuals and re-subsume them into comparable value systems; the vanishing of the 'career of space' is, however, a concern. See Kuwako (2005) regarding 'career of space.'
13 However, 'dwelling' here traces back to the Heideggerian expression of 'being,' which 'signifies "to reside alongside [...]", "to be familiar with [...]"' (Heidegger 1962: 80) but it is used in connection with the multitiered

disjunctive structure of globalization in order to avoid a communitarian bias.

Chapter Four

1 Here, articulation means that various areas of professional 'knowledge' in different positions constitute 'collective knowledge' as they transform their identities, rather than a particular body of professional 'knowledge' existing as a 'privileged subject.'
2 Regarding 'virtual community,' see Delanty (2003: ch. 9). See also Castells' formulation mentioned below.
3 However, Marshall's exposition is more or less limited to citizenship concerning ordinary White subjects and overlooks the fact that gays and lesbians, for example, are still treated as 'half citizens.' This has undeniably fallen to the evil of turning a blind eye to gender and sexuality-related inequalities.
4 This refers to an array of a wide variety of gadgets, machines and technologies which dramatically compress or contract time-space, ranging from optic fiber to military technologies, not to mention computer networks.
5 Diaspora used to imply such meanings as 'victims of persecution,' 'forceful persecutors' and 'the inwardly wounded.' Now, the existing form of diaspora is generating discussion in terms of its compatibility with global flows and networks.
6 The medieval world was characterized by indefinable national borders and the absence of 'society.' Each empire containing a 'center and periphery' was comprised of diverse cross zones, competing powers and multiple linguistic areas. Today, various competing institutions with such 'medieval' multitiered sovereignty and identities are said to be emerging under globalization.
7 Here, the neoliberal position is the view that globalization is relentless and practically unstoppable, therefore it has to be accepted rather than resisted. The communitarian position is the view that the local is a field tied down to an identity or a field of regression to the 'past' such as the reactionary politics of aesthetisized space (Yoshihara 2004: 176–177).
8 Today, people are said to identify themselves in global terms on the basis of brand-name products and advertisements.
9 This term immediately invokes such entities as large corporate organizations and industrial complexes but it also includes organized religions such as Christianity, Islam and Messianic movements.
10 They refer to fractional and peripheral groups and minority groups which oppose state power structures in their attempt to maintain the power of their sections of society.
11 Even though new electronic media are readily used to obtain information about others, people do not know/are not informed of the full picture of virtual communities created by these electronic media. This state is giving rise to a widespread situation in which human beings are now managed through computer-controlled 'surveillance' and 'systems.' It is curious that the following behavior, which Lyon calls 'participation in social orchestration' is being observed widely under this situation.

Within surveillance societies power seems to flow along a variety of channels. No central watchtower dominates the social landscape, and few people feel constrained, let alone controlled, by surveillance regimes. Most of the time, most people comply cheerfully with requests to show their identification, or acknowledge that they divulge personal data to companies, believing that the benefits are greater than the costs, or that if they have done nothing wrong they have nothing to hide or to fear. I shall suggest that this compliance with surveillance systems can be seen as participation in a kind of social orchestration. For those who are not for some reason marginalized or excluded, social participation generally means active involvement in the mechanisms that keep track of and monitor their everyday lives. Conductors try to ensure that different sections of the social orchestra play together at the appropriate moment. But they still depend on the willing and usually conscious activity of the social "players," whose participation ensures that the system as a whole works and is perpetuated. (Lyon 2001: 7–8)

12 Decartes geometricized the world through a monocle and established the foundation for a position that views space as perspectivist spaces. He treated time as absolute time which can be represented by length and numbers.
13 See Yoshihara (2004: 152–155) for the characteristics of this perception of place as 'place' (*Ort*) with locality and distinctiveness.
14 According to Harvey (1989), this concept attributed to Marx refers to the reorganization of time-space through which capitalism overcomes a crisis and reaches a new stage of capital accumulation.
15 'Visualism' relies solely on visual sensation, separates the world from the parent body of lived experience, and regards it as one 'sphere.'
16 This may sound like a very common problematization but we have reached the stage where we must reexamine old yet new themes such as 'community-association' ('*chonaikai* (neighborhood association)-NPO/VA') based on the measurement of global locational values of sociations in the meantime.
17 In order to avoid this risk, it is necessary to develop communities 'where both the criticism of national beings and the resistance to globalization can take place,' as pointed out by Iyotani (1998: 235).
18 It goes without saying that the appearance of the so-called gated community all over mega cities in the Third World as well as global cities is noteworthy in this context (see Chapter 7 for the case of Jakarta). For that matter, the gated community notably constitutes the reverse side of the aforementioned 'surveillance society.'

Chapter Five

1 Since my systematic argument on local governance (Yoshihara 2000), various people have discussed it based mainly on Rhodes' assertion. I have not yet seen any attempt for standard generalization but, for example, *The Dictionary of Human Geography, 4th ed.*, summarizes Rhodes' formulation into four points: interdependence between organizations, continuing interactions between network members, game-like interactions, and autonomy from the state. An attempt to understand the evolution of governance theory in relation to the social complexity argument as well as the 'policy network' approach and actor-network theory is quite interesting

(Painter 2000: 317). In my view, the argument about social complexity is the key to the development of governance in the future.

2 According to Held, 'the contemporary paradox involves, in short, a situation in which the tension level of collective issues to be dealt with is rising and their scope is widening but the available means to deal with them are weak and incomplete' (2007: 81). This is why 'collective cooperation' and the 'construction of appropriate governance for that purpose' to deal with this situation is required and Held stresses solidarity, social justice and democracy.

3 Incidentally, Held states that 'it was assumed in the formative period of the nation-state that geography, political power and democracy were firmly bound together; it was also considered that political power, sovereignty, democracy and citizenship came into existence by being partitioned into a certain territorial space and that it was a reasonable arrangement' (Held 2007: 101–102).

4 The pluralistic and multitiered structure of local governance has been understood rather heterarchically in the past. Conversely, it appears that there has been some reluctance to introduce spatial scales and time deviations. Certainly, the principle of subsidiarity has been argued alongside governance (Endō 2003, for example). However, it does not necessarily appear to have been organically associated with governance. I believe that the possibility of conceptual utilization and empirical application of the principle of subsidiarity should be explored in the introduction of spatial scales and time deviations.

5 Kaneko describes unsuccessful intervention by the state and involvement by the market in these issues as the 'failure' of hierarchical and market solutions (1999). Apart from the question of how effective the alternative community-based solution proposed by Kaneko would be for these issues, the scope of his thinking almost certainly extends to the base of local governance.

6 This is precisely what the principle of subsidiarity is about. According to Endō, 'the crux of this principle lies in the problematic by which each unit takes its share of responsibility as it pursues the fulfillment of its reason for being without becoming an absolute existence' (2003: 262). The question is, 'through the imported concept of subsidiarity, what society is specifically imagined and what issues is it trying to address by realizing it?' (Endō 2003: 268). See also Note 4 above.

7 In fact, the situation appears to have moved on from the stage of conflict between so-called social democracy and neo-conservatism to the stage of the former being enveloped by the latter. Here, the view that government activity is wasteful has resulted in arbitrary acceptance of the market economy. A range of discourses relating to welfare state reform have lost substance, and the view that 'the reach of the organizational resources of a group, political party and even a state will be narrower than that of a market' (Bartolini 2003: 52–53) has become the commonly accepted assumption.

8 I have already mentioned that heterarchy and the principle of subsidiarity form the conceptual pillars in the explanation of pluralistic and multitiered structures of governance. In the case of a network or cooperation, it is important that all the constituent subjects articulate their respective orga-

nizational resources in a rhizomatous manner, and the key concepts here are self-organization and 'emergence.' These concepts are often used interchangeably with 'spontaneity' by the communitarian camp today. This trend is not followed here. Self-organization and 'emergence' referred to here go with social complexity described by Jessop as follows: 'this discovery [discovery of "governance"] could well reflect the dramatic intensification of societal complexity which flows from growing functional differentiation of institutional orders within an increasingly global society, with all that implies for the widening and deepening of systemic interdependencies across various social, spatial and temporal horizons of action' (1997: 59).

9 Especially notable in relation to this is the role played by the non-profit sector, and the position occupied by it, in local governance. The non-profit sector, which is considered to 'possess mobility and flexibility to deal with new needs' (Miyamoto 2005: 11), has the possibility of not only exercising its 'privity' but also assuming a leading role in mediating between various subjects by strengthening its cooperation with administration and community. Nevertheless, the intermediary role referred to here is supported solely by autonomy at the site of activity and will not be absorbed into the so-called 'public and private mix' theory, which is a subspecies of modernistic dichotomy. Regarding a theoretical pitfall of the theory of the concatenation of public and private matters in relation to NPOs, see Kageyama (2005).

10 The breadths of Harvey's and Castells' theories are extremely wide. For this very reason, it is inevitable that their theories attract both praise and censure. One thing we can say about this, however, is that their theories are influenced by extremely diverse sources and that these sources of influence rise and fall with the ebb and flow of the current of thought. From another angle, it means that they have always had their eyes on the predominant current of the times in the background of their theoretical perspectives. See Yoshihara (2008a) for Harvey's theoretical transition.

11 I relied heavily on Mizuguchi (2007) in developing my discussion in this section, especially in my extensive reading of documents and organization of issues. I am writing separately about a systematic survey of theories of 'open urban space,' especially theoretical rearrangement in relation to the arguments of Jacobs and Sennett. For example, Haraguchi (2005) raises interesting points about Jacobs' theoretical perspective.

12 Today, we are in what can be called the state of governance inflation. In addition to overuse of the word governance, non-conceptual use is noticeable. Although this phenomenon itself may be an expression of a certain aspect of the spirit of the times, we need to establish the theoretical and practical necessity underlying the use of the term governance deliberately as I mentioned in this chapter. I cannot help but feel that there are some peculiar political and social factors behind the manipulative use of governance (in such areas as organizational theory, for example). If we neglect the aforementioned task, we will overlook these political and social contexts. In any case, we need to examine the climate of the age surrounding the discourse of governance.

13 It goes without saying that the key to this detour is the 'concrete circuit to public' (Kōichi Hasegawa). Hasegawa considers that the success or

failure of the 'new public sphere' is effectively contingent on the state of governance (2004).

Chapter Six

1. According to Koyasu, 'the phrase "oriental despotism" had been cast over Asia by the West as a clear indicator of the oriental which refers to a political/state regime [that has been] left behind the forward march of civilization and remained in a primitive form from the beginning of history' (2003: 57).
2. This way of thinking is characterized by the so-called East-West dualism— a dichotomy between the West and the East or the West and the non-West— under which the West is considered as a 'messenger' of civilization who illuminates 'the world in the dark' while Asia is despised as a narrow-minded bigot who resists civilization.
3. What comes into view here is what Hiroyuki Kotani calls 'internalized orientalism'/'postcolonial difficulty' which has existed throughout the colonial system and the de-colonial system. According to Kotani, de-colonization (independence from colonialism) does not immediately lead to a break from orientalism/colonial situations and orientalism continues to define politics/society/cultural situations that are supposed to have been de-colonized (2003: 32). The following discussion will reveal that globalization, which is the greatest decisive factor in the morphological change of Asian cities from primate cities to megacities, is in the end reinforcing and supporting the aforementioned 'continuous horizon.'
4. The origin of the primate city is clearly found in the colonial city and many of the primate cities are said to have appeared at the end of the nineteenth century and the early twentieth century. In particular, large Asian cities grew from multifunctional harbor cities as in the example of Jakarta. A brief commentary about Batavia's development into a primate city can be found in Yamamoto (2005: 509–511).
5. Appearing contemporaneously with this argument was urban involution theory. Based on the primary meaning of the term, it refers to an urban population increasing in a geometric progression while the economic system is fundamentally unchanged, but it also contains another aspect which Geertz looked at with keen interest, namely so-called 'shared poverty' in which kinship and hometown networks are reorganized in the city, traditional mutual aid is practiced and work and earnings are endlessly fractionalized in order to accept the ever-increasing number of new arrivals (Geertz 1963). However, we must not forget that this practice to accept the ever-increasing number of new arrivals, maximize the number of jobs and share in common poverty continued because the Kampung was left behind by the colonial empire as a 'backyard community' densely populated by tradesmen, laborers and servants as it was a source of cheap labor (Ishizawa 1989: 59) and that this condition was maintained even after independence.
6. The term 'colonial' is usually used in the context of an external ruling colony. However, 'internal colony' here is used in the sense that a colony exists within this colonized place from the beginning. In other words, it

refers to the preservation of the colonial/postcolonial system by keeping the informal sector under an unstable and low-wage condition and imposing 'subhuman habitation of very poor quality' on the slums as has often been pointed out.
7 The question about the original form of Kampung arises here. In order to understand it, we must be informed about the following characteristics of urban habitation in plural society peculiar to a colonial city.

> The central district has a landscape dominated by large stone buildings and a Western European style in terms of the type, scale and structure of its institution and culture which is in stark contrast with districts of Chinese or indigenous culture.
>
> Adjacent to the central district are enclaves of retail shops or small industries operated by Chinese or Indians. These people have superior commercial and industrial skills than those of the indigenous population and are suited to urban living, and they have put themselves in a monopolistic position in the city by operating wholesale, brokerage, money lending, precious metal, clothing and food businesses and small industries. Their shops differ from labor-saving Western-style shops with minimal numbers of employees in that they operate as mutual aid organizations in which large numbers of people, including family, relatives and connections from the same native place, work for low wages.
>
> Businesses and industries operated by indigenous families are found everywhere and shopless stall keepers and street peddlers are selling their wares on the street, but it is difficult for them to even maintain subsistence. The market is at the apex of the bazaar economy where there are no fixed prices and bargaining and haggling are the ways to do business. (Yazaki 1988: 51–52)

In the case of Batavia, Kampungs began amongst this prevailing mixed habitation from the formation of 'residential quarters surrounded by fences or mounds containing groups of tree-lined residential compounds' (Funo 2005: 115) by various ethnic groups (except the Chinese and slaves) who migrated from other regions to the areas outside of the central city walls.
8 On this point, it is logical to consider, as Douglass does, that megacities are the command centers for accumulation and circulation of global capital at the local level and play a part in the hierarchical system between world cities (1995). In other words, megacities are linked to the global network beyond society.
9 KIP was implemented from 1974 as community improvement planning with the participation of residents and divided into four main types: 'resident-driven,' 'municipality-driven,' 'World Bank KIP' and 'UNEP-type KIP' (Ishizawa 1989: 88). From the 1990s, post-KIP large-scale development went into full swing and reportedly made some progress as far as slum clearance was concerned. Some have pointed out, however, that all it achieved was slum removal because of its 'stopgap measure' nature.
10 The 'return to tradition' phenomenon is one example. One background factor is the fact that globalization is threatening people's lives in some ways. As well as bringing about the instability of employment and social mobilization, globalization is destroying the substance of 'communality'

which people have preserved in the life-world and putting them in a state of bottomless anxiety. In this circumstance, an increasing number of people see globalization as a threat.
11 According to Maotani, *rukun* refers to 'the pattern of behavior in the case of conflict of interests to give way to one another to reach a compromise and settle the conflict amicably through bid collusion which does not create bitter feelings, and also the situation which results from this behavior' (1983: 143). This is the pattern/state of so-called *zenin icchi* (common assent), which is considered vital to 'the formation of organizations and dynamism to jointly manage the community' (Satō 2005: 143).
12 Analysis of RT/RW is essential if we are to examine the changing state of local community via the effect of interactions between individual actions on change at the level of people's daily living while keeping our eye on the effect of structural factors 'from outside.' See Yoshihara (ed.) (2005) for the modes of RT/RW, including the role they played in nation building under the postcolonial regime.
13 In Indonesia, approximately fifteen percent of men in employment as of 1997 had lost their jobs by August 1998 and economic devastation was particularly serious in Jakarta. The size of the poor class reportedly doubled. Indonesia's GDP dropped 13.1 percent from the previous year and its GDP three years after the Currency Crisis was still seventy-five percent lower than the pre-crisis level (Harvey 2005).
14 Street furniture on the street from Glodok to Blok M in Kebayoran Baru, described as the 'street dazzling with electric lights,' is not very different from that of any global city. The only difference is the use of local emblems such as Sanskrit and old Javanese writings on postmodern buildings all over the place which appears to be intentionally emphasized. Of course, the landscape is completely different in nature from that of a capital city which represents national integration.
15 I shall quote my description of it here.

> Asia, which is situated on the land called Eurasia to begin with, was formed by a diverse and non-convergent developmental process as East Asia under the Chinese civilization, South Asia under the Hindu civilization and West/Southeast Asia under the Islamic civilization went down the path of "coevolution" through competition and imitation. During the process, wide-area networks for commercial and financial transactions created by Islam played the central role (Hara 2003: 3–11). Of course, this polyphyletic developmental process appears to have been once denied by "top down" industrialization policy, under the developmentalist regime. However, as the "age of development" ends, intercommunity relations and interpersonal networks, which cannot be converged with international relations and contain their own conflicts and frictions, begin to sprout. At the same time, domestically, as the nation-state system unravels, segmented society that has been locked in under "competitive nationalism" is rearing its head, together with self-assertiveness of the provinces and the emergence of religious organizations. And pluralistic identities floating about in all sorts of directions are adding vivid colors to people's life-worlds. (Yoshihara 2006a: 334–335)

Chapter 7

1 The process of shift between geographical areas in which one initially settles in a 'zone in transition' and gradually moves to outer rings is at once a process of social mobility. Burgess' zonal model is an ecological description of this dual process (1925). However, it conceals the grand narrative of filtering down within it. The equilibrium theory of change was unable to extract this narrative. It appears that assimilation to America was encouraged by the impregnation of the WASP-led 'American dream.'
2 'Shared poverty' was originally referred to as urban involution. Involution literally means that something 'continues to increase its internal complexity and never reaches a new evolutionary stage' and it is usually used in a negative sense. However, Geertz used the term in a positive sense in a Javanese rural village setting. He argued that paddy cultivation could absorb a large labor force and a mutual aid custom enabled fractionalization of work opportunity and distribution, thus making it possible to support many people without changing social mechanisms (1963). By analogically applying this logic, it is argued that a large inflow population shares poverty by mainly engaging in the tertiary sector and fractionalizing work in the condition of urban involution, or 'shared poverty.'
3 Kitano et al. point out that this low-cost housing supply plan does not satisfactorily achieve 'its original aim of helping the low-income class acquire their own homes' and comment as follows:

> The maximum price and specifications under the forward mortgage at a fine rate program were set by the Ministry of Public Works for each category (very simple house, core house and simple house). [Interest rates were 8.5 percent for a very simple house, eleven percent for a core house and fourteen to twenty-one percent for a simple house.] A difference in the maximum price between the provinces and major cities was only about twenty percent and developers could only build relatively expensive simple houses in major cities in most cases due to higher land prices. Consequently, more middle-income earners than low-income earners received forward mortgages at preferential rates, which would continue for a period of up to twenty years. (Kitano et al. 2001: 95)

4 In one RT in Menteng Atas adjoining the CBD where I conducted my fieldwork, 'shared poverty' was functioning as a safety net in its own way up until the economic crisis. For example, when one section of land within the RT was bought up by a developer as part of urban restructuring and left untouched, a *karang taruna* (youth association) and other locals prepared the ground and converted it to a children's playground (Yoshihara 2000). This was a good example of reinterpretation *from below/inside* of restructuring *from above/outside*. However, as many of these young people who were the key players in the local community became unemployed and got involved in drugs and other problems amid the economic crisis, the foundation of 'shared poverty' began to crumble. The decline of community is clearly under way in these places.
5 Informal sector workers who are eligible for social welfare include those who 'operate street stalls, sell goods to cars stopped at traffic lights, direct

traffic at intersections without traffic lights, get into cars as "*kaedama* (jockey-three-in-one)" so that they carry a minimum of three people when entering the main street between the periods of 7 a.m. and 10 a.m. and 4:30 p.m. and 7 p.m. stipulated by law and receive money as soon as they enter the main street, drive the rickshaw and so on' (Dwianto 2006: 86–87). Small (petty) merchants such as *pedagang keliling* discussed in this chapter are not eligible for social welfare.
6 Here, the new middle class are treated as identical to the new rich. Some are of the opinion that they should be separated. For example, they can be told apart by the car they drive according to Ziv, who is an observer of the streets of Jakarta (2000:101): 'the new rich cruise around in a sparkling Maserati or S-class Mercedes past pattering *bajai* (compact tricycles) and beggars playing a half-broken guitar, which have been poetic features of Jakarta since the time of primate city. On the other hand, the new middle class clog every street with their cars bearing Honda and Toyota emblems especially in mornings and evenings and invite frowns of disgust all over Jakarta.'
7 More specifically, land development became part of the Master Plan of the DKI Jakarta for 1985–2005 that was established under the 1981 Jabotabek Metropolitan Development Plan. However, there was hardly any systematic land development by municipal authorities and this process was mainly led by conglomerates of Overseas Chinese who saw it as a business opportunity and went on a land-buying spree. These conglomerates were weeded out during the subsequent economic crisis but it can be said that they played a substantial role in urban restructuring in the sense that they provided gated communities to customers according to their own intentions.
8 The 'communality' which was created surrounding the establishment of *syskamrin* (civil defense groups) at the time of the May 1998 riot in Pesona Kayangan, Depok in the outskirts of Jakarta, satisfied the need for 'an arena to empower residents and formulate public opinion' and at the same assumed the character of the gated community as a highly homogeneous and 'privatistic' space. Faced with a threat, residents identified 'our world' among themselves. This prompted the development of local community. Whether it has formed a highly exclusive space or not, it clearly represents a paradigm of the gated community led by the urban middle class. See Dwianto (1999) for details of this case.

Chapter 8

1 Balinese society was originally characterized by a two-dimensional construction consisting of the *adat* and *dinas* (local government). It began when Bali Hindu was placed outside the system under Dutch colonial rule, and was consolidated when it was incorporated into the system in the post-colonial era. However, as the overwhelming wave of urbanization that goes hand in hand with the advance of global tourism hits the community, it also creates a situation where the *adat* is being encroached upon by the *dinas* (refer to Yoshihara (2006c) regarding this point).
2 Incidentally, Geriya (2002) posits that tourism in Bali prior to this was in a sporadic introductory stage. He argues that the roads were built with the opening of the Ngurah Rai Airport, thus spurring on the development of

tourism both in quantity and quality. It was then that Bali entered into its so-called concentrated period (Geriya 2002: 15–7).
3 Tourists were later required to obtain visas in the midst of a sharp decline in their numbers due to the impact of the terrorist bombings. Some voiced opposition to this, saying that the number of tourists would fall even further, but so far it has contributed to increased revenue.
4 In 2000 the Bali provincial government began to take measures against batik factory waste fluids. Specifically, starting in 2002 a reservoir was built in each factory under the instruction of the provincial government. Furthermore, factories were required to use chemicals to dilute the wastewater color. However, none of this succeeded in reducing the damage done to the surrounding areas, and the factories suffered even greater criticism. Incidentally, volume 29 of the 'Purnama' newsletter published by the PPB (Persatuan Purnama Batik) association set up by batik factory managers described the decisions it made on 14 August 2003 as follows:

1. Regulations members must comply with:
   a) Do not rinse batik in the rivers
   b) Do not dump batik waste fluid without filtering it first within the factory
   c) Do not dry batik in public areas
2. Penalties for violators:
   a) Members who do not comply with the regulations will be expelled from the association
   b) Members who violate the regulations will be penalized by the *desa* (administrative village).

5 Presently, the number of batik factories is on a downward trend due to a lack of vacant land as a result of the rising population, steep rises in land prices and the intensifying competition with China. As for the employees, they return to Java. However, because they cannot find employment in Java, they end up coming back to Bali, after which many move to other batik factories. Therefore, they effectively settle in Balinese society.

Incidentally, some of the owners of the batik factories are starting to devise new business strategies, such as manufacturing a wide variety of products in small quantities (for example, the manufacturing of beach sarongs and bedcovers), or focusing on the artistic aspect of batik and the value in handicrafts. There are also owners who are attempting to work out new management strategies by moving the factories to Java, while maintaining a distributing agent in Bali.
6 Although, as mentioned in Note 1, Balinese society is formed from a two-dimensional construction consisting of the *adat* and *dinas*, this framework applies even in the *banjar*, the lowest level of administration. Balinese community is then constructed from a combination of the *banjar adat* and *banjar dinas*. Moreover, this community is characterized by a pluralistic group composition consisting of various *sekas* (prescriptive group or voluntary association). Up until now, there was a clear cut raison d'etre in which the *banjar adat* was responsible for traditional festivities and events, while the *banjar dinas* was responsible for secular administrative duties. Today, however, we can see cases where the former is becoming

formalized, particularly in areas where urbanization is progressing, and being incorporated into the latter (refer to Yoshihara 2006c for details). Even if it does not go this far, we cannot deny the fact that on the whole both parties are mutually penetrating each other. It is amidst this trend that the division of roles between the *banjar adat* and *banjar dinas* is starting to blur (in fact, in some cases the same person may have a position in both the *banjar adat* and *banjar dinas*).

Incidentally, although new movements, which are riding on the back of the decentralization policy in their pursuit to increase autonomy for the *banjar adat* in the name of the protection of Bali's traditional society, are appearing, in general they are not changing the abovementioned trend.

7 At this *banjar* the following measures are taken in response to KIPEM who are unable to pay the administrative fees. First, they are allowed to pay in three installments. Furthermore, if, for example, both husband and wife are KIPEM, the administrative fees would total 200,000 rupiah. In such a case, they are allowed to first register the husband, and then register the wife three months later. Also, the responsibility for registration is placed in the hands of the employers in the case of KIPEM employed by batik factories, and so the employers are required to carry out the registration collectively. Additionally, if someone registered as a KIPEM returns to Java before the three-month validity period expires, the manager is given unspoken permission to use that name for a KIPEM who has yet to be registered.

8 The loud call made by *ajeg Bali* to promote local culture was already incorporated into the government policies under colonial rule and was also an indispensable part of the post-colonial strategy of global tourism. Undoubtedly, the local culture that *ajeg Bali* is trying to revive is deeply rooted in Bali Hindu. However, its difference to the local culture that appeared in relation to globalization is not always clear. Indeed, it even appears as if it has been completely drawn into the flow of globalization.

9 While this may sound like a repeat of Note 8, it can be noted that *ajeg Bali* may perhaps be posited as one of the new types of anti-globalization movements seen in various places today. Furthermore, it can perhaps be considered in an analogical light with the neonationalistic movement spreading across Europe, which rejects immigrant labor and has, in a way, hijacked the notion of cultural relativism. What is important here is how the *ajeg Bali* movement perceives the progress of global tourism to be undermining the social order created on the basis of 'race.' In relation to this, it is perhaps also necessary to point out that *ajeg Bali* is, on the one hand, trying to faithfully restore the doctrines of Bali Hindu. Refer to the *Bali Post* (2004) for the time being regarding this point.

10 The 'emergent' referred to here is not something that spreads without limit, or that arises from some sort of bottomless source. The debate regarding self-organization and spontaneity that is presently spreading has a tendency to take on such characteristics. The 'emergent' that I am suggesting is that which arises from the multilayered network created through relationships that real life people living in the day-to-day world make with the 'other,' and not that which exists in and of itself. Refer to Yoshihara (2005c) for details.

Chapter Nine

1 Cohen makes the following comment on diasporas:

> Deterritorialized, multilingual and capable of bridging the gap between global and local tendencies, diasporas are able to take advantage of the economic and cultural opportunities on offer. [...] As diasporas become more integrated into the cosmopolis, their power and importance are enhanced. (1992: 176)

Conversely, Urry states, 'Nomads characterise societies of de-territorialisation, constituted by lines of flight rather than by points or nodes' (2000: 27). I would like to point out that diasporas and nomads are used as metaphors for movement and travel here.

2 Sociation here means collective participation = community 'premised upon...a kind of horizontal extension of the networks of civil society, both within and especially beyond the boundaries of nation-states' which 'is conscious and freely chosen on the basis of mutual sentiment and emotional feeling' (Urry 2000). I have made brief mention of some examples of the actual forms of sociation in Chapter Four.

3 See Konno's studies (chapters 2 and 3) in Yoshihara (ed.) (2008b) about the development of global tourism in Bali. Regarding the state of global tourism observed by local researchers, see Geriya's study (2002) using the Parsonian model, also mentioned in Note 4 below.

4 According to Geriya, the phenomenon of *kawin campur* (mixed marriage) in Bali is not new. There was marriage between a Balinese King and a Chinese Queen in the seventh century and marriages between Balinese and Americans, Dutch, Germans and Australians were common under the colonial regime. Then, marriages between Balinese and Japanese increased markedly in the 1990s (there were about 300 cases of marriage between a Balinese man and a Japanese woman in 1997). According to Geriya's definition, the 1990s was the third phase of Bali tourism during which Bali's intrinsic attractions (e.g., natural beauty, hospitable people, village community values etc.) were placed at the center of tourism strategies and venture and family businesses were actively developed to take advantage of them. This state of tourism captured the hearts of Japanese female tourists (Geriya 2002).

5 Figure 9.2 (see the next page) shows the numbers of long-stay people over the age of fifty by age group for 1999–2006 as estimated by the LongStay Foundation. The overall rising trend is evident but trends for individual countries are not clear. According to the ranking of preferred host countries by age group for 2006, Indonesia is ranked eighth amongst those in their 50s, ninth for the 60s age-group, eighth for the 70s and second for the 80s. It is the third most popular destination in Asia after Malaysia and Thailand (except for the 80s age group) (LongStay Foundation 2007). I must avoid a hasty conclusion but it appears that long term residence in Indonesia, especially Bali, is becoming a trend.

6 As at the end of August 2007, fifty-one issues of *Tile Book Print Kecak* have been published. It is published by the public relations section of the Japan Club. Its fifty-first issue contains the latest reports on members, Japan Club's budget, section activity, operating committee, event information,

Figure 9.2: Changes in the estimated long-stay population (by age group)

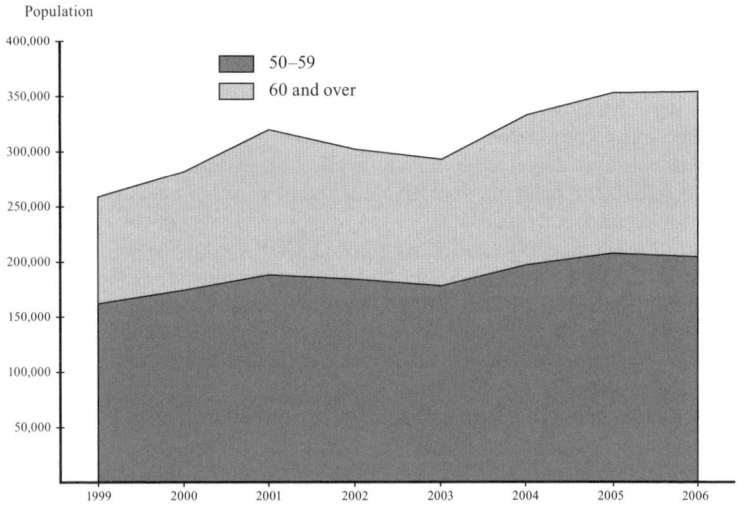

Source: LongStay Foundation (2007: 49).

    latest news from the Japanese School, and corporate and individual membership, serial commentary, yellow pages, message board, messages from the consulate, and notices from the secretariat and so on. It clearly fulfills the role of 'information center' but that is not the only role it plays, as discussed below.
7 The *bale banjar* functions as a medium ('arena') for everyday activities of the *banjar*. Various *banjar* meetings are held and members enjoy activities such as table-tennis, TV and cockfighting. Some people gather there simply for a chat or a break. Some *bale banjar* are used as a venue for literacy classes or a service outlet of petty loans associations for the public such as *simpan pinjam* of Java, or are equipped with a kitchen for large banquets or a storeroom to keep costumes and musical instruments for Balinese dance. Bazaars and small markets are held in some cases.
8 The house in which T lives was purchased with her own savings, sales proceeds of her husband's land and a contribution from her father. Her money and that of her father covered ninety percent of the purchase price. Under Indonesian law, only Indonesian nationals are permitted to register house and land ownership in their names. Accordingly, T has made a notarized deed certifying 'joint ownership' of the house and land by herself and her husband. She anticipates an increase in the number of disputes over land and house ownership as the number of Japanese migrants increases.
9 I's husband has two younger brothers. His parents sent him to Japan for university education, their second son to the U.S. and third to France.

Notes 205

10 Indonesia issues a retiree visa for one year (renewable annually up to four times, then the person can apply for a residency permit) to foreigners over the age of fifty-five who can prove the receipt of at least US$1500 per month (US$2500 for the fist year) in pension or other income (from investments etc.).
11 Drawing on Kelsky's theory (2001), Mari Shimamura points out the existence of latent Japanese-style orientalism in the desire to gain superiority by entering a relationship or marriage with a Westerner and the preference for Asian men (2007: 98).

Chapter Ten

1 Well-known regional communities at the global level include the European Union (E.U.) that is widely supported on the western side of the Eurasian Continent and the East Asian Community and Asia-Pacific Region discussed below. Interestingly, these regional communities are constructed on the equilibrium between an upward vector beyond the nation-state and a downward vector toward the nation-state (see Iwanaga 2008). In other words, the basis of the formation of regional communities today is the advancement of the regional integration and differentiation that is taking place while some sort of balance is maintained between them. Movements for the revival of local regional identities can be regarded as an acute manifestation of localism on this basis. Yet, it is difficult to deny the existence of latent intention behind such movements to reconstruct ethnicity/nationality or reorganize the state and local government.
2 During the period of predominance of 'new urban sociology,' the Keynesian welfare state (i.e., interventionist state) was yet to face a serious crisis. The central interest of 'new urban sociology' at that stage was the question of how the city was defined and redefined by major external forces. The major external force was bureaucracy (urban managerialism) in the eyes of neo-Weberian R. E. Pahl, and capitalism (collective consumption) in the eyes of structural Marxist Manuel Castells. This fact itself is an indication of the pluralistic and contentious nature of 'new urban sociology,' but what draws our attention here is that both bureaucracy and collective consumption were within the framework of the interventionist state, or in other words, they were completely enveloped by the mechanism of Fordistic capitalism. It is now clear that 'new urban sociology' was fixated on the subattributes of the nation-state as well as a transition from Fordism to post-Fordism.
3 In relation to this point, see Note 2 for the theoretical trend of 'new urban sociology.' The main feature of Chicago sociology, which was the subject of criticism by 'new urban sociology,' was that it was underpinned by a methodological position to study the city to understand it, or in other words, a theoretical posture to assume a 'self-contained urban area' (i.e., treating the city as an independent variable). This methodological position or theoretical posture was a sharp reflection of the 1920s (the Chicago world) seen by Chicago sociologists. It appears that this point was rarely considered in 'new urban sociology.' See Yoshihara (1983) for details.
4 To orthodox (dare I call it) sociology, distinction between urban theory with affinity for economic geographic arguments and 'new urban sociology'

appears to have been outside of its interest. It appears to have regarded that both were leaning toward the political economic arguments. Above all else, the central interest of orthodox sociology was to draw a sharp line between itself and political economic argument. This methodological distinction was also applied to the notion of 'spatial turn.' Although I shall not discuss 'spatial turn' in detail here due to space limitations (see Yoshihara 2002 for details), I would like to reiterate that orthodox sociology scarcely took notice of the primary feature of the 'spatial turn' concept, which is the gaze at the ambiguity of modernity. This appears to have had something to do with the subsequent 'internal group' tendency of orthodox sociology.

5 According to Bauman, 'Instantaneity (nullifying the resistance of space and liquefying the materiality of objects) makes every moment seem infinitely capacious; and infinite capacity means that there are no limits to what could be squeezed out of any moment—however brief and "fleeting"' (2000: 125). By the way, Bauman describes 'liquid' modernity as follows, using this 'instantaneity' as the key concept.

> If "solid" modernity posited eternal duration as the main motive and principle of action, "fluid" modernity has no function for the eternal duration to play. The "short term" has replaced the "long term" and made of instantaneity its ultimate ideal. While promoting time to the rank of an infinitely capacious container, fluid modernity dissolves—denigrates and devalues—its duration. (2000: 125)

6 In short, they are norms based on neoliberal principles. They arrive in as a three-piece set: market economy, 'limited government,' and deregulation. Adoption of these norms by individual countries advances the reorganization of Pax Americana and develops economic spaces which not only depend on the 'permeability of national borders' but also increase it further. At the same time, cities 'begin to make a frantic effort to provide more favorable conditions for creating surplus value for flexibly acting capital' (Tasaka 2005b: 11). In other words, they 'emerge as "competitive agents" who compete for locational supremacy and attraction of enterprises and industries' (Tasaka 2005b: 8). What plays a crucial role in driving cities as 'competitive agents' to a fierce intercity competition is the 'competitive state' peculiar to the post-Fordism stage. I shall discuss this point later.

7 I have stated in Chapter Two that these networks symbolically represent the contemporary nature of globalization, namely, its state of existence as fluid rather than region. It basically comes through the lightness of footwork of global capital, but there is more than that. Hybridity found in the networks also include collectivity at the 'civic' level. If cities are not unilaterally defined by site selection by corporations and 'site procurement' by the 'competitive state' fully supporting it but they reinterpret such site selection/ 'site procurement' by associational activity of the citizens, then it becomes extremely important to examine the nature of this collectivity.

8 While the 'class problem' is associated with national citizenship, the secondary citizen problem is mainly linked with 'differential multi-tiered citizenship' (Yuval-Davis 1997: 12) or what Urry (2000) calls the 'citizenship of flow.' Both the secondary citizen problem and the 'class problem' are certainly intricately linked with social marginalization.

However, marginalization is prevented from moving toward the center by multiple divides in the former case whereas it is drawn toward the center again in the latter case. It is particularly important today to identify the undercurrent to this difference but, in order to do so, it is firstly necessary to clearly understand 'the present' of modernity in which there is a definite separation of citizenship and nationality.

9 The 'competitive state' is peculiar to the post-Fordism stage. Hirsch places the 'security nation,' which is a mixture of the welfare state and the surveillance state, in opposition to this. It is a form of state compatible with the Fordism stage and concentrates on deploying its huge financial power and coordinating the interests of various actors. By contrast, the 'competitive state' attacks the welfare state and pushes a shift toward 'limited government' vigorously based on neoliberalism. The action agenda of the 'competitive state' is said to be 'to increase the level of economic liberalization and bring the public domain into line with market-based systems and processes, whether at the local, national or global level' (Held 2007: 87). At the same time, the 'competitive state' plays the role of the interventionist state by way of 'site procurement,' although it criticizes the interventionist state.

10 In 'economies of scale,' the most important task was to minimize production-related costs. Now that globalization has made the acquisition of factors of production easier, cost reduction in production has become secondary. Or rather, the question of how to utilize and execute factors of production and where to site the operation in order to do so has become more important. In other words, it is a question of the productivity of individual corporations itself. Corporate productivity is largely determined by the total accumulative environment offered by the city. This is a question of what Tasaka calls the business climate. According to Tasaka, it consists of four elements: 'condition of factors (input resources), corporate strategy and competition, demand condition, and industry cluster (industry accumulation)' (2005b: 5).

11 It has become apparent to everyone that the greater the degree of global integration, the greater the degree of differentiation (i.e., division), particularly multidimensional and multilayered division. This condition can be regarded fundamentally as an indication of the paradox/ambiguity of globalization as modernity (or even postmodernity), but it is notable that this condition is manifesting today as 'self-differentiation' of the city, which is an attempt to highlight differences between itself and others according to the requirements of the instinctual drive of capital. I would like to point out here that such 'self-differentiation' ultimately denies the foundation for the city's 'creativity' = 'emergence' which controls the self from the perspective of the 'citizens.' This means turning a blind eye to the paradox of globalization which is the very act of 'self-denial.'

12 It of course manifests itself in various ways. The composition of gated communities and slums in Tokyo and Denpasar is not as highly segregated as in Jakarta. From a different point of view, Jakarta's position is markedly different from that of Tokyo or Denpasar in that the both are woven together in a mixed configuration via Kampungs despite a high degree of segregation between them. The aforementioned two-layer constitution

prominently exhibited a side that did not correspond to class segregation due to differences in ethnic origin or cultural traditions to start with, and globalization is further accentuating this side. However, this is one of the aspects of globalization and, on the other side, the aforementioned two-layer constitution is acting to create underlying class segregation in each city. However, class segregation referred to here is not limited to segregation marked by revenue raising activity.

13 As I explained in Chapter Six, it means that the prestige structure formed under colonial rule has been built in deep within the postcolonial spatial composition. As pointed out earlier, the spatial composition under colonial rule was characterized by the mechanism to form the prestige system on one hand and preserve/incorporate indigenous customs (*adat*) on the other, and this mechanism cast a complex shadow over the subsequent urban development process. Based on the premise of concentric zone hypothesis of E. W. Burgess, for example, it clearly acts as a distortion factor. Even the spatial restructuring faithfully executed according to the Washington Consensus principles has failed to destroy the structure of intricately intermingling prestige and *adat* systems in a strict sense. Or rather, it steered around it. From the increasing trend toward EMR in recent years, however, it is obvious that the postcolonial landscape is showing greater conformity to the aforementioned globality.

14 Some point out that the Washington Consensus, especially the Washington Security Agenda, 'break many of the central arguments of international politics and international agreements since 1945' and others argue that 'the end of the Cold War and the geopolitical upheavals that followed could become major geopolitical factors' (Held 2007: 88–89). In any case, it can become the 'global standard' for the very reason that American hegemony is being maintained. However, global governance led by the U.S. is not necessarily rock-solid. This is evidenced by the fact that 'alliances based on anxiety' are appearing in every city exposed to the 'global standard,' and they are even presaging a move toward intercity governance. Nevertheless, it is too hasty to think that this is an indication of a countermodel against global governance steeped in the neoliberal mechanism. In reality, it is highly likely that it will be captured by global governance. Again, there is an urgent need to actualize 'civic' control here.

15 Shigeto Sonoda points out that as far as the emerging middle class of Jakarta, especially the new middle class, is concerned, their sense of 'national pride' is stronger compared with the laboring class (2007: 293). According to our survey on the street, however, a very low awareness of nationality goes hand in hand with its extravagant lifestyle among members of the new rich segment of the middle class which has been growing steadily after surviving the Orde Baru era and the economic crisis (Yoshihara 2006). Conversely, the new middle class, who used to enjoy the benefits of Orde Baru before being forced to drop out due to the economic crisis, are highly critical of the Indonesian government as a 'competitive state.' However, the fact that this critical perception has encountered neo-nationalism in part instead of completely turning to transnationalism demonstrates the complexity of the situation. The *ajeg Bali* movement discussed in Chapter Eight is symbolic of this complexity.

16 Needless to say, the key question in this case is how to reveal the aforementioned interchangeability and emergence. Although I have partially elaborated this point in Part I, I shall discuss it systematically in relation to place in the final chapter.

Epilogue

1 According to Kiyoshi Nakamura (2009), contemporary anthropology has a strong tendency to treat certain cultures in the singular while asserting the plurality of culture. It is undeniable that 'racism based on difference theory' discussed below has an aspect of 'plagiarism' of structuralist anthropology, but it may have been the case that it has a logical composition which is prone to resonate with, or is archetypal of, the aforementioned tendency peculiar to today's anthropology.
2 It appears that Nakamura's argument has been strongly influenced by Anderson's 'imagined communities' (1983), which is clearly detected in the following comment, in addition to the argument of Rapport and Overing. Nakamura develops his argument as the issue of culture 'entwined with the conflict between tradition and modernity.' See Nakamura (2009) for details.
3 Heidegger grasps 'dwelling' in terms of its unity/isomorphy with 'building' and states that 'dwelling'/'building' shows that the person who is to die is on the ground (1954). Incidentally, Shizuteru Ueda interprets this world of Heidegger's developed from 'dwelling' as 'living in all quarters of the world by (people who are) supported by the earth, blessed by the heavens, encounter the gods and can complete death together with other mortals' (1992: 61). To Heidegger, '"dwelling" means transforming a homogeneous infinite space, which is plain and without any symbolization and marked only by distance and direction, into "place" (*Ort*) which possesses locality and distinctiveness' (Yoshihara 2004: 154). This means that Heidegger's 'dwelling' contains 'taking root'/'enclosing' a priori, but at the same time, it partially resonates with the 'practical occupancy of the world by five senses' of young Marx as glanced at in Chapter Four.
4 Lefebvre (1991) comments elsewhere, by substituting the society-wide rule of abstract space with that of clock time, that it has completely banished *kairos* time. However, what is important for Lefebvre is not the fact that abstract space has colonized 'lived space' but the fact that it has created *another social space*, namely 'heterotopy/differentiated space.' Therefore, 'heterotopy' can be considered as a product of the dialectical mechanism of space and place in the main.
5 The growth of megacity Jakarta into the Extended Metropolitan Region is in itself a result of spatial restructuring prompted by advancing globalization, but it maintained organic linkage to the industry by distributing the CBD, industrial areas and residential areas functionally according to the need of export processing-oriented industrialization. However, spaces of exclusion and isolation were being created on a massive scale behind this functional space segmentation. Chapter Seven has scrutinized the state of the city of exclusion and isolation in the multilayering process of class conflict and individual isolation.

6 This corresponds to what Massey calls a 'progressive sense of place' mentioned in Chapter Four. It appears as a theoretical trend to '"draw a line around a place" which is conspicuous in the argument emphasizing a sense of homecoming (at-homeness) or aboriginal identity of people toward the "lived world"' (Yoshihara 2004: 180). What is interesting is that this theoretical trend sympathizes with the '"neoliberal stance" to consider that globalization is relentless and virtually unstoppable and therefore has to be accepted rather than resisted' (Yoshihara 2004: 176) since it has not fully grasped the dialectical momentum contained in the conflict between global and local. The 'far, but near relation' between the communitarian and the neolibertarian is one characteristic of today's theoretical stance on place.

7 What is notable about this landscape is the invisibility of the public sphere in civil society (intermediate space). Some level of institutional mediacy still remains between the individual and the market but the problem is that such mediacy is instead promoting direct confrontation between the two. Because state intervention aggravates the risk management-type landscape which serves the instinctual drive of capital, the direct confrontation between the individual and the market leaves the latter as the 'sole winner.'

8 The gated community originally had the connotation of 'isolation' from different others. Now it carries the connotation of 'exclusion' of different others. At the same time, the base of the gated community has extended from the super wealthy class to the middle class. This in itself is symbolic of a society-wide spread of neoliberalism, but what is notable is that the gated community has become a point of sharp intersection of neoliberal and communitarian values. It points to a highly compatible relation between the neolibetarian and the communitarian today. See also Note 6.

9 The mentality to feel comfortable in a space filled with watchful eyes is spreading today. This frame of mind resonates with that which yearns for clean space. However, these mentalities are surprisingly indifferent to the social mechanism which materializes these comfortable and clean spaces. In fact, they appear to actively join in the change of society's perception of surveillance from negative to positive. At any rate, the spreading of these mentalities is accompanied by the 'overextension of security' that is under way especially in gated communities.

10 'Non-place' specifically refers to 'spaces of circulation (freeways, airways), consumption (department stores, supermarkets), and communications (telephones, faxes, television, cable networks)' (Auge 1994: 110). According to Auge, 'non-place' is highly interchangeable/complementary and '[w]hat is a place for some may be a non-place for others, and vice versa' (1994). He considers that '[n]on-places... are characteristic of the state of supermodernity, defined in opposition to modernity' and states as follows:

> [S]upermodernity corresponds to an acceleration of history, a shrinking of space, and an individualizing of references, all of which subvert the cumulative processes of modernity. (Auge 1994: 111)

11 Berque explains this relationship from a lexical point of view as follows:

> "Trajection (*trajet*)" responds to "subject (*sujet*)" and "object (*objet*)" succinctly and eloquently. This word generates derivative forms in the same way as the other two do: *trajet, trajectif, trajection, trajectivité, trajective-*

ment and so on. The derivation of "trans- (*tra-*)" [meaning "beyond…" or "across…"] conveys the concepts of (dualistic) "transcendence" and "relationship" (between two extremes in dualism such as the subject and the object) well. Moreover, trans- does not connotate intrinsic centralization (from the subject as the starting point) which is assumed in the case of pro- (forward) in projection. On the other hand, *trajectivité* is distinguished from *intersubjectivité* in that the former is involved in the whole milieu whereas the latter excludes the object and belongs only to the social psychological domain. (Berque 1986: 153)

12 There is much to learn from Hirotaka Itō's argument on this point. According to Itō (2007), this type of interactionism fails to find the significance of collective practices inherent in interactive networks because it overemphasizes the subjectivity = activity of people living in community and views community living as highly homogeneous. By the way, Itō applies this critical viewpoint to a series of self-organization theories as well.

13 In my view, spontaneous development assumes something that exists a priori in a 'gap' between persons or person and object (fixed traditions in a sense). It focuses on 'the thing that appears from there.' It seems homological with the emergent whole at first glance but it is not the same as the emergent whole that appears from the 'gap' as a *process*. In this sense, spontaneous development may rather resonate with a 'progressive sense of place' coined by Massey, who is particularly concerned with 'internalized origin.'

14 In this case, it would be necessary to take account of the fact that developmental despotism has always captured and spoiled creativity and activity inherent in the life-world *from above* in the form of 'expressions of spontaneity.' There has been no proliferation of 'gaps' between persons or person and object that promote the formation and development of the emergence system there. However, it is likely that the precondition for this situation was created at the colonial stage. Because the sociocultural potential of such creativity and activity was ignored then, postcolonialism gave rise to the formation of a field in which they were treated as tools.

15 Needless to say, the greatest challenge at the theoretical level in an attempt to reformulate place today is the question of how to decipher the Lefebvrian matrix surrounding 'spatial practices' in the 'production of space' (Lefebvre 1991). In fact, Harvey has been working on this task for years and many people in Japan, especially in the fields of architecture and urban design, have written monographs with this task in mind in recent years. Since I was unable to grapple with this question here, I am hoping to address this issue in due course.

Bibliography

Abe, K. (2006) 'Kōkyō kūkan mo kaiteki—kiritsu kara kanri e (Comfort in public space—from discipline to control),' in K. Abe and H. Narumi (eds) *Kūkan kanri shakai—kanshi to jiyū no paradokkusu* (Spatial control by society—the paradox of surveillance and freedom): Shinyōsha.

Adam, B. (1995) *Timewatch*: Polity.

Albrow, M. (1996) *The Global Age*: Polity.

Albrow, M., J. Eade, J. Dürrschmidt and N. Washbourne (1997) 'The impact of globalization on sociological concepts,' in J. Eade (ed.), *Living the Global City*: Routledge.

Amako, S. et al. (eds) (1999) *Iwanami gendai chūgoku jiten* (Iwanami encyclopedia of contemporary China): Iwanami Shoten.

Anderson, B. (1983) *Imagined Communities: Reflections on the Origin and Spread of Nationalism*: Verso.

Appadurai, A. (1996) *Modernity at Large: Cultural Dimensions of Globalization*: University of Minnesota Press.

Arendt, H. (1958) *The Human Condition*: University of Chicago Press.

Armstrong, W. and T. G. McGee (1985) *Theatres of Accumulation: Studies in Asian and Latin American Urbanization*: Methuen.

Auge, M. (1994) *An Anthropology for Contemporaneous Worlds*: Stanford University Press.

Bachelard, G. (1957) *La poetique de l'espace*: Presses Universitaires de France.

Bali Government Tourism Office (1997) *Bali 97, Bali Tourism Statistics*.

Bali Post (2004) 'Ajeg Bali: sebua cita-cita.'

Balibar, E. and I. Wallerstein (1990) *Race, Nation, Class*: Éditions La Découverte.

Barber, B. R. (2001) 'Malled, mauled, and overhauled: Arresting suburban sprawl by transforming suburban malls into usable civic space,' in M. Hénaff and T. B. Strong (eds), *Public Space and Democracy*: University of Minnesota Press.

Bartolini, S. (2003) 'Chūō-chihō kankei no tenkan (Changing the center-region relationship),' translated by Y. Ogawa, in J. Yamaguchi and K. Endō et al. (eds), *Gurōbaruka jidai no chihō gabanansu* (Local governance in the age of globalization): Iwanami Shoten.

Baudelaire, C. (1981) *Selected Writings on Art and Artists*: Cambridge University Press.

Baudrillard, J. (1999) *L'echange impossible*: Galilee.

Bauman, Z. (1987) *Legislators and Interpreters*: Polity Press.

Bauman, Z. (2000) *Liquid Modernity*: Polity Press.

Beauregard, R. A. (1995) 'Theorizing the global-local connection,' in P. L. Knox and P. Taylor (eds), *World Cities in a World-System*: Cambridge University Press.

Beck, U., A. Giddens and S. Lash (1994) *Reflexive Modernization*: Polity Press.

Bell, C. and H. Newby (1976) 'Communion, communalism, class and community action: The sources of new urban politics,' in D. Herbert and R. Johnston (eds), *Social Areas in Cities*, vol. 2: Wiley.
Bergson, H. (1889) *Essai sur les données immediates de la Conscience*: Félix Alcan.
Berman, M. and T. Sakai et al. (2005) 'Kōkyōsei no genzai—komyuniti no tameni (Publicness now—for community),' *Gendai shisō* (Contemporary thoughts), May: 48–55.
Berque, A. (1986) *Le sauvage et l'artifice—Les Japonais devant la Nature*: Gallimard.
Billig, M. (1995) *Banal Nationalism*: Sage.
Bourdieu, P. (1977) *Algerie: structures economiques et structures tempor*: Edition de Minuit.
BPS (1996) *Bali Dalam Angka 1996*.
BPS (2001) *Bali Dalam Angka 2001*.
BPS (2005) *Bali Dalam Angka 2005*.
BPS (2006) *Bali Dalam Angka 2006*.
Braidotti, R. (1994) *Nomadic Subjects*: Columbia University Press.
Breckenridge, C. and P. van der Veer (eds) (1993) *Orientalism and the Postcolonial Predicament*: University of Pennsylvania Press.
Brodie, J. (1998) 'Global citizenship: Lost in space,' *Rights of the City Symposium*, University of Toronto, June.
Burgess, E. W. (1925) 'The growth of the city: An introduction to a research project,' in R. E. Park and E. W. Burgess (eds), *The City*: University of Chicago.
Canetti, E. (1973) *Crowds and Power*: Penguin.
Castells, M. (1972) *La question urbaine*: Maspero.
Castells, M. (1989) *The Informational City: Information Technology, Economic Restructuring, and the Urban Regional Process*: Blackwell.
Castells, M. (1996) *The Rise of the Network Society*: Blackwell.
Castells, M. (1997) *The Power of Identity (The Information Age: Economy, Society and Culture, Volume II)*: Blackwell.
Castells, M. (2001) *The Internet Galaxy*: Oxford University Press.
Castells, M. (ed. by I. Susser) (2002) *The Castells Reader On Cities and Social Theory*: Blackwell.
Castells, M. and J. H. Mollenkopf (1991) *Dual City: Restructuring of New York*: Sage.
Chambers, I. (1990) *Border Dialogues: Journeys in Postmodernity*: Routledge.
Cohen, J. (1997) 'Deliberation and democratic legitimacy,' in J. Bohman and W. Rehg (eds), *Deliberative Democracy: Essays on Reason and Politics*: MIT Press.
Cohen, R. (1992) *Global Diasporas*: UCL Press.
COHRE (1998) *Violations of Human Rights 1994–1995*.
Cooke, P. (1990) *Back to the Future: Modernity, Postmodernity and Locality*: Routledge.
Covarrubias, M. (1937) *Island of Bali*: KPI.
Dahl, R. (1973) *Size and Democracy*: Standford University Press.
Davidoff, P. (1965) 'Advocacy and pluralism in planning,' *Journal of the American Institute of Planners*, 31(4): 331–337.

Deguchi, Atsushi (2005) 'Ajia toshi eno apurōchi (An approach to Asian cities),' in A. Deguchi (ed.), *Ajia no toshi kyōsei—21-seiki no seichōsuru toshi wo tankyūsuru* (Coexistence of Asian cities—an exploration of growth cities of the 21st century): Kyūshū Daigaku Shuppankai.
Delanty, G. (2003) *Community*: Routledge.
Deleuze, G. and F. Guattari (1986) *Nomadology*: Semiotext.
Douglass, M. C. (1995) 'Global interdependence and urbanization: Planning for the Bangkok mega-urban region,' in T. G. McGee and I. M. Robinson (eds), *The Mega-Urban Regions of Southeast Asia*: UBC Press.
Dürrschmidt, J. (1997) 'The delinking of locale and milieu,' in J. Eade (ed.), *Living the Global City*: Routledge.
Dwianto, R. D. (1999), 'Toshi bōdō to jikeidan—1998-nen 5-gatsu Jakaruta bōdō wo megutte (Urban riots and civil defense groups),' *Tōhoku toshi gakkai kenkyū nenpō* (Annual bulletin of Tōhoku Association of Urbanology), 1: 34–51.
Dwianto, R. D. (2005) 'Kanpon to pudagan kuririn (Kampung and pedagang keliling),' in N. Yoshihara (ed.), *Ajia megasiti to chiiki komyuniti no dōtai—Jakaruta no RT/RW wo chūshin ni shite* (An Asian megacity and the dynamics of local community—centering on RT/RW in Jakarta): Ochanomizu Shobō.
Dwianto, R. D. (2006) 'Bunsetsuka to tasōka no naka no infōmaru sekutā (The informal sector in segmentation and multilayering),' *Ajia yūgaku* (Intriguing Asia), 90: 76–87.
Endō, K. (2003) 'Nihon ni okeru hokansei genri no kanousei (The possibility of the subsidiarity principle in Japan),' in J. Yamaguchi and K. Endō (eds), *Gurōbaruka jidai no chihō gabanansu* (Local governance in the globalization era): Iwanami Shoten.
Erawan, I. Nyoman (1994) *Parawisata dan Pembangunan Ekonomi*: Upada Sastra.
Fabian, J. (1992) *Time and the Work of Anthropology: Critical Essays, 1971–91*: Harwood.
Firman, T. (1997) 'Land conversion and urban development in the northern region of West Java, Indonesia,' *Urban Studies*, 34: 1027–1046.
Firman, T. (2000) 'Rural to urban land conversion in Indonesia during boom and bust periods,' *Land Use Policy*, 17: 13–20.
Foucault, M. (1982) 'Space, knowledge and power,' *Skyline*, March.
Fujita, S. (1995) *Zentaishugi no jidai keiken* (The experience of the totalitarian era): Misuzu Shobō.
Funo, S. (1991) *Kanpon no sekai—Jawa no shomin jūkyo-shi* (The world of Kampung—a record of popular dwellings in Java): PARCO Shuppankyoku.
Funo, S. (2005) 'Kindai shokumin toshi no keifu—seiō rekkyō to kaigai shokuminchi (A history of modern colonial cities—the western powers and their colonies abroad),' in S. Funo (ed.), *Kindai sekai shisutemu to shokumin toshi* (The modern world-system and colonial cities): Kyoto Daigaku Gakujutsu Shuppankai.
Furnival, J. S. (1956) *Colonial Policy and Practice: A Comparative Study of Burma and Netherland India*: New York University Press.
Gault, R. (1995) 'In and out of time,' *Environmental Values*, 4: 149–66.

Geertz, C. (1963) *Agricultural Involution: Processes of Ecological Change in Indonesia*: University of California Press.
Geertz, C. (1984) 'Culture and social change: The Indonesian case,' *Man*, New Series, 19 (4): 511–532.
Geriya, I. Wayan (2002) *International Marriage: Tourism, Inter Mrriage and Cultural Adaptation in the Family Life of Balinese-Japanese Couple in Bali*: Center for Japanese Studies, University of Udayana.
Giddens, A. (1984) *The Constitution of Society: Outline of the Theory of Structuation*: Polity Press.
Giddens, A. (1990) *The Consequences of Modernity*: Polity Press.
Gilroy, P. (2005) *Postcolonial Melancholia*: Columbia University Press.
Goldblum, C. and T. C. Wong (2000) 'Growth, crisis and spatial change: A study of haphazard urbanization in Jakarta, Indonesia,' *Land Use Policy*, 17: 29–37.
Grabow, S. and A. Heskin (1973) 'Foundations for a radical concept of planning,' *Journal of the American Institute of Planners*, 39: 106–114.
Gregory, K. (1985) *The Nature of Physical Geography*: Edward Arnold.
Guinness, P. (2000) 'Contested imaginings of the city; city as locus of status, capitalist accumulation and community: Competing cultures of southeast Asian societies,' in B. Gray and W. Sophie (eds), *A Companion to the City*: Blackwell.
Hall, P. (1993) 'When was the "Post-colonial"?' in I. Chambers and L. Curti (eds), *The Post-Colonial Question, Common Skies, Divided Horizons*: Routledge.
Hamnett, C. (1991) 'The blind men and the elephant: The explanation of gentrification,' *Transaction of the Institute of British Geographers*, NS 16: 173–189.
Hara, Y. (2003) 'Ajia-gaku no hōhō to sono kanousei (The methods of Asian studies and their possibilities),' in Tokyo Daigaku Tōyō Bunka Kenkyūjo (ed.), *Ajia-gaku no shōraizō* (The future of Asian studies): Tokyo Daigaku Shuppankai.
Haraguchi, T. (2005) 'Kōkyō kūkan no henyō—jentorifikēshon kara hōfuku no toshi e (Changing public space—from gentrification to the city of revanchism),' *Gendai shisō* (Contemporary thoughts), May: 142–155.
Harvey, D. (1973) *Social Justice and the City*: The Johns Hopkins University Press.
Harvey, D. (1985) *The Urbanization of Capital: Studies in the History and Theory of Capitalist Urbanization*: The Johns Hopkins University Press.
Harvey, D. (1989) *The Condition of Postmodernity: An Enquiry into the Origin of Cultural Change*: Blackwell.
Harvey, D. (1996a) *Hybrids of Modernity*: Routledge.
Harvey, D. (1996b) *Justice, Nature and the Geography of Difference*: Blackwell.
Harvey, D. (2005) *A Brief History of Neoliberalism*: Oxford University Press.
Hasegawa, K. (2004) *Constructing Civil Society in Japan*: Trans Pacific Press.
Hassan, I. (1985) 'The culture of postmodernism,' *Theory, Culture & Society*, 2(3): 119–131.
Hegel, G. W. F. (1900) *The Philosophy of History*: Colonial Press.

Hegel, G. W. F. (1928) *Vorlesungen über die Philosophie de Geschichte*: Fr Frommann.
Heidegger, M. (1929) *Sein und Zeit*: M. Niemeyer.
Heidegger, M. (1954) 'Bauen Wohnen Denken,' in *Vorträge und Aufsätze*: Neske.
Heidegger, M. (1962) *Being and Time*: Harper.
Heidegger, M. (1971) *Poetry, Language, Thought*: Harper & Row.
Held, D. (2000) *A Globalizing World?*: Open University Press.
Held, D. (2007) 'Gurōbaru gavanance no saikōchiku (Reconstruction of global governance),' in Y. Nakatani (ed.), *Gurōbaruka riron no shiza—puroburematīku & pāsupekutibu* (The perspective of globalization theory—problematique & perspective): Hōritsu Bunkasha.
Held, D. and A. McGrew (1999) *Global Transformations*: Polity.
Hirsch, J. (1996) *Der nationale Wettbewerbsstaat: Staat, Demokratie und Politik im globalen Kapitalismus*: Edition ID-Archiv.
Hitchcock, M., I. Putra and D. Nyoman (2007) *Tourism, Development and Terrorism in Bali*: Ashgate.
Hosaka, M. (2005) 'Fukushi shakai kaihatsu-gaku eno hōhōronteki kōsatsu (A methodological consideration of the study of social welfare and development),' in Nihon Fukushi Daigaku COE Suishin Iinkai (ed.), *Fukushi shakai kaihatu-gaku no kōchiku* (The construction of the study of social welfare and development): Minerva Shobō.
Hotta, I. (2002) *Modaniti ni okeru toshi to shimin* (The city and the citizen in modernity): Ochanomizu Shobō.
Hozelitz, B. F. (1955) 'Generative and parasitic cities,' *Economic Development and Cultural Change*, 3: 278–294.
Husserl, E. (1966) *Zur Phänomenologie des inneren Zeitßbewubtseins (1908–1917)*: M. Nijhoff.
Ingold, T. (1993) 'Globes and spheres: The topology of environmentalism,' in K. Milton (ed.), *Environmentalism*: Routledge.
Ishizawa, H. (1989) 'Jakaruta no kanpon to kyojū seisaku ni tsuite no ichi kōsatsu (A study on kampungs and housing policy in Jakarta),' *Tōkeidai ronshū* (Tokyo Keizai University bulletin), 10: 53–92.
Itō, H. (2007) 'Gurōbaru sekai ni okeru "basho" to sōhatsu no shakaigaku (Sociology of "place" and emergence in the global world),' Ph.D. dissertation, Tohoku University.
Iwaki, S. (2005) *Gurōbarizēshon to chiiki shakai hendō* (Globalization and changing local community): Kantō Gakuin Daigaku Shuppankai.
Iwanaga, S. (2008) *Gurōbarizēshon, shiminken, toshi* (Globalization, citizenship, city): Shumpūsha.
Iwasaki, N. (2003) 'Gurōbaru na imin ryūdō to nihon (Global mobility of migrants and Japan),' in N. Iwasaki et al. (eds), *Kaigai ni okeru nihonjin, nihon no naka no gaikokujin* (Japanese overseas and foreigners in Japan): Shōwadō.
Iyer, P. (1989) *Video Night in Kathmandu*: Vintage Books.
Iyotani, T. (1998) 'Gurōbarizēshon to nashonarizumu no sōkoku (Conflict between globalization and nationalism),' in T. Iyotani, N. Sakai and T. Morris-Suzuki (eds), *Gurōbarizēshon no naka no Ajia—karuchuraru sutadīzu no genzai* (Globalization and Asia—the current state of cultural studies): Miraisha.

Iyotani, T. (2007) 'Hōhō toshite no imin (Immigration as a method),' in T. Iyotani (ed.), *Idō kara basho wo tou* (A question of motion and place): Yūshindō.
Jacobs, J. (1965) *The Death and Life of Great American Cities*: Penguin Books.
Jefferson, M. (1939) 'The Laws of the primate city,' *Geographical Review*, 2: 226–232.
Jessop, B. (1997) 'The governance of complexity and the complexity of governance: Preliminary remarks on some problems and limits of economic guidance,' in A. Amin and J. Hausner (eds), *Beyond Market and Hierarchy: Interactive Governance and Social Complexity*: Edward Elgar.
Jessop, B. (1998) 'The rise of governance and the risks of failure: The case of economic development,' *International Social Science Journal*, 155: 29–45.
Jones, S. (1995) 'Understanding community in the information age,' in S. Jones (ed.), *Cybersociety*: Sage.
Kageyama, M. (2005) 'Chūkan soshiki toshite no NPO no shisutemu rironteki imi to rōdō seikatsu seisaku (The systems-theoretical significance of the NPO as the intermediate organization and working life policy),' *Yokohama Shiritsu Daigaku ronsō (shakai dagaku keiretsu)* (Bulletin of Yokohama City University, social science), 56(3): 143–163.
Kaneko, I. (1999) *Komyuniti soryūshon—borantarīna mondai kaiketsu ni mukete* (Community solution—toward voluntary problem solving): Iwanami Shoten.
Kellner, D. (2002) 'Theorizing globalization,' *Sociological Theory*, 20(3): 285–305.
Kelsky, K. (2001) *Women on the Verge*: Duke University Press.
Kidokoro, T. (1998) 'Ajia-gata toshi seichō kanri moderu kōchiku eno tenbō (The prospect for constructing an Asian urban growth management model),' in K. Takeuchi and Y. Hayashi (eds), *Iwanami Kōza chikyū kankyō-gaku 8 chikyū kankyō to kyodai toshi* (Iwanami lectures on global environmentology 8, the global environment and megacities): Iwanami Shoten.
Kitano, N., K. Mizuno and T. Kidokoro (2001) 'Tōnan Ajia jūtaku sekutā no kadai—Indoneshia, Tai, Firipin, Marēshia (The challenge for the Southeast Asian housing sector—Indonesia, Thailand, the Philippines and Malaysia),' *Kaihatsu kinyū kenkyūjo-hō* (Bulletin of the JBIC Institute), 8: 88–113.
Klosterman, E. (1978) 'Foundation for normative planning,' *Journal of the American Institute of Planners*, 44: 37–46.
Konagatani, K. (1999) 'Toshi kōzō (Urban structure),' in K. Miyamoto and K. Konagatani (eds), *Ajia no daitoshi 2 Jakaruta* (Asian megacities 2 Jakarta): Nippon Hyōronsha.
Konagaya, K. (1997) 'Ajia toshi keizai to toshi kōzō (Asian urban economy and urban structure),' Osaka Shiritsu Daigaku Keizai Kenkyūjo, *Kikan keizai kenkyū* (The quarterly journal of economic studies), 20(1): 61–89.
Konno, H. (2006) 'Toshi chūkansō no dōkō (Orientations of urban middle classes),' in K. Niitsu and N. Yoshihara (eds), *Gurōbaruka to Ajia shakai—posutokoroniaru no chihei* (Globalization and Asian societies—postcolonial perspective): Tōshindō.
Kotani, H. (2003) 'Posutokoroniaru Ajia-shi kenkyū no sekai (The world of postcolonial Asian history studies,' *Shisō* (Thought), 949: 23–41.
Koyasu, N. (2003) *'Ajia' wa dō katararetekitaka—kindai Nihon no orientarizumu* (How 'Asia' was depicted—the orientalism of modern Japan): Fujiwara Shoten.

Kuwako, T. (2005), *Fūkei no naka no kankyō tetsugaku* (Environmental philosophy in the landscape): Tokyo Daigaku Shuppankai.
Lakoff, G. and M. Johnson (1980) *Metaphors We Live By*: Chicago University Press.
Lash, S. and J. Urry (1994) *Economics of Signs and Space*: Sage.
Latour, B. (1987) *Science in Action*: Open University Press.
Lefebvre, H. (1984) *Everyday Life in the Modern World*: Transaction Publishers.
Lefebvre, H. (1991) *The Production of Space*: Blackwell.
Leisch, H. (2002) 'Gated community in Indonesia,' *Cities*, 19(5): 341–350.
Lo, F. C. and Y. M. Yeung (eds) (1996) *Emerging World Cities in Pacific Asia*: United Nations University Press.
Long, N. (1962) *The Polity*: McNally and Co.
LongStay Foundation (2007), *Rongusutei chōsa tōkei 2007* (Long-stay survey statistics 2007).
Lyon, D. (2001) *Surveillance Society: Monitoring Everyday Life*: Open University Press.
Lyotard, J.-F. (1979) *La condition postmoderne*: Les editions de Minuit.
Ma, L. J. C. and L. Cartier (eds) (2003) *The Chinese Diaspora: Space, Place, Mobility and Identity*: Rowman & Littlefield Publishers.
Machimura, T. (1994) *'Sekai toshi' Tokyo no kōzō tenkan* (The structural transformation of 'world city' Tokyo): Tokyo Daigaku Shuppankai.
Maffesoli, M. (1991) *Le Temps des tribus*: LGF.
Maotani, S. (1983) *Gendai Indoneshia kenkyū* (A study of contemporary Indonesia): Keisō Shobō.
Marshall, J. (2005) 'Megacity, mega mess…,' *Nature*, 437: 312–314.
Marshall, T. H. and T. B. Bottomore (1992) *Citizenship and Social Class*: Pluto.
Marx, K. (1844) *Ökonomisch-philosophische Manuskripte*: MEW, Erg. Ed. 1.
Marx, K. (1959) *The Economic and Philosophic Manuscripts of 1844*: Foreign Language Publishing House.
Marx, K. and F. Engels (1964) *The German Ideology*: Progress Publishers.
Massey, D. B. (1993) 'Power-geometry and a progressive sense of place,' in J. Bird et al. (eds), *Mapping the Futures: Local Cultures, Global Change*: Routledge.
Massey, D. (1994) *Space, Place and Gender*: Polity Press.
Matoba, A. (2007) '"Ōkina monogatari" no saihen to posutomodan (Re-organization of "master narrative" and postmodernism),' *Kanagawa daigaku hyōron* (Kanagawa University review), 57: 33–39.
Matsubara, H. (1998) 'Hashigaki (Preface),' in H. Matsubara (ed.), *Ajia no toshi shisutemu* (Urban systems in Asia): Kyushu Daigaku Shuppankai.
McGee, T. G. (1991) 'The Emergence of desakota regions in Asia: Expanding a hypothesis,' in N. Ginsburg, B. Koppel and T. G. McGee (eds), *The Extended Metropolis: Settlement Transition in Asia*: University of Hawaii Press.
McGee, T. G. and I. M. Robinson (eds) (1995) *The Mega-Urban Regions of Southeast Asia*: UBC Press.
Mckay, G. (1996) *Senseless Acts of Beauty*: Verso.
Mead, G. H. (1959) *The Philosophy of the Present*: Open Court.
Meyrowitz, J. (1985) *No Sense of Place: The Impact of Electronic Media on Social Behavior*: Oxford University Press.

Mita, M. (1984) *Miyazawa Kenji*: Iwanami Shoten.
Mitchell, D. and H. Molotch (1997) 'Talking city trouble: Interactional vandalism, social inequality, and the "urban interaction problem",' *American Journal of Sociology*, 104(5): 1263–1295.
Miyamoto, T. (2005) 'Sōsharu gavanansu (Social governance),' in J. Yamaguchi and T. Miyamoto (eds), *Posuto fukushi kokka to sōsharu gavanansu* (Post-welfare state and social governance): Minerva Shobō.
Mizuguchi, N. (2007) *Toshi to iu shudai—saiteii ni mukete* (The city as a theme—toward a reformulation): Hōritsu Bunkasha.
Mol, A. and J. Law (1994) 'Regions, networks and fluids: Anaemia and social topology,' *Social Studies of Science*, 24(4): 641–671.
More, T. (1989) *Utopia*: Cambridge University Press.
Morris-Suzuki, T. (2000) 'For and against NGOs: The politics of the lived world,' *New Left Review*, March/April.
Mumford, L. (1953) *The Highway and the City*: Harvest.
Nagano, Y. (2007) 'Indoneshia Bari-tō ni okeru gurōbaru tūrizumu ka deno ijūsha no zōka to dentōteki seikatsu yōshiki no kaitai (Increasing immigrants and disintegrating traditional lifestyles under global tourism in Bali, Indonesia),' *Yamagata Daigaku kiyō (shakai kagaku)* (Bulletin of Yamagata University, social science), 37(1): 161–208.
Nakamura, K. (2009) 'Bari ni okeru dentō to kindai (Traditions and modernity in Bali),' in A. Kurasawa and N. Yoshihara (eds), *Kawaru Bari, kawaranai Bari* (Changing Bali and unchanging Bali): Bensei Shuppan.
Negri, A. and M. Hardt (2000) *Empire*: Harvard University Press.
Negri, A. and M. Hardt (2004) *Multitude: War and Democracy in the Age of Empire*: Penguin.
Nietzsche, F. (1993) *Thus Spake Zarathustra*: Prometheus Books.
Nikkei Architecture (2007) 850, 11 June.
Nishio, M. (1975) *Kenryoku to sanka* (Power and participation): Tokyo Daigaku Shuppankai.
Nishiyama, Y. and Y. Nishiyama (2008) *Igirisu no gabanansu-gata machizukuri* (Governance-type town planning in England): Gakugei Shuppansha.
O'Conner, J. (1973) *The Fiscal Crisis of the State*: St. Martin's Press.
O'uchi, M. and T. Yogo (1985) 'Role of social organizational resources in local level development,' *Regional Development Dialogue*, 6(1): 156–179.
Onjō, A. (1998) 'Toshin chiku no suitai to "machizukuri" katsudō wo megutte (Declining urban center and "town planning"),' in M. Arayama and N. Ōshiro (eds), *Kūkan kara basho e—chirigakuteki sōzōryoku no tankyū* (From space to place—searching for geological imagination): Kokon Shoin.
Ōtsuka, K. (2000) *Kindai isurāmu no jinruigaku* (Anthropology of modern Islam): Tokyo Daigaku Shuppankai.
Painter, J. (2000) 'Governance,' in R. J. Johnston and D. Gregory (eds), *The Dictionary of Human Geograph (4th ed.)*: Blackwell.
Picard, M. (1996) *Cultural Tourism and Touristic Culture*: Archipelago Press.
Pinches, M. (ed.) (1999) *Culture and Privilege in Capitalist Asia*: Routledge.
Polanyi, K. (1968) *Primitive, Archaic, and Modern Economics*: Beacon Press.
Poster, M. (1990) *The Mode of Information*: Blackwell.
Power, M. (1994) *The Audit Explosion*: Demos.

Pringle, R. (2004) *A Short History of Bali: Indonesia's Hindu Realm*: Allen & Unwin.
Rapport, N. and J. Overing (2000) *Social and Cultural Anthropology: The Key Concepts*: Routledge.
Rawls, J. (1971) *A Theory of Justice*: Harvard University Press.
Redfield, R. and M. Singer (1954) 'The cultural role of cities,' *Economic Development and Cultural Change*, 3: 53–73.
Relph, E. (1976) *Place and Placelessness*: Pion.
Rhodes, R. A. W. (1996) 'The new governance: Governing without government,' *Political Studies*, 44: 652–667.
Robison, R. (1992), 'Indonesia: An autonomous domain of social power?,' *Pacific Review*, 5(4): 338–349.
Rose, N. (1996) 'Refiguring the territory of government,' *Economy and Society*, 25: 327–356.
Said, E. W. (1993) *Culture and Imperialism*: Alfred A. Knopf.
Saitō, H. and S. Iwanaga (1996) *Toshi no bigaku* (Urban aesthetics), (Korekara no sekaishi 13): Heibonsha.
Saitō, J. (2000) *Kōkyōsei* (Publicness): Iwanami Shoten.
Saitō, J. (2005) 'Toshi kūkan no saihen to kōkyōsei (Urban spatial reorganization and publicness),' *Iwanami kōza toshi no saisei wo kangaeru 1* (Iwanami lectures on urban renewal 1): Iwanami Shoten.
Sassen, S. (1991) *The Global City, New York, London, Tokyo*: Princeton University Press.
Satō, H. (2005) 'Shakai kaihatsu no seido to ninaite (The system and participants of social development),' in Nihon Fukushi Daigaku COE Suishin Iinkai (ed.), *Fukushi shakai kaihatsugaku no kōchiku* (The establishment of the study of social well-being and development): Minerva Shobō.
Savage, E. and A. Warde (1993) *Urban Sociology, Capitalism and Modernity*: Macmillan.
Scannell, P. (1996) *Radio, Television and Modern Life*: Blackwell.
Scholte, J. A. (1996) 'Identifying Indonesia,' in M. Hitchcock and V. T. King (eds), *Images of Malay-Indonesian Identity*: Oxford University Press.
Schwendinger, H. & J. (1974) *The Sociologists of the Chair*: Basic.
Sennett, R. (1974) *The Fall of Public Man*: Cambridge University Press.
Shimamura, M. (2007) 'Ajia e mukau onna tachi—Nihon karano kankō (Women heading for Asia—tourism from Japan),' *Ajia yūgaku* (Intriguing Asia), 104: 92–99.
Simmel, G. (1900) *Philosophie des Geldes*: Duncker & Humblot.
Simmel, G. (1957) *Brücke und Tür, Essays des Philosophen zur Geschichte, Religion, unst and Gesellschaft*: Im Verein mit Margarete Susmann herausgegeben von Michael Landmann.
Smith, M. P. (2001) *Transnational Urbanism*: Blackwell.
Smith, N. (1996) *The New Urban Frontier: Gentrification and the Revanchist City*: Routledge.
Soja, E. (1989) *Postmodern Geographies: The Reassertion of Space in Critical Theory*: Verso.
Sonoda, S. (2007) 'Toshi chūkansō no taitō to aratana aidentiti no keisei? (The emergence of the urban middle class and the formation of a new identity?),' in J. Nishikawa and K. Hirano (eds), *Kokusai idō to shakai*

henyō (International mobility and social change) (Higashi Ajia kyōdōtai no kōchiku 3): Iwanami Shoten.
Soysal, Y. (1994) *Limits of Citizenships*: University of Chicago Press.
Stewart, I. (1989) *Does God Play Dice?: The Mathematics of Chaos*: Blackwell.
Stoker, G. (1998) 'Governance as theory: Five propositions,' *International Social Science Journal*, 155: 17–28.
Sugiura, S. (2003) *Toshi keizai-ron* (Urban economic theory): Iwanami Shoten.
Suzuki, E. (1957) *Toshi shakaigaku genri* (The principle of urban sociology): Yuhikaku.
Swift, J. (1965) *Gulliver's Travels*: Rinehart Editions.
Takahashi, S. (1993) 'Manyueru Kasuteru to "toshiteki na mono"—"toshi no imi" no henyō wo megutte (Manuel Castells and "the urban"—surrounding change in the "meaning of city"),' in N. Yoshihara (ed.), *Toshi no shisō* (The history of urban thought): Aoki Shoten.
Takei, T. (2007) *Shūgō jūtaku to nihonjin—aratana 'kyōdōsei' wo motomete* (Group housing and the Japanese—toward new 'cooperativity'): Heibonsha.
Tasaka, T. (1998) 'Bankoku sekai toshika kasetsu (The hypothesis of world city Bangkok),' in T. Tasaka (ed.), *Ajia no daitoshi (1) Bankoku* (Asian megacities (1) Bangkok): Nippon Hyōronsha.
Tasaka, T. (1999) 'Kankō ni atatte (On publication),' in K. Miyamoto and K. Konagaya (eds), *Ajia no daitoshi (2) Jakaruta* (Asian megacities (2) Jakarta): Nippon Hyōronsha.
Tasaka, T. (2005a) 'Maegaki (Preface),' in T. Tasaka (ed.), *Higashi Ajia toshi-ron no kōsō—Higashi Ajia no toshi-kan kyōsō to shibiru sosaeti kōsō* (The concept of East Asian urban theory—Intercity competition in East Asia and the concept of civil society): Ochanomizu Shobō.
Tasaka, T. (2005b) 'Higashi Ajia toshi-kan kyōsō-ron no wakugumi (The framework for East Asian intercity competition theory),' in T. Tasaka (ed.), *Higashi Ajia toshi-ron no kōsō—Higashi Ajia no toshi-kan kyōsō to shibiru sosaeti kōsō* (The concept of East Asian urban theory—Intercity competition in East Asia and the concept of civil society): Ochanomizu Shobō.
Tayama, K. (1981) *Tōkyō no sanjūnen*: Iwanami Shoten.
Tomlinson, J. (1999) *Globalization and Culture*: Polity Press.
Tomosugi, T. (1999) 'Maegaki (Preface),' in T. Tomosugi (ed.), *Ajia toshi no shosō—hikaku toshi-ron ni mukete* (The aspects of Asian cities—toward comparative urbanology): Dōbunkan Shuppan.
Tsuji, K. (1954) 'Keikaku (A plan),' in T. Nakamura and K. Tsuji, *Seijigaku jiten* (The encyclopedia of political science): Heibonsha.
Tuan, Y.-F. (1990) 'Realism and fantasy in art, history, and geography,' *Annals of the Associations of American Geographers*, 80(3): 435–446.
Tuan, Y.-F. (1977) *Space and Place: The Perspective of Experience*: University of Minnesota Press.
Ueda, S. (1992) *Basho* (Place): Kōbundō.
Ueki, Y. (2000) 'Rōkaru gavamento kara rōkaru gavanansu e (From local government to local governance),' in N. Yoshihara (ed.), *Toshi keiei no shisō—modaniti, bunken, jichi* (Thoughts on urban management—modernity, decentralization, self-government): Aoki Shoten.
Urban Poor Consortium (UPC) (2005) *Kampung Masalarh*.
Urry, J. (1995) *Consuming Places*: Routledge.

Urry, J. (2000) *Sociology beyond Societies: Mobilities for the Twenty-first Century*: Routledge.
Urry, J. (2003) *Global Complexity*: Polity.
Wallerstein, I. (1966) *Open the Social Sciences: Report of the Gulbenkian Commission on the Restructuring of the Social Sciences*: Stanford University Press.
Webber, M. (1978) 'A difference paradigm for planning,' in W. Burchell and G. Sternlieb (eds), *Planning Theory in the 1980s*: Center for Urban Policy Research, Rutgers University.
Wong, R. B. (2001) 'Entre monde et nation: les regions braudelienne en Asie,' *Annales, Histoire, Sciences Socials*, 56(1): 5–41.
Wright, T. and R. Hutchinson (1997) 'Socio-spatial reproduction, marketing culture and the built environment,' in R. Hutchinson (ed.), *Research in Urban Sociology*, 4: JAI Press.
Yamachita, S. (2007) 'Rongusutei, aruiwa kurasu yōni tabisuru koto (Long-stay, or residential-type travel),' *Ajia yūgaku* (Intriguing Asia), 104: 108–116.
Yamamoto, N. (2005) 'Sekai toshi Jakaruta (world city Jakarta),' in S. Funo (ed.), *Kindai sekai shisutemu to shokumin toshi* (Modern world system and colonial cities): Kyoto Daigaku Gakujutsu Shuppankai.
Yamashita, S. (1999) *Bari—kankō jinruigaku no ressun* (Bali—A lesson in tourism anthropology): Tokyo Daigaku Shuppankai.
Yazaki, T. (1963) *Nihon toshi no shakai riron* (A social theory of Japanese cities): Gakuyō Shobō.
Yazaki, T. (1988) *Kokusai chitsujo no henka katei ni okeru hatten tojōkoku no toshika to kindaika—Tōnan Ajia no jirei* (Urbanization and modernization of developing countries in the changing process of international order—the case of Southeast Asia): Keiō Tsūshin.
Yoshihara, N. (1983) *Toshi shakaigaku no kihon mondai* (Basic problems in urban sociology): Aoki Shoten.
Yoshihara, N. (1988) 'Daitoshi kūkan no saikōzōka to chiiki mondai (Restructuring of metropolitan space and community issues),' in S. Takauchi, T. Okuchi (eds), *80-nendai nihon no kiki no kōzō* (The crisis structure of Japan in the 80s) II: Hōritsu Bunkasha.
Yoshihara, N. (1993) 'Robāto E Pāku to hyūman ekorojī—seiseiki no toshi shakaigaku shisō (Robert E. Park and human ecology—urban sociological thought in the formative stage),' in N. Yoshihara (ed.), *Toshi no shisō* (The history of urban thought): Aoki Shoten.
Yoshihara, N. (2000) *Ajia no chiiki jūmin soshiki—chōnaikai, kaibōkai and RT/RW* (Neighborhood associations in Asia—chōnaikai, kaifong and RT/RW): Ochanomizu Shobō.
Yoshihara, N. (2002) *Toshi to modaniti no riron* (The city and modernity): Tokyo Daigaku Shuppankai.
Yoshihara, N. (2004) *Toshi to kūkan de yomu kindai no monogatari—sengo shakai no suimyaku wo saguru* (The narrative of modernity read in time and space—exploring the vein of postwar society): Yūhikaku.
Yoshihara, N. (ed.) (2005) *Ajia megashiti to chiiki komyuniti no dōtai—Jakaruta no RT/RW wo chūshin ni shite* (An Asian megacity and the dynamics of local community—centering on RT/RW in Jakarta): Oshanomizu Shobō.

Yoshihara, N. (2005a) 'Gurōbaruka shakai ni okeru kakusa fubyōdō no kōzō to basho no sonzai keitai (The structure of disparity and inequality and the form of place in globalized society),' *Chiiki shakai gakkai kaihō* (Annals of the Japan Association of Region and Community Studies), 132.

Yoshihara, N. (2005b) 'Toshi no kaisō bunka (Urban hierarchical division),' *Iwanami kōza toshi no saisei wo kangaeru 3* (Iwanami lectures on urban renewal 3): Iwanami Shoten.

Yoshihara, N. (2005c) 'Ajia megashitī no isō—chiiki komyuniti zō no saishin ni mukete (The topography of Asian megacities—toward a reexamination of the image of local community),' in N. Yoshihara (ed.), *Ajia megashiti to chiiki komyuniti no dōtai—Jakaruta no RT/RW wo chūshin ni shite* (Asian megacities and the dynamics of local community—centering on RT/RW in Jakarta): Oshanomizu Shobō.

Yoshihara, N. (2006a) 'Modaniti to Ajia shakai (Modernity and Asian societies),' in K. Niitsu and N. Yoshihara (eds), *Gurōbaruka to Ajia shakai—posutokoroniaru no chihei* (Globalization and Asian societies—a postcolonial perspective): Tōshindō.

Yoshihara, N. (2006b) 'Midoru kurasu to gēteddo komyuniti (The middle class and the gated community),' *Ajia yūgaku* (Intriguing Asia), 90: 141–144.

Yoshihara, N. (2006c) 'Urban Banjar no ichi sonzai keitai—Denpasāru-shi no aru jirei bunseki kara (One form of urban banjar—from the study of a case in Denpasar City),' *Hesutia to kurio* (Hestia and Clio), 3: 52–75.

Yoshihara, N. (2007) *Hiraite mamoru—anzen anshin no komyuniti zukuri no tameni* (Open security—to create a safe and secure community): Iwanami Shoten (Booklet).

Yoshihara, N. (2008a) 'Hāvei wo dō yomuka—hitotsu no oboegaki (How to read Harvey—a note),' *Jōkyō* (Situation), July: 103–114.

Yoshihara, N. (ed.) (2008b) *Gurōbaru tūrizumu no shinten to chiiki komyuniti no henyō—Bari-tō no banjāru wo chūshin to shite* (Advancing global tourism and the changing of local communities—centering on banjar in Bali): Ochanomizu Shobō.

Yoshimi, S. (1995) *"Koe" no shihonshugi* ("Voice" capitalism): Kōdansha.

Yoshimi, Shunya and K. Sang-jung (2001) *Gurōbaruka no enkinhō* (A perspective on globalization): Iwanami Shoten.

Young, I. M. (1990) *Justice and the Politics of Difference*: Princeton University Press.

Yuval-Davis, N. (1997) *National Space and Collective Identity: Borders, Boundaries, Citizenship and Gender Relations*: University of Greenwich.

Ziv, D. (2002) *Jakarta Inside Out*: Equinox.

Zohar, D. and I. Marshall (1994) *The Quantum Society*: William Morrow.

Zorbaugh, H. W. (1929) *The Gold Coast and the Slum*: University of Chicago Press.

Zukin, S. (1991) *Landscapes of Power: From Detroit to Disney World*: University of California Press.

Zukin, S. (1996) 'Space and symbols in an age of decline,' in A. D. King (ed.), *Representing the City*: Macmillan Press.

Name Index

Adam, B. 3
Albrow, M. 32–3, 38, 55
Anderson, B. 15, 104, 138, 209
Appadurai, A. 4, 15, 17–20, 22, 32–3, 36–7, 65, 140, 188, 191
Arendt, H. 51
Aristotle 13

Bachelard, G. 18, 185
Balibar, E. 174
Barber, B. R. 46
Baudelaire, C. 12, 185
Baudrillard, J. 24
Bauman, Z. 59, 160, 189, 206
Beck, U. 12
Bergson, H. 3, 18, 185
Berque, A. 179–81, 210–11
Bourdieu, P. 15, 22, 188
Braidotti, R. 45
Brenner, N. 29
Brodie, J. 57
Burgess, E. W. 190, 199, 208

Castells, M. 2, 32–4, 39–41, 44–5, 57, 59, 62–3, 67, 80–1, 94, 161, 176, 189, 192, 195, 205
Cohen, J. 44, 56, 79, 141, 203

Dahl, R. 72
Davidoff, P. 82–3
Deleuze, G. 38, 60–1
Descartes, R. 13
Douglass, M.C. 197

Dwianto, R.D. 113–14, 200
Dürrschmidt, J. 33–4

Endo, K. 26, 61, 111, 124
Engels, F. 42, 66

Fabian, J. 66
Foucault, M. 80
Friedmann, J. 162
Fujita, K. 162
Fujita, S. 178–9

Geertz, C. 90, 108, 141, 196, 199
Geriya, I. 201–1, 203
Giddens, A. 12, 22–3, 58, 184, 186, 189
Gilroy, P. 32
Gregory, D. 4
Guattari, F. 38, 60–1
Gus Dur 126

Hall, P. 4, 97
Haraguchi, T. 49, 190, 195
Hardt, M. 25, 28, 39, 190
Harvey, D. 184–5, 187–8, 195
Hegel, J. W. F. 90
Heidegger, M. 18, 56, 64, 175, 177–8, 191, 209
Held, D. 25–7, 72–3, 170, 194, 207–8
Hirsch, J. 166, 207
Husserl, E. 18
Hutchinson, L. 191

Name Index

Ingold, T. 32, 63–5
Itō, H. 78, 211
Iyotani, T. 141, 183, 193

Jacobs, J. 72, 195
Jefferson, M. 92
Jessop, B. 74–5, 195
Johnson, M. 36
Jones, S. 56

Kaneko, I. 194
Kellner, D. 28
Kelsky, K. 205
Kitano, N. 112, 199
Klosterman, E. 84
Konagaya, K. 93, 116
Kotani, H. 196
Koyasu, N. 196

Lakoff, G. 36
Langton, C. 190
Lash, S. 15, 20, 189
Lefebvre, H. 3, 5–6, 11, 18, 46, 65, 177, 209, 211
Lo, F. C. 95
Long, N. 82
Lyon, D. 192–3
Lyotard, J. -F. 14, 24

Machimura, T. 163
Maotani, S. 99–100, 198
Marshall, I. 6, 37
Marshall, J. 111
Marshall, T. H. 54, 192
Marx, K. 64, 66, 162, 179, 184, 186, 193, 205, 209
Massey, D. B. 5, 19, 64–5, 95, 175, 183–6, 210–11
Mckay, G. 57
Mead, G. H. 18
Merton, R. K. 15

Miyamoto, K. 78–9, 195
Mol, A. 31, 34
Mollenkopf, J. H. 2

Nakamura, K. 175, 209
Negri, A. 25, 28, 39, 190
Nishio, M. 84, 157

O'uchi, M. 101

Pahl, R. E. 205
Park, R. E. 6
Poster, M. 16–7, 22, 164
Power, M. 61
Prigogine, I. 37, 190
Rapport, N. 174–5, 209
Rawls, J. 84
Relph, E. 64, 80
Rhodes, R. A. W. 74, 193
Rose, N. 32, 62

Saitō, H. 174, 176–7
Saitō, J. 46, 51, 71
Sassen, S. 39–41, 162
Scholte, J. A. 124
Sennet, R. 51–2, 71, 195
Shimamura, M. 144, 205
Simmel, G. 72, 162, 176
Smith, N. 2, 95, 162, 191
Soja, E. 16, 49, 188
Sonoda, S. 208
Sorokin, P. 15
Soysal, Y. 55
Stewart, I. 27
Sugiura, N. 164
Suharto 124–5

Tasaka, T. 89, 164, 168–9, 206–7
Thompson, E. P. 15
Tomlinson, J. 19, 27, 32, 36–7

Tuan, Y. -F. 64, 184
Tuji, K. 82

Uchida, R. 165
Ueda, S. 209
Urry, J. 3, 6–8, 15, 17–18, 25,
    27–31, 35–8, 42, 45–6, 55,
    57–8, 63, 65–8, 183–5, 187,
    189–91, 203, 206

Wallerstein, E. 1, 7, 174
Webber, M. 84
Weber, M. 162, 205

Yamashita, S. 143–4
Yazaki, T. 42, 190, 197
Yeung, Y. M. 95
Yoshimi, S. 45, 165
Young, I. M. 71–2, 165
Yuval-Davis, N. 55, 206

Ziv, D. 96, 200
Zohar, D. 6, 37
Zorbaugh, H. W. 106
Zukin, S. 191

Subject Index

absence of legitimacy 77–8
absolute time 15–16, 18–21, 187, 193
abstraction of space 5, 185
abstraction of the subject 45–6, 48
adaptation 26, 81
advocacy planning 82
aesthetical distance 4
Ajeg Bali 137–8, 175, 202, 208
alliances based on anxiety 208
alternative globalization 189–90
alternative understanding of place 183
American century 29
anti-globalization 202
arisan 108
Asia 60, 87, 89, 90–5, 97–9, 101, 103, 104–7, 112, 114, 117–18, 121–2, 125–6, 155, 159–61, 166–73, 182, 184, 187, 196, 198, 203, 205
  Asia Pacific Region 205
  Asian megacities 87, 92, 94–5, 98, 105–7, 112, 121–2, 161, 166–7, 169, 182
  Asian NIES 95
  of despotism and stagnation 91
association 32, 42, 59, 68, 75, 95, 101, 108, 130, 159, 178–9, 182, 188, 193, 199, 201, 204, 206

audit society 61

backyard community 196
Bali Beach Hotel 125
Bali Hindu 138, 200, 202
Banjar 116, 134–6, 138, 149–50, 154–5, 157, 201–2, 204
  adat 136, 201–2
  dinas 136, 201–2
Batavia 98–9, 124, 196–7
batik 128–32, 201, 202
bias towards time without space 16
bleak urban landscape 47
Botabek 102, 116, 118, 200
Buruh Lombok 131

champ 188
cities beyond society 38–9, 41, 43–5, 47, 49–52, 190
cities within society/the state 41–4, 190
citizen of the world 4, 62
citizenship 5, 38, 44, 53–6, 59, 63, 73, 152, 159, 192, 194, 206–7
  national 38, 44, 54–6, 206
  performative 38, 55
city of conventions 127
civic public sphere 42–3
civility 52
clean cities 113
collective consumption 81, 161, 205

communion 65, 67–9
communities of the emotional and affective dimensions 20–1
community 2, 20, 32–3, 54, 63, 67–9, 71–2, 94, 98, 101–2, 106–9, 111, 113, 115, 117–22, 133, 135–6, 138, 141, 144, 147, 152, 154, 156, 158, 160, 169, 175, 178, 188, 192–201, 203, 205, 210–11
  closed 71–2
competitive agents 168, 169, 170, 206
competitive states 166–9, 171–3
complexity 1, 4, 6, 7, 31, 51, 75, 184, 189, 193–5, 199, 208
concrete sense of place 177
continuous space of geometry 15–6, 19–21, 187
corporate emigrants 142–3, 158
counterturn of globality 165–6, 169, 171
creativity 7, 207, 211
critical infrastructure 47
cultural imperialist 63
cultural studies 14, 62, 187

defensive safety net 102
degradation of collectivity 6–7
de-Japanese 156, 159
deliberative democracy 79, 84
democracy 26, 56, 72–3, 79, 84, 100, 194
  transnational 56
de-nationalization of the state 167
dependent integration 91–2, 95
  theory of 91
de-territorialization 11, 17, 30–4

de-territorialized 32, 34, 46, 61, 76
de-totalise 31
developmental despotism 100, 102, 103, 104, 105, 169, 211
diasporaization 44, 56
diasporic/diasporas 5, 56–7, 141, 188, 192, 203
  global diasporas 141
dinas 136, 200–2
division of labor between monopoly capital and the state 43
dual city 2, 106
duality of structure 189
dureé 3, 185
dwelling 32, 50, 52, 65–6, 89, 99, 175, 178–9, 182, 191, 209

East Asian Community 160, 205
East Asian urban cloister 167–72
edge of chaos 8
efficiency issues 78, 95
enclosing 177–9, 181–2, 209
end of geography 4
end of history 25, 39
Enlightenment knowledge 16, 20, 22, 186–7
Enlightenment rationality 16
equilibrium theory of change 186, 199
equivalence principle 76
ethnoscape 33, 140–1, 159
excluded regions 168
expression of spontaneity 195, 202, 211
extended metropolitan region 96, 169, 209

external time 18, 21
extinguishing boundaries and differences 175

familiarity 34
flexible specialization 184
Fordism 2–3, 6, 164, 168, 184, 205–7
  post-Fordism 168, 184, 205–7
friction of distance 164, 168

gamekeeper 44, 59–60
gardening state 44
gated community 106–7, 109, 111, 113, 115, 117–22, 169, 178, 193, 200, 210
Gattungswesen 179
gem of the Lesser Sunda Isles 124
gentrification 48–9, 191
Gleichschaltung 187
global cities 2, 40–1, 43–4, 48, 94–5, 161, 165, 171, 193
  global city theory 162
  paradox of 165
  post-global 160–1, 163, 165, 167, 169, 171, 173
global citizenship 54–5, 159
global civil society 53–7, 59, 61, 63, 65, 67, 69–70
global diasporas 141
global tourism 123–4, 127, 131–2, 136, 138–9, 142, 149, 189, 200, 202–3
Golden Triangle 95, 102
gotong royong 98–101, 103, 150
government 42, 48, 54, 72–8, 82–4, 86, 108–9, 114, 124–5, 133, 135–7, 142, 170, 175, 191, 194, 200–2, 205–8

failure 77–8
graveyard of the orient 99
great civilization 179

habitus 20, 22, 188
half citizens 192
hegemony politics 77–8, 80, 82, 85
heritage industry 189
heterarchy 74, 194
heterotopy 36, 177, 209
high modernity 20, 23
human ecology 6, 186
human nature 6–7, 186
hyperglobalist 26

ideoscape 33
imagined communities 138, 209
individualism 20, 33, 49
  possessive 49
individualization 178–9
informational city 171
informational mode of development 40
instantaneous time 3–7, 185, 187
integral institution 42–3, 190
intercity competition 160–1, 167–70, 172–3, 206
intercity governance 168, 208
internal colony 196
internal time 18
Island of the Gods 123, 138

Japan Club of Bali 144–7, 152, 155–6, 203
kairos time 3, 209
Kampong 138
Karawaci 116, 118–21
KIPEM 130, 133–7, 202

laissez faire city 107
Lefebvrian matrix 211
life politics (biopolitique) 39
lifestyle emigrants 142–3, 158, 159, 172
liminality 46
limited government 206–7
linear time 20
Lippo Karawaci 116, 118–20
lived space 19–20, 49, 209
lived time 17–19, 187
lived world 64–5, 210
local government 42, 48, 72, 74–5, 83–4, 108, 136, 200, 205
localism 205
long-stay 143, 149, 156, 203–4

Madonnaization 95, 122
malling 46
master narrative 1, 4, 12, 14, 21–2, 24, 188
McDonaldization 7, 95, 122
mediascape 33, 165
megacities 91–2, 95, 97–8, 104–7, 112–13, 121–2, 160–1, 166–7, 169, 182, 196–7, 209 *See also* Asian megacities
metaphor 3, 22, 25, 27, 29, 30–1, 33–7, 42, 54, 58–9, 63, 65, 173, 181, 183, 188, 203
  fluids metaphor 37, 59, 65
  of network 30, 58
metropolitanization 95–7
microhistory 14, 187
milieu 33–4, 180, 211
military police of the liberalist world 163
mobilization of the subject 44–5
modern west 11, 58, 101

multiple sensitivity 36, 66
multitude 5, 25, 39, 63, 189

national citizenship 38, 44, 54–6, 206 *See also* citizenship
national identity 38, 54, 56, 102, 163
national narrative 77, 104
nationalism 71, 102, 104, 198, 208
  competitive 198
  top-down 104
nationalization of civil society 42
natural 3, 7, 16, 18, 29, 103, 106, 118, 121, 127, 139, 152, 154–5, 179, 186, 203
  area 106, 121
nature 5–7, 11–12, 16, 28, 30, 36, 56, 59–60, 71–2, 75, 82, 99, 105, 115, 117–18, 120–1, 127, 133, 150, 161, 167, 175, 181, 186, 190, 197–8, 205–6
  second 186
neighborhood 7, 19, 75, 94, 100–1, 108, 120, 158–9, 193
neoliberal urbanism 48
neo-medieval society 38
neo-nationalism 208
new empires 39
new international division of labor 23, 40, 91, 102
  theory of 23
new middle class 95, 97, 102, 114–15, 191, 200, 208
new pocket of order 190
new rich 115, 200, 208
new urban sociology 162, 205
nodal institution 42, 190

nomads 141, 164, 203
non-manual new middle class 114
non-place 19, 31, 179–81, 210
  See also placeless

open urban space 71–73, 75, 77, 79–81, 83–5, 195
Orde Baru 98, 115, 117, 124–6, 137–8, 208
  post- 98, 117, 126, 137
oriental despotism 90, 196
orientalism 14, 91, 93, 101, 158, 187, 196, 205
  internalized 196
  radical 14
orientation to de-nationality 142
overextension of security 178–9, 210
overurbanization 89, 91–2, 97–8, 101, 104, 113
  post-overurbanization 97, 101
  theory of 91, 104

Pancasila Democracy 100
patron-client relation 100
Pax Americana 206
pecalang 135
pengajian 150
people who cross borders 141–2, 159
permeability of national borders 164, 166, 206
place
  alternative interpretation of 5, 65
  consuming place 189
  place without power 176–7
  placeless flow 176
  space of 33, 176
  variations of 2, 5, 7, 64, 185–6, 188
placeless 4, 34, 36, 62, 64, 80, 176 *See also* non-place
plural society 92, 98–9, 197
postcolonial 25, 89, 92–4, 97, 101–4, 107, 121–2, 183, 188, 196–8, 200, 208, 211
post-development 98, 101, 103, 106
post-Fordism 168, 184, 205–7
primate city 92–3, 97, 107, 112–13, 169, 196, 200
principle of subsidiarity 194
privatization 46, 48–9, 51, 121, 191
progressive sense of place 64, 185–6, 210–11
promotional culture 184
propinquity 2, 7, 19, 40, 63, 67–9, 178–9, 186
public space 46–7, 49
  privatized 46
public sphere 5, 38, 42–3, 45, 53, 56, 79, 187, 196, 210

quantum reality 6
Queen of the orient 99

racism based on difference theory 174, 209
rational dialogue 84
regulatory state 31
reinforced placeness by capital 185
relocation 109
resistance identities 32, 34, 62, 189
re-territorialization 31, 33–6, 141
right to difference 174

risk 35, 50, 55, 58, 68, 102, 104, 173, 193, 210
ruko 132
rukun 98, 99, 100, 101, 103, 198

secondary citizen problem 166, 206
security nation 207
self-differentiation 165, 168, 207
service intensive mode of production 40, 42
shanty town 107, 132
shared poverty 101–2, 108, 112–13, 196, 199
shock city 106
shrinkage of distance 160–1, 163–4, 168
skepticism toward globalization 70
sociation 32, 35, 42, 57, 59, 68, 75, 95, 101, 105, 108, 130, 141, 147, 159, 178–9, 182, 188, 193, 199, 201, 203–4, 206
societal power 31
societies beyond society 141
sociological particularities 102
space
  compensatory 49
  production of 103, 211
  of flow 40, 43
  of the commons 182
spatial fetishism 186, 188
spatial restructuring 168–70, 208–9
spatial semiotics 190–1
spatial turn 1, 11, 23–4, 87, 160, 162, 172–3, 184, 186, 206
spatiality 16–17, 19, 56

spontaneous development 182–3, 211
strange attractor 28
street dazzling with electric lights 198
strengthening and replay of play 64
structural adjustment program 101, 112
structural duality 40
structuralist anthropology 174, 209
subak 130
subculture of poverty 93
sweatshop 130
system failure 74

taking root 177–9, 181–2, 209
technician of value 81–4
technoscape 33
territorial trap 29
textual action theory 23
the emergent 1, 6, 18, 37, 94, 181–3, 190, 211
  of the present 18
the Japanese never learn 157
the territorial 1, 17, 76
theory of structuration 22, 189
theory of totalization 11, 22, 23
time
  annihilation of space by time 64
  new experience of time and space 2
  of becoming 18, 185
  spatial time 17, 19, 20, 185
  time-space compression 2–3, 62, 164, 178, 184
Tokyo Midtown 49–50, 191
traditional non-west 101
trajectivité 179–81, 210–11

Subject Index

trap of linearity 27
tyranny of intimateness 71

unity in diversity 137–8, 175
unthinking social science 1
urban cloister 95, 167–72
urban crisis 191
urban entrepreneurialism 48
urban impoverishment theory 92–3
urban involution theory 196
urban middle class 113–15, 117–18, 120, 200
urban restructuring 39, 95, 104, 107, 108, 121, 199, 200
urban–rural dichotomy 92, 96
urban space 1, 9, 45–6, 48, 51, 71–3, 75, 77, 79–81, 83–85, 101, 104, 112, 115, 165, 168, 171–2, 177–8, 184, 191, 195
urban underclass 102
urbanization 89–92, 94, 97–8, 101, 103–4, 113, 118, 200, 202
  distorted 90
  without industrialization 89–90

visualism 66, 193

waiting culture 184
Washington Consensus 169–70, 172, 208
web of meaning 6
Western European modernity 13–14, 21, 187
world
  de-severance of the world 56
  factory of 163
  practical possession of the world 66

World Bank 97, 108, 170, 197
world cities 40, 42, 162–7, 197
  downward explosion of 42
  hypothesis of 162
  World City of Tokyo 162–7

zero tolerance 71
zone of transition 42